I Remember It Well

I Remember It Well

Fifty Years of Colonial Service
Personal Reminiscences

Edited By
David Le Breton

Foreword By Anthony Kirk-Greene

Librario

Published by
Librario Publishing Ltd.

ISBN : 978-1906775186

Copies can be ordered from retail
or via the internet at :

www.librario.com

or from :

Brough House
Milton Brodie
Kinloss
Morayshire
IV36 2UA

Tel / Fax : 01343 850178

Cover design & layout by Steven James
www.chimeracreations.co.uk

Front cover image :
*Schoolboy Nathaniel Pemberton climbing the
Union Jack flag pole, St Kitts, Leeward Islands 1955*
Courtesy The Imperial War Museum

Back cover image :
*Colonial Service plaque, Westminster Abbey Cloisters
(unveiled by H M The Queen on 23 March 1966)*
Tariq Chaudry, 115 Elmscott Road, Bromley, Kent BR1 4RJ

Printed and bound in Great Britain

Contents

Foreword by Anthony Kirk-Greene		9
Preface		11
Note on Copyright		15
The Overseas Service Pensioners' Association		17
Map of The Colonial Empire 1947		18

PART 1 : ADMINISTRATION, POLICE & SECURITY

1.1	**Vacancy Tanganyika** by J Lewis-Barned	21
1.2	**A Course of Fun (the First Devonshire)** by B D Wilson	25
1.3	**Checking the Books** by R E N Smith	28
1.4	**The White Man's Grave** by FG (Pat) O'Dwyer	31
1.5	**The Solomon Islands in the 1930s** by R A Lever	36
1.6	**Emergency Days, Malaya 1948-50** by R R H Horsley	40
1.7	**Fish Bombs and Copra** by Peter Burbrook	44
1.8	**A New Town Plan for Zuru** by N C McClintock	49
1.9	**Lamu Town** by Peter Lloyd	53
1.10	**Malayan Opium Tales** by David Brent	56
1.11	**The Day's Work and Odd Jobs : Rescue up the Niger** by Ronald Bird (Dogon Yaro)	59
1.12	**The Day's Work and Odd Jobs : No Tax? No Bridge!** by Ronald Bird (Dogon Yaro)	64
1.13	*"Vive Le Royaume Uni!"* by R E N Smith	67
1.14	**Signed, Sealed and Delivered** by John Gullick	71
1.15	**Africa Past and Present** by Kenneth J Forder	74
1.16	**Signing Off** by B D Wilson	78
1.17	**Two Knights and a Chief in Central Africa** by Brian Reavill	79

PART 2 : PROFESSIONAL & TECHNICAL

2.1	**Reminiscences of the Leeward Islands, 1931-34** by Winifred K O'Mahony	85
2.2	**The Making of a Colonial Agriculturalist** by Justin Trevor Moon	91

2.3	**Children of Arabia, 1944-46** by Mary Fletcher	97
2.4	**A War Effort in Tanganyika** by John H Harris	99
2.5	**How Government Officers Became Official Opium Dealers in the Old Federated Malay States** by J S A Lewis	103
2.6	**Season of Green Leaves** by Kuldip Rai Moman	107
2.7	**A Woman Education Officer on the Niger** by Joan Russell	111
2.8	**Magnet Brand** by J D Kelsall	116
2.9	**Dura Camp** by James Lang Brown	118
2.10	**Resettlement of Suspected Mau Mau Sympathisers in Tanganyika** by J M Ainley	121
2.11	**Rain Stimulation in East Africa** by B W Thompson	126
2.12	**First Foot** *Ulendo* by Ted Wilmot	130
2.13	**Train to Iganga** by Kuldip Rai Moman	133
2.14	**A Learning Experience** by Eric Cunningham	137
2.15	**A Matter of Understanding** by Simon Templer	139

PART 3 : TOURING, TRAVEL & TRANSPORT

3.1	**Journey to Yola, 1929** by B A Babb	145
3.2	**First Footsteps** by John Cooke	149
3.3	*Ulendo* by R E N Smith	153
3.4	**Jungle Trip from Grik to Temengor** by Mrs M C Barkway	158
3.5	**Lake Victoria Passage** by J D Kelsall	165
3.6	**Karamoja Journey** by S Nicholl	169
3.7	**Massa Gets Transport** by R R Yearley	174
3.8	**Journeying to Cape Guardafui** by Colin Everard	178
3.9	**Anuta – An Island from Paradise?** by James L O Tedder	184
3.10	**Not a Wisdom Tooth** by Jane Shadbolt	189
3.11	**Journey in the Hadhramaut** by Mary Reid	193
3.12	**Journey to Mongu** by B H	200
3.13	**Stomach Ache in the Solomons** by James L O Tedder	205
3.14	**A Kenya Journey** by B W Thompson	210
3.15	**On Being a Pacific Sea-Dog** by R E N Smith	216
3.16	**By Motorcycle in Uganda** by S Nicholl	221
3.17	**The Silver Handshake** by J D Kelsall	225
3.18	**Railways and Motive Power** by Don Owens	227

PART 4 : DOMESTIC

Home Life

4.1	**The Lap of Luxury** by R E N Smith	233
4.2	**A Nigerian Garden** by Muriel Barnett	239
4.3	**It's a Dog's Life** by Duncan McCormack	243
4.4	**Mail Day** by James L O Tedder	246
4.5	**Supermarket – Island Style** by James L O Tedder	250
4.6	**Bumps in the Night** by J S A Lewis	253

Wives

4.7	**Who's Afraid?** by Janet Wimbush	256
4.8	**One Christmas in the Gold Coast** by Faith Dennis	260
4.9	**Hurricane Janet, Barbados 1955** by Winifred K O'Mahony	262

PART 5 : LANGUAGE & LOCAL CUSTOMS

Language

5.1	**How Do You Do?** by PC 49	269
5.2	**Massa Gets to Speak Propa** by R R Yearley	272
5.3	**How Not to Learn Swahili** by John H Harris	275

Local Customs

5.4	**Witchcraft** by R E N Smith	277
5.5	**He Needs a White Cloth** by A S Webb	280

PART 6 : SPORT & WILDLIFE

Sport

6.1	**Golf in the Nigerian Bush, 1948-65** by Iddo Hudo	285
6.2	**Cricket in Sarawak** by L J Holliday	288

Wildlife

6.3   **The Lion** by E W Bult   291
6.4   **Good Advice Will Defeat Your Enemy** by G R P Henton   295

PART 7 : PERSONALITIES

7.1   **A Tribute to Captain A Gibb, DSO, DCM**
       District Commissioner, British Somaliland by Roland A Hill   299
7.2   **Berkeley of Upper Perak** by Anon   303
7.3   **Serving Mallam Abubakar Tafawa Balewa,** *Nigerian*
       Minister of Works and Transport in 1951 by R L Armstrong   306
7.4   *"Wote Timamu, Effendi"* **("All Present and Correct, Sir")**
       by Ian D St G Lindsay   311

Appendix I : Colonial Emblems and Badges   319
Appendix II : British Colonial Territories   321
Contributors   327
Territories Index   333
Subject Index   337
About the Editor   343

Foreword

The Overseas Service Pensioners' Association (OSPA) is now approaching its 50th birthday, and with it the 50th anniversary of the launching of its hugely appreciated journal, *the Overseas Pensioner* (OP). In addition to ensuring that the journal fulfils its primary purposes of keeping members in touch with policies, problems and decisions about Colonial Service pensions and of providing them with a detailed account of the proceedings of OSPA's Annual General Meetings, our last two Secretaries, Douglas Stenton and David Le Breton, have each introduced a notable and much valued addition to the contents of the OP, thereby converting its status from a basic newsletter to that of a respected magazine.

The first innovation was the ready acceptance by Douglas Stenton in 1980 of my suggestion that the OP should regularly carry short reviews of books about the Colonial Service. This developed into including a few members' own memoirs. The second was David Le Breton's practice in the 1990s deliberately to encourage more members – and their wives – keen to submit short accounts of aspects of their service, such as recruitment, first tour, touring and travel, their work and their leisure activities, and many other personal recollections of their days in the Colonial Service. Without a doubt such pen-portraits of events and personalities, some of them rendered all the more historically valuable when they focused on the experiences of pre-war Colonial Service life, provide a positive contribution to a fuller understanding of what we did and how we lived and worked. It was thus that David Le Breton succeeded in the eyes of many members in recapturing much of the spirit and readability of the Colonial Service's one-time own Journal, *Corona*, which appeared monthly between 1948 and 1962 (and from which an extensive anthology was published by I B Tauris in 2001 under the title of *Glimpses of Empire*). In this respect the OP may be said to have proved both a welcome and a worthy successor to *Corona*.

It is from these 'recall' articles in the OP that the editor has assembled the collection which comprises this excellent book. In reading and enjoying them, it is important to remain aware that these articles were not intended to be profoundly researched or meticulously reconstructed recollections of the type that make up the splendid, published, book-length memoirs of many of our members. Rather they represent the instant memory reflex of when, if you like, we are asked, "What is it that comes to mind first when you think back on your life in the Colonial Service?" The result, then, is principally a matter of immediacy rather than of refinement, of what is uppermost in the writer's instant recall. It is the reaction accurately described by several of the contributors themselves, who talk about how "some of these odd jobs are still quite vivid in one's memory", "a flight of fancy", "stirred memories", or Kuldip Rai Moman's "I look back . . . A longing comes over me to see once again long-forgotten faces and places from the dim, hazy past". Mercifully, none of the contributors seems to have been faced with that proverbial question put, I am told, by one infamous, immature (but in no way, let me assure you, imagined) student researcher who, armed with his tape-recorder but little else by way of preparation for the occasion, allegedly commented to the interviewee, "Wow! Twenty-five years in Africa! And did you learn African?"

The selection assembled by the editor dexterously achieves a wide coverage of territories as well as of services. The focus is deliberately on the personal, not policy, on occasions recalled rather than events reconstructed. The result is a brilliant and telling insight into the kind of incidents that remain almost instantaneous in the mind when one is asked about those years in the Colonial Service. Together with the full-length and studiously crafted insider's memoirs and with some of the academic studies, generally written from the outside, these vignettes successfully round off the total picture of life (rather than just work alone) as it was lived by members of the Colonial Service and HMOCS.

OSPA's numbers are steadily but inevitably falling year by year, from 25,000 in the 1970s to under 5,000 today, a decline propelled by the fact that by definition it was always an Association built on a limited and non-replacing membership created between the winding down of the Colonial Service in the 1960s and its final closure in 1997. The admission of public service pensioners from Southern Rhodesia / Zimbabwe in 1980 and from Sudan in 2009 slowed but could not halt that trend. Thus we should all welcome the appearance of these 'last generation' personal recollections as a unique contribution to the recording and the understanding of many moments of life in the Colonial Service. Those who have shared that experience will surely gain as much from these narratives as those to whom the Colonial Service moment is something that they can only read about.

Anthony Kirk-Greene
(*N Nigeria 1950-65*)
Oxford, March 2010

Preface

As Secretary of the Overseas Service Pensioners' Association since 1992, in succession to Douglas Stenton who had filled that position since 1979 (sadly he died on 29th December 2009), it has been my duty – and my pleasure – to be the Editor of the Association's bi-annual journal, *the Overseas Pensioner*.

The idea for this book came from an OSPA member, Ian Lindsay, now living in Australia, one of the contributors herein – see his very suitable closing piece, No 7.4 on page 311. He suggested that a number of the 'general interest' articles that have appeared in the journal over the last nearly 30 years deserved publication in some more regular and accessible form.

To set it going, he scanned a large number of the articles onto his computer and sent them on a CD to me in the OSPA office in Tonbridge. That initiative deserved to be followed up, so with the patient and absolutely vital supportive help of my secretary, Marjory Mackay, I began to select, edit and adapt the material to make it suitable for a marketable publication. It turned out to be a more demanding task than I had expected, having to be slotted in among other jobs – whether priority or regular work – in the OSPA office.*

Starting with over 150 items, I reduced the number to the present 72 contributions. They cover a wide range of members' recollections, a diversity of topics and a good spread of territories. Many of the pieces had to be made shorter, either by omitting certain passages or by just selecting an extract, but they have not been 'condensed' à la *Readers Digest*. They are arranged into seven groups, shown as Parts on the Contents page. The largest Part covers touring, travel and transport, as members seem to have found their journeys among their most vivid and memorable experiences.

There are 50 named contributors, and four more whose names are not known. Some of them have written more than one piece, with the late

---

*Ian Lindsay was opposed to these processes of selection and editing. He wanted all the articles to be reproduced in their original form. He has now printed his own collection of all those from 1986 to 2006, unedited, bound into an A4 size volume. He is willing to send copies to anyone interested, at a price to be decided when he sees how many requests he receives. His address is : 19 Kewarra Street, Kewarra Beach, Cairns, QLD 4879, Australia.

Mr R E N Smith being the most prolific. They come from many professions in the Service, thus countering a common impression that colonial rule chiefly involved civil administrators. There are least 25 different occupations represented :

accountant	geology
administration	judiciary
agriculture	locust control
air traffic control	medical
audit	meteorology
cartography	metallurgy
chemist	mining
customs	police
education	postal services
engineering	railways
entomology	surveys
fisheries	water development
forestry	

There are others that have not been covered. For example, it is a pity that there are none dealing with animal husbandry / veterinary, maritime, nursing, or prisons. Although books dealing with those subjects have been written by OSPA members and reviewed in *the Overseas Pensioner,* there have been no journal articles about them.

That fact emphasizes the patchy, almost random, nature of this collection. The articles must not be regarded as constituting a balanced description or representation of Colonial Service as a whole. This is very evident from a look at the Territories Index. Only 19 colonial territories and institutions are mentioned, whereas there are 37 territories in the 1949 Colonial Office List, and that excludes the three "South African High Commission Territories" of Basutoland, Bechuanaland and Swaziland where HMOCS people served. Some of the missing ones are sizeable, like British Guiana; some are notable for other reasons, like Cyprus and Malta; and others are of lesser rank, like St. Helena and the Falkland Islands.

Naturally there are more articles dealing with the larger territories, but some smaller ones – Nevis for example – are included. All the major regions are represented – West, East and Central Africa, South and South East Asia, Pacific and the Caribbean.

It is a sad and unfortunate fact that most of the contributors have died. Looking back with hindsight, the present collection would have been fuller and richer if it had been possible for *the Overseas Pensioner* to have carried more such general interest articles at an earlier stage. The earliest one in this selection was in *the Overseas Pensioner* No. 42, November 1981 (*Journey to Mongu*). The journal was slimmer in those days, and coverage had to be given for many different pensions issues, leaving few pages available for the book reviews and general memoir articles. The journal number and date are given at the end of each article herein.

In publishing these articles, my thanks are of course due first to the authors who were sufficiently inspired by their memories of Colonial Service days to take the trouble to write up their recollections and send them to the editor of the journal. More immediately, I have to thank Marjory Mackay, my Personal Secretary in the OSPA office since 2001, for all the exact and often repetitive computer/word processing work involved in setting up and printing out of every word in these pages, as well as for her often helpful advice. Also Andrea Fryatt of the OSPA staff, who gave much valuable help, particularly over the colonial badges. Nick Baxter, the Deputy Head of the Overseas Pensions Department of the Department for International Development, helped me find details of many of the contributors, for the purpose of the Index. I am especially grateful to Tony Kirk-Greene, the frequent and authoritative contributor to *the Overseas Pensioner* on matters of Colonial Service history, who read the initial 150 contributions selected and then the final 72 as well as the indexes and made helpful suggestions on the text and format. He also suggested the title, from Maurice Chevalier's acclaimed duet with Hermione Gingold in the 1958 musical *Gigi*, disregarding the lyric's theme that personal recollections can be faulty (but none of those herein!). More generally, I am indebted to the OSPA Council for sanctioning the idea of the book, and making the publication possible. Above and beyond all these, my acknowledgement and thanks are due to the many thousands of OSPA members, past and present, who first created the Association in 1960, and have supported it for half a century. While OSPA's primary objective was the practical one of protecting the value of our Colonial Service pensions, it was at a time when interest in and understanding of Britain's colonial record in the 20th century were becoming diminished. The Association in more recent years has striven to preserve and present that record in forms that successive generations can study, assess and appreciate in whatever way they wish. My hope is that these recollections may contribute to that process.

David Le Breton
Overseas Service Pensioners' Association
138 High Street
Tonbridge
Kent TN9 1AX
March 2010

Note on Copyright

The legal position is that the copyright of articles published in *the Overseas Pensioner* belongs to the author, not to OSPA. Successive editors have thought it not necessary, nor desirable, to require a member who chose to send in an article for the journal to make a written assignment to transfer the copyright to OSPA, or to provide a written licence allowing the article to be used. The consequence is that re-publication of an article in any altered form could infringe the author's exclusive right over his literary work. I have written to each of the authors still living and whose address is known, to obtain their consent to use their article for this book, often in an edited or shortened form. In the case of an author who has died, the copyright passes to the heirs of the estate for a period of 70 years after the date of death. I have no means of knowing who would be the heir of a deceased member (unless the spouse happens to be an OSPA member too). If there is anyone who claims to own the copyright of any article published herein, and wishes to have due acknowledgement, please contact me accordingly. The same applies to any author still living who I have not been able to contact for any reason.

David Le Breton

The Overseas Service Pensioners' Association

The Overseas Service Pensioners' Association (OSPA) was founded in October 1960. Its members were and are people who served in Her Majesty's Overseas Civil Service (HMOCS) or its predecessor the Colonial Service, or a similar service, in British colonial territories (including Sudan since 2009) and who receive a pension or have entitlement to a deferred pension in respect of such service. Also widow pensioners and some wives. Associate membership is open to non-pensioners who were in colonial Government service, or anyone who has interest in Colonial Service matters, and their wives and children. There are nearly 4,500 members, of whom about a quarter live outside Britain.

OSPA's primary objects are to represent, safeguard and promote the interests of its members and their dependants in all matters relating directly or indirectly to their pensions. It persuaded the British Government to take over responsibility for the payment of Overseas Service pensions (including widows' pensions), and to protect their value through the SPOS (Supplementary Pension for Overseas Service). It is recognised by the British Government as the only body representing such pensioners.

Secondly, OSPA serves as the focal point for HMOCS (and other) officers and widows who wish to belong to an organised body of colleagues having unique shared experiences and background, understanding the special nature of service in the colonial territories, and being capable of representing their common interests and expressing their views when necessary. OSPA aims to be a guardian, as far as resources permit, of the good name and reputation of HMOCS and its antecedents and as an enquiry point about the Colonial Service. It also gives encouragement and support to institutions which promote understanding of Colonial Service matters, such as the British Empire & Commonwealth Museum and University Libraries in London, Oxford and Cambridge.

The Overseas Pensioner journal is issued free to members twice yearly, with news about current pension matters, articles and book reviews and letters relating to general Colonial Service topics.

Application to become an ordinary or associate member of OSPA should be sent to :

Overseas Service Pensioners' Association
138 High Street
Tonbridge
Kent TN9 1AX

Tel : 01732 363836
Int : (+) 44 1732 363836

Email : mail@ospa.org.uk
Website : www.ospa.org.uk

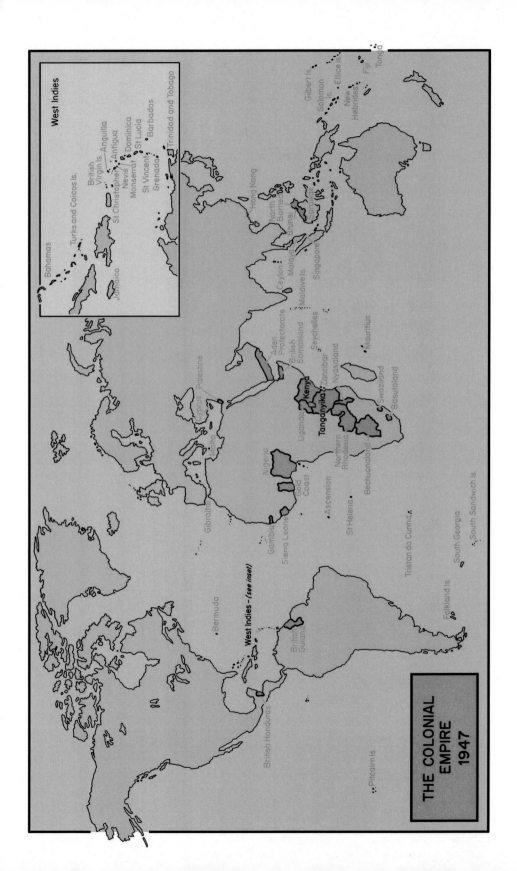

West Indies

Bahamas
Turks and Caicos Is.
Jamaica

British
Virgin Is. Anguilla
St Christopher Antigua
Nevis Dominica
Monserrat St Lucia
St Vincent Barbados
Grenada
Trinidad and Tobago

Pitcairn Is

British Honduras

West Indies – (see inset)

Bermuda

Falkland Is.

South Georgia

South Sandwich Is.

Tristan da Cunha

St Helena

Ascension

British Guiana

Sierra Leone

Gambia

Gold Coast

Nigeria

Gibraltar

Malta

Cyprus Palestine

Aden Protectorate

British Somaliland

Bechuanaland

Swaziland

Basutoland

Northern Rhodesia

Nyasaland

Tanganyika Zanzibar

Kenya

Uganda

Seychelles

Mauritius

Maldive Is.

Ceylon

Malaya Brunei

Singapore

North Borneo

Sarawak

Hong Kong

Gilbert Is.

Solomon Is.

Ellice Is.

New Hebrides

Fiji

Tonga

THE COLONIAL EMPIRE
1947

Part 1
ADMINISTRATION, POLICE & SECURITY

Vacancy Tanganyika

by J Lewis-Barned

Like many others, I left the Army in 1949 with no very clear idea of what to do next. I scanned the daily newspapers, went for interviews with the Ministry of Labour and sundry agencies, and made enquiries from friends and acquaintances. There was the possibility of going to University, but perhaps foolishly, I fought shy of going back to being *in statu pupillari* and to study for examinations after seeing something of the great world outside.

I had no trade or professional qualifications, nor a degree, and I felt that my field was accordingly limited. I was rather attracted by an article which appeared in the *Sunday Express* headed *Sanders of the River, still the best job for a British Boy*, describing in romantic terms the 'key men' who carry forward the work of the Empire. 'There are still boys', said that great newspaper, 'with the same idea as their fathers and grandfathers who see themselves in jungle or desert helping primitive tribesmen towards progress, keeping law and order in a district as big as Yorkshire . . . ' Qualities demanded were 'a sense of vocation, an urge for adventure, and a response to the call of duty, initiative and almost above all, a sense of humour and an ability to return the affection of the people who you are serving'. 'Empire Builder', the article concluded, 'still the best job for a British Boy!'

As a matter of fact the Colonial Service had been in my mind for some time. I consulted an old standby called *Every Boy's Book*, published in 1938 and describing itself as '*An Epitome of Information Covering all the Interests and Activities of the Modern Boy*'. The careers section of this admirable compendium advised intending applicants for the Colonial Service to apply to a long since defunct address for '*Colonial Service Recruitment Pamphlet No 1*', and this I accordingly did. On receipt of this document, I found that recruits did not necessarily have to have a degree but should be able to show 'academic capacity equivalent to 1st or 2nd Class Honours' and this sounded hopeful. I had a fairly good Oxbridge Matriculation and thought I could cope with the interview so I applied.

I was required to produce typewritten, and in original, reports from head-masters and employers under whom I had worked since the age of nine. These were all satisfactory as far as I could see except the last which declared emphatically that the writer did not think that I was suitable for the Colonial

Administrative Service. Concerned about this, I called at the Colonial Office and handed in the papers personally. They told me not to worry and in due course I attended three interviews. The first was clearly intended to separate sheep from goats, and I conclude that I must have been classified as one or other of these because a little later I was summoned to appear before a Board.

As I sat in the lobby waiting to be interviewed – feeling rather groggy about the knees – the door swept open and out came a Scotsman resplendent in kilt and sporran. He was kind enough to tell me that the most tricky question that he had been asked was 'Why do you consider that you have sufficient sympathy and understanding to deal with Africans?' Accordingly I had my answer prepared to the effect that I had always assiduously looked after the welfare of my soldiers and had a genuine interest in people, which seemed to satisfy the Board.

When I went in, a number of interviewers were ranged along a table and they asked the searching sort of questions that are usually asked at interviews with Boards. I remember in particular that I was asked to comment on the merits or demerits of the fagging system then in force at Public Schools, and when the Board learned that I had begun my military career in the ranks of the Grenadier Guards, at Caterham Depot, they wanted to know how I had enjoyed it. I think I replied negatively, but I remember that they burst into laughter and looked at the Chairman, whose tie looked to me vaguely like a Guards tie.

A short while after I went for the third interview. This was with a younger man who leant back in his chair and puffed a pipe. Among other things he was keen to know what I thought of the Groundnut Scheme. I had studied *The Times* with care every day for some months before my interviews and so was able to assure him that it was a failure. This answer seemed to please him. I did not know at the time that this was also the view of the Africans who lived in the areas concerned who never understood (until recently perhaps) the illogical ways of the white men who were trying to grow groundnuts where it was known that groundnuts simply would not grow.

In August I received a telegram from the Colonial Office (who presumably imagined that Maidstone was some remote bush station with a doubtful postal service) which stated 'Vacancy Tanganyika. Formal Offer Follows'. Next day there came a letter from someone who had been directed by Mr Secretary Griffiths to offer me a probationary appointment in the Colonial Administrative Service preceded by a course of instruction at Oxford University.

Accordingly I found myself up at Oxford for a year commencing in October 1950 with four other people bound for the same destination. Although the

Colonial Office decreed that the Oxford terms were to be extended at both ends to make them longer than the normal undergraduate term, it was a pleasant year. We studied Field Engineering in the Parks with Mr Longland, whose book on the subject is still a bible to me, and attended courses in Colonial History with Professor Harlow, Geography, Tropical Agriculture (Geoffrey Masefield), Colonial Accounts, Anthropology (Professor Evans-Pritchard), Law (Professor Cross), and Swahili. The latter was particularly well taught by Bobby Maguire and Ali Jahadmi, an Arab from Zanzibar, helped by a dictaphone. If only languages had been taught like that at school!

Anyway we satisfied our examiners and embarked on 2nd August 1951 on the *Llanstephan Castle* to travel round the Cape to Dar es Salaam on the East Coast. Apparently the Colonial Office had left the booking too late and all the vessels of the Union Castle Steamship Navigation Co going via Suez were full. In my pocket I had a telegram from an aunt which read 'Best hopes that budding Governor will bloom'. We were on half-pay with comfortable 1st class accommodation and a six week cruise ahead of us. In due time we were in the harbour in Dar es Salaam when I woke up in the morning with the palm trees, bright sunshine and busy movement of the town around us.

Not long afterwards, I found myself sitting in a compartment of the Central Line train. This is not at all the same as its namesake in London. It is called the Central Line because it runs almost straight for 600 miles across the centre of the country – a single metre-gauge track – over miles and miles of uninhabited bushland. It was built in 1910 by the Germans, and virtually no more railway lines had been laid in the country since they left.

We alighted at Itigi where, in the absence of an hotel, we stayed at a rest house and later boarded a bus in which we spent an entire day travelling over some of the most beautiful country I had ever seen, climbing up into the Southern Highlands over the dusty murram and earth road to 6,000 feet and down to 5,000, to where lies the attractive township of Mbeya, 360 miles from the railhead, and administrative centre and capital of the Southern Highlands Province.

I was put into an hotel after the usual sort of friendly welcome from my District Commissioner, Alan Scott. I was introduced to the office side of the job. I found that I was secretary of the Board of Film Censors, Passport Officer, Executive Officer for the Housing Committee and a Class III Magistrate. A steady stream of visitors came through my ever-open door in the course of the day – some seeking employment, some tax exemption, the latter given for old age or infirmity, others with very intricate and complicated legal, domestic or matrimonial problems which I found at first very hard to untangle. Kyanda, the office messenger with 28 years service, was a friend indeed at this time, patiently repeating the Swahili slowly and methodically as I scampered through my dictionary. I shall never forget Kyanda carrying a stone on his head on foot safari.

"Whyever," said I, "do you carry a stone on your head?"

"Because," said he, "I am used to carrying my baggage that way and I don't feel right without it".

I ought perhaps to mention the domestic side of life. It certainly occupied my mind to some extent for I had never hitherto had to manage for myself on my own. Unfortunately even the District Commissioner wielded no substantial power with the Housing Committee, so it was a little time before I was able to move out of the hotel into my own house. This turned out to be an old German-built bungalow with a corrugated-iron roof and mud-brick walls technically still vested in the Custodian of Enemy Property. It had one bedroom, and reasonable ancillary services and the usual allocation of Public Works Dept furniture, but no electricity. They put the electricity in the same day that the candlesticks arrived as a gift from my grandmother. A bare house with a cement floor can be depressing, so my first purchase was two rush mats. I bought a spear to hang in the lobby and wrote home about curtains. The biscuit-type chair cushions had no covers but I had made a start. I had a few pictures from home to hang on the walls, a traditional wind-up gramophone and *Mad Dogs and Englishmen* among other 78s.

Finally Alan sent me on foot safari for a week on my own. This was the custom with a new cadet so that he learned the language. No one was there who could speak English. After it had all been arranged it occurred to me that he had not told me what to do. I sent him a note on Sunday evening and the reply came saying I was just to see that the contour ridging was going ahead and check the books and cash at the Courthouses. I took 18 porters up the hills and walked for miles. I had not yet learned that in spite of being in the Highlands, where it is cool, the sun can do damage, and I suffered accordingly, until I bought a hat about which I have been teased ever since. I chucked it into the Atlantic Ocean at the Equator on the last journey home like the British Army used to do with their topees years ago when a regiment came home from India.

OP 51 (April 1986), OP 52 (October 1986)

A Course of Fun
(the First Devonshire)

by B D Wilson

On the 'First Devonshire Course' in 1948 *(officially, the Devonshire 'A' Course)* we were a relaxed group of over 100 lads, mostly wartime ex-Service, impatient to be done with lectures and to get on with the job in our respective territories. One humourless young man attending at Oxford who tried to press his Communist views on lecturers ceased to appear one day, and was presumed to have been quietly sacked. An amiable African on the course said he found the content unappealing and dropped out.

The vast majority of us were destined for African territories and this was reflected in the content of the lectures. One man named Coffin was going to a Pacific territory, giving rise to a string of jokes about cannibals, big cooking pots and deadly diseases. Donald Luddington (later Sir Donald, and Governor of the Solomon Islands) and I were due to go to Hong Kong. For me, this choice of destination was somewhat round-about. Having been born in Penang, I had opted for the Malayan Civil Service, but was instead offered Uganda. Finding that Uganda was well inland and far from the coast, I asked the Colonial Office to reconsider. They offered Hong Kong. I looked it up on the map, thought it sounded all right and said "yes".

At the London School of Economics, Donald and I grew increasingly bored with the continual stream of lectures on Africa. Its colonial history, anthropology, economics, and geography were of little interest to us. We complained, and were told that special arrangements would be made for us to learn about the administration of a comparable waterfront community. This consisted of attending a meeting of the Stepney Borough Council which turned out to be a splendid slanging match between Councillors, vying with each other in invective and insults. The politest Councillor present was a West Indian.

The other students at the LSE were almost all younger than ourselves, perhaps less mature and certainly more prone to silly ideas. Notice-boards and corridors were plastered with posters on the lines of *Hands off Malaya, Down with Colonialism, Freedom for All*. The Devonshire men felt themselves a cut above this nonsense, believing that our job in our posted territory was to educate its people to their own eventual self-government. Needless to say, we made little contact with the remainder of the LSE, although out of curiosity I did attend a lecture by Harold Laski, a well-known left-winger to the point of communist. To my disappointment, he stuck strictly to the lecture's stated title.

The frustration of the Devonshire men at being back at school when they wanted to get on with the real work in their territory led to increasing bolshiness. One lad who had served in the Coldstream Guards always appeared in a blue suit and a bowler hat. Another was a racing fan and spent his time at lectures reading *Raceform over the Sticks*. Having made his daily selection, he would discreetly slip out, ostensibly to go to the toilet, in reality to the nearest telephone to place his bets. A group of crossword devotees, with heads down, would get on with the puzzle as if making notes, calling perhaps to neighbours, "Have you got 5 across?"

"No, but I can help with 10 down if you're stuck".

Tired of this lack of attention, one lecturer actually asked us to get our newspapers turned to the right page before the lecture started, as the rustling was too distracting for him. When the lecturer on colonial history described the establishment of African colonial territories as a disgraceful episode, he was roundly booed, much to his surprise. He kept a more discreet tongue thereafter. When the time came for an examination at the end of the course no one had any worries. We were not competing with each other. We simply passed notes round and whispered answers to those who had paid even less attention than ourselves. One young man felt the need to be fortified during the long hours of examinations, so he armed himself with numerous bottles of ink (only fountain pens in those days, no ballpoints). But they contained sherry which he was kind enough to share with neighbours.

The one really useful piece of information came from a visiting Colonial official who said that if you find yourself in some distant posting and you tear off a strip of black velvet, for God's sake send her elsewhere when your DC comes to visit. Otherwise you may be in real trouble.

All this sounds as if we were the most useless bunch of larrikins about to be let loose on an unsuspecting colonial public. In reality, it was nothing of the sort. These were serious young men, but tired of academic study and anxious to get on with the practical side of their chosen profession. The real learning probably came overseas on the job. It's a sad reflection that few of us actually served our full time in HMOCS. The majority probably became redundant in mid-career as their territory reached independence, forcing them to seek other employment, often in a quite different field.

Were we better administrators after completing the Devonshire Course? I doubt it, but ever since I've always enjoyed crossword puzzles.

OP 76 (Autumn 1998)

Checking the Books

by R E N Smith

As a humble Probationer Cadet I attended the 'First Devonshire Course' at Oxford and London in 1948-49. This, the last of the long courses, was intended to prepare me and other hopefuls in all the essentials of a District Officer's life and works, and on the whole it succeeded quite well. It was perhaps rather biased towards West Africa in general and Nigeria in particular (one lonely unfortunate rose to his feet and cheered on the only occasion the Gilbert and Ellice Islands were mentioned), but the content was on the whole sufficiently catholic to suit most tastes. Many grey-haired veterans will remember with affection the lively and hilarious lectures in criminal law from that ace of dais performers, Professor Davidge, and Mr Longland's detailed and solid lectures on simple engineering, illustrated by almost incomprehensible sketches drawn on newsprint. Looking at the lecture list I see that we studied Colonial Government, Religion and Administration, the Law of Evidence & Tort, Land Utilization, Problems of the British Empire, Land Tenure and Native Law, Imperial Economic History, Geography, Social Anthropology, Forestry, and the other two already mentioned, Criminal Law and Field Engineering. After Oxford we went on (with the Cambridge course members) to a joint five-month course at SOAS and LSE (where we were known derisively and unlovingly as the 'White Masters') and here we studied not only the language of the territory for which we were destined, but also its geography, history, agriculture and economics. The eighteen month course covered a formidable breadth of study, but the one thing missing was training in the most practical and vital basic subject that would bedevil us all from the moment of our arrival in any district in any colony.

I am referring to simple book-keeping. From my earliest days as a very junior ADC at Port Herald in Nyasaland, to my more mature years as Senior District Commissioner in the Gilbert and Ellice Islands, I had ample opportunity to bemoan my lack of basic book-keeping skills. In 1950 there I was, green but keen, foot-slogging from one Native Authority Headquarters to the next, followed by an impressive train of porters carrying my tent and baggage in the most romantic Sanders of the River style, but coming face to face with reality on arrival at the chief's court, where I found myself struggling to check the Court Clerk's accounts for both the court and the Native Authority itself. Twenty years and more later, there I still was, sailing the wide Pacific in the best Grimble manner, from one Island Council office to the next, endeavouring to make sense of their receipts and expenditure and trying to produce annual budgets. In the interim I had perforce learned a great deal, but it would have helped if I had been trained in book-keeping to begin with.

I suppose that basic accounting is really very simple, but as the years have gone by, colonial accounting seems to have become more abstruse and complicated. I came across an ancient and long superseded system in Nyasaland that I still feel has much to commend it in unsophisticated societies. On the upper back verandah of the four-roomed Boma in Port Herald, an appallingly hot building stinking of old and new bat droppings and plagued with the largest mosquitoes in Africa, was a stack of abandoned ancient court records. As the DC (himself new to the job) tried to keep all the reins in his own hands and gave me far too little to do (a kindness bad for both my education and my reputation), I found myself studying not only the obligatory volumes of the Colony's Laws but also the old records.

These were fascinating in the insight they gave to the administration of the district in the days when District Officers were often locally recruited; not that these officers were necessarily inferior to their successors, but they were often men of strong character, with a chequered history and highly individualistic habits. From the court books it seemed that the bane of their workaday lives was the ineradicable habit of the local African of picking up his spear and going walkabout – usually down to South Africa or Rhodesia for work. There was no official disapproval of this practice (except insofar as it deprived the country of the man's 'hut' tax), but the travellers were supposed to obtain a pass to leave the country. Never greatly impressed by the magic of Western legal thinking, the requirement was generally ignored by Africans, and the DCs of old appear to have spent much time in court fining the offenders ten shillings or a pound for their delinquency.

Now this is where the accounting was solved by a stroke of genius. In my time there would have to have been a clerk or three, receipt books in triplicate or quadruplicate, and pages of accounts, the money then paid into the treasury and yet more accounting carried out and columns of figures balanced and reconciled with the receipts, with many possibilities (too often seized upon) for chicanery. In the bad old days the DC as District Magistrate heard the case in his court room (another name for his office), entered it in his court case book in longhand, and then sent the offender down to the Post Office, which, together with an enormous and steadily growing termite mound, occupied one of the Boma's other three rooms. There he would buy a stamp for the amount of his fine, take it back to the DC, who would then ceremonially stick it alongside the court record, obliterate it with his office 'District Magistrate' stamp and that was that. The only actual accounting was done by the Post Office clerk, who had to balance his own accounts however many or how few stamps he sold, and, even if so inclined, he could not pass off a ten-bob stamp as a pound one, as it had to go back to the court record. The process was simplicity itself, and I still cannot see any flaw in it. The court record said 'Fined £1', there was the £1 stamp, duly cancelled, alongside it, and no mass of receipt books to be checked – the court record said it all. The only document the auditor needed was the court record, and he merely checked that each 'fine' entry had the appropriate cancelled stamp alongside it, as an army of green ink ticks testified. Perhaps the system was too simple and too foolproof, for any self-respecting and ambitious Assistant Financial Secretary could easily dream up a more complicated one, and be on his way to great heights in the colonial hierarchy. Innovation, however unnecessary, can be sold to one's superiors if you wear the right air of modest omniscience, imply that the inspiration came from them in the first place, and promotion is yours!

OP 74 (Autumn 1997)

The White Man's Grave

by F G (Pat) O'Dwyer

I got into the Colonial Service in 1932 and was sent up to Cambridge by the Government on the Colonial Service course for a fourth year to study those subjects which it was considered would help us to run the Empire. I went out to Freetown (Sierra Leone) by Elder Dempster ship in 1933 and was met in Freetown by my brother who had been seconded from his Regiment, the Inniskilling Fusiliers, to whom I had been attached in the Supplementary Reserve for the four years I had been up at Cambridge. He had been seconded to the Royal West African Frontier Force (RWAFF) and it was good to meet one of my own family on first setting foot on foreign soil.

I was sent up-country as an Assistant District Commissioner, on probation, to Makeni under the District Commissioner, Humpherson. He soon went out on trek and left me in charge of the Station HQ with an African staff of three literate clerks, to keep records and interpret if necessary, and about 35 Court Messengers. These were all ex-soldiers of the RWAFF of exemplary character, with military ranks from Private to Sergeant Major, a very much respected force throughout the country, who wore distinctive uniform and were the maid-of-all-work for the DC.

A much decomposed body was brought into the District Office by a messenger from a Paramount Chief and I was required to ascertain the cause of death. I sent the body down to the Medical Officer who reported that he thought that the body had died as a result of being mauled by a leopard. I held an enquiry such as I was able, and brought in a verdict that the body had died as a result of being mauled by a leopard. I was quite ignorant of African ways of thought, but I sensed from murmurings amongst the Court Messengers that my verdict was incorrect, though of course they were too polite to make an open objection.

You see, from the African standpoint there were three ways in which that body could have met its end. One was being mauled by a leopard; the second was by murder, for there was a Leopard Society in which malefactors combined and took binding oaths of secrecy, covered their bodies with leopard skins and tied on to their hands and feet iron claws made by local blacksmiths, then lay in wait for their chosen victim, pounced on him and clawed him to death. Then the Africans thought there was a third way, by which a man could put

31

his spirit into that of a leopard, which would then be conducted to attack his chosen victim, and thus though the leopard had actually killed the person, the guilty party was he who had put his spirit into the leopard. In African eyes this was murder. In this case I gathered that the Court Messengers thought that number three of the alternatives was the correct one – which we know is impossible, and thus I gained the first insight into the African mind, about which as time went on I began to learn a little more.

Later, still in my first tour, I was transferred to Port Loko as Asst. DC to the DC who was 'Baby' Taylor. There was no proper house for the Asst. DC in the HQ station, so my permanent house was just a Rest House as it would be on trek. The government decided that there should be a permanent house for the Asst. DC and allotted £60 for its construction. Even in those days of cheap labour and material, £60 was very little. I chose the site and in the evenings I cut down the bush on this site to clear the area. As I was cutting down a tree with a great axe I felt a piercing stab in my head, and as I looked up a green snake fell from the tree on to my shoulder and on to the ground. I realised that this snake had bitten me, but I had no idea of the variety. I went to 'Baby' Taylor and told him, but he was writing a report and I remember him saying, "Are you sure it wasn't a mosquito?" So I went back to my Rest House and told my boys.

"Oh, Massa, that is a very bad snake, you must have some native medicine."

I had been warned against native medicine but I recalled my tuition on the Colonial Service course up at Cambridge in Tropical Hygiene. We were taught that when bitten by a snake you should rub pot permanganate into the area after having cut open the part bitten. I did not feel very much like doing that on my head.

But the other instruction was to apply a tourniquet at a point nearer to the heart. This would mean putting a strangle-hold round my neck, and I didn't think that was much good either. The final remedy was to drink some spirits, so I asked my boy, or rather intimated to him, to bring me some whisky. I put this in my mouth, but I was quite unable to swallow. The liquid just came down my nose. I could not talk for I was unable to articulate. My eyes remained closed for there were no muscles able to lift my eyelids. I could not even get rid of my saliva. I was completely paralysed from the neck up. My head swelled right up and as I pressed my finger into it left a great hole, showing it to be oedematous. 'Baby' Taylor did come along finally and saw me in this poor shape and he sent off to the nearest doctor, who was at Makeni, 80 miles away. He came the following evening, when the effects of the venom of the green mamba, as the snake turned out to be, had begun to wear off. He gave me an anti-venom injection, for what it was worth at that late hour, but he said that I really was lucky at being bitten on the head, for the venom had to go through my thick hair, which must have absorbed some, and then the blood vessels in the scalp are very small and so comparatively little of the venom got into my system at a time and the body defence mechanism was able to deal with it. He said that if I had been bitten in the arm or leg I would surely have been a goner!

Owing to the white corpuscles which are the body's mechanism for fighting infection having been excessively over-produced by the lymphatic gland I got quite sick and was sent home after a year instead of 18 months which was the normal tour. I also got a lot of malaria. However I got perfectly well on leave and came back for my second tour when I acted for a spell as ADC to the Governor.

Another incident was when I was acting as DC in Nkolili District and was out on trek. I had fetched up at a Rest House and the Doctor from my HQ, Bill Quin, happened to arrive at this same Rest House, he also being out on trek, a coincidence which never occurred again. After having supper together we went to bed and in the middle of the night I was awakened by a messenger from a Paramount Chief asking me to come to his town immediately as a European had killed one of his subjects. If a dead body was concerned I thought that this was right up the doctor's street, so I asked my boys to waken the doctor so that he could accompany me to the scene of the shooting. There was a man called Opey, an engineer from a Mining Company, whom the Chief said had shot the African, so I asked him about it. He said that all he had been doing the previous evening was to shoot at tins which he had chucked in the river Sewa, a very big river, and as the swift-flowing stream carried the tins down he shot at them to practise his accuracy. He had a .22 rifle.

The dead body of a young African was laid out on the verandah of a house, so I asked Bill Quin if he could find the bullet which had killed the boy, and he set to work to carve the body up. I was fascinated with the meticulous manner in which he did this, and he could see where the bullet had gone through the heart. He then put his hand to the back of the African and just under the skin he could feel the bullet. The bullet matched the rifle which Opey had been using. Bill Quin was at that time working for his FRCS and I wondered whether he purposely did his dissection in the front to get some practice. The bullet matched Opey's .22 rifle, so it was clear how the African had met his end. The evening before, he had been lying up on the steep bank in thick bush which came right down to the river, with a string tied on to his big toe, on the other end of which was a baited hook. He would lie up there, invisible to anyone on the opposite bank, and probably go to sleep until he felt a tug at his toe when he would wake up and play the fish. The chances were millions to one against, but somehow one of Opey's shots must have ricocheted off either a tin or the water itself and bored its way through the bush into the African's heart. I had to hold an enquiry and it was clear that there was no guilt on Opey's part, but a young African had been killed whose dependants must be compensated. I decided that Opey, or his Company, should pay to the African's family the sum of £20 with which all agreed. That was in 1937.

Early in 1939 I was out on trek collecting tax and hearing complaints when I got an urgent message from an iron ore mining company, Sierra Leone Development Co, to come to their HQ at Lunsar because 4,000 of their labourers had gone on strike and things were looking very bad. I left all the tax, several thousand pounds, for the clerk to get back to my HQ, Port Loko, and with four Court Messengers set off to walk to the nearest motor road, 10 miles away, to get a lorry and then drive on the 40 miles to Lunsar. As I approached the mine I saw a large band of Africans, all armed with sticks and looking bellicose. I then noticed that they had felled the palm trees on the side of the road, thus preventing any vehicles getting up to the mine. The DC always wore a blue band round his topi, and the Africans knew that he was impartial and when I got out of the lorry and they saw this they became more friendly. I asked them to pull the palm trees off the road so that we could get up to the mine, and this they did. There were 40 Europeans up at the mine and the Manager said that the Company would not parley under duress and if they would go back to work they might consider the increase in pay the labourers were demanding. The Company wanted to give them more rice to improve their diet and thus get more work out of them, but the labourers wanted more money. Then I got a message from the Government in Freetown to the effect that I must get the labourers back to work, for the iron ore which the company produced was needed in England for armaments which were then being built up in preparation for the War. I asked the Government to let me have 30 more Court Messengers from other Districts, which they provided. Each morning I used to hold a meeting on the football field and ask the labourers to go back to work and then the company would consider increasing their pay, with or without more rice. Each time they refused to go back to work.

I had to do something so I asked the Army to let me have a platoon of troops to be kept in reserve. Col Woolner, the OC of the Battalion of RWAFF, came up and said to me, "You know, Pat, if you call us in, a soldier shoots to kill." Oh Gosh, I thought, this is reminiscent of my namesake, Sir

Michael O'Dwyer, Governor of the Punjab, and of General Dyer before the First World War. I asked the Court Messengers to get as many labourers as they could on to the football field the next morning and I would ask them finally to go back to work, after which the Company would talk. I made the plan that if they continued to refuse, then each of the 34 Court Messengers should grab the labourer standing next to him and frog-march him up the hill to the alluvial iron ore mine and set him to work. If this plan failed, and there was chaos, then the RWAFF troops, hidden out of sight in the adjoining bush would be called in to keep order. Well, they would not go back to work: I gave the signal, the Court Messengers frog-marched each adjacent African up the hill and put a shovel in his hand, to put the iron ore onto a conveyor belt, thence onto a railway which went down through the country to the shore at Pepel and onto a ship bound to England. All the other labourers seemed so stunned at seeing their colleagues going up the hill and starting to work that they followed and the strike was over.

OP 54 (October 1987)

Sierra Leone

The first badge for Sierra Leone, dating from 1889, depicted an elephant standing under a palm tree, with the letters SL below. The same badge was introduced for the Gold Coast and for Gambia but with the letters GC and G respectively instead. In 1914 a new badge was used, being a shield divided into three parts. The top third was the union flag, as it had been prior to 1801, with only the cross of St. George for England and the saltire for Scotland – before the addition of St Patrick's cross. The lower part of the shield had two upright sections, one showing a liberated slave sitting by the sea-shore with a ship beyond, and the other showing a palm tree. Underneath the shield is the motto in Latin "Auspice Britannia Liber" (Free Under Britain's Protection).

The Solomon Islands in the 1930s

by R A Lever

Fifty years ago the capital of the then-styled British Solomon Islands Protectorate was concentrated on the southern end of the small island of Tulagi, itself tucked into the larger Florida island. The site had been chosen in 1893 on account of its more or less central position and the possession of a good harbour with depths of up to 27 fathoms. On an Empire cruise in the early 'twenties, Admiral Lord Jellicoe was looking for a site for a Far Eastern Naval base for which, of course, the final choice was Singapore – but one cannot help wondering how events would have gone had the giant graving dock been constructed in the Solomon Islands.

Tulagi was virtually destroyed during its capture from the Japanese by the United States Marine Corps in 1942 and a large hutted camp on Guadalcanal was developed into the new capital of Honiara which has since spread from the coast into the adjacent foothills. The first residency there was built out of the remains of a disused casualty clearing station left behind by New Zealand forces – it had to be content with a thatch roof made from palm fronds.

Although Tulagi had the usual complement of hospital, post office, prison, wireless station, Lands, Survey and Public Works Department (under one roof) and Treasury, Customs and Excise (under another one), yet by 1935 there was no lunatic asylum, or schools. This probably unique set-up for the capital of a dependency was simply due to the system adopted whereby grants were made to the missions (there were five brands of Christianity) in return for non-sectarian education in addition, of course, for propagation of their particular religious beliefs. This anomalous system was soon changed and both schools and an asylum were in operation just before the last war.

As in most, if not all, tropical colonies, after-office activities were centred on the golf and tennis club, a timber building perched on concrete piles built for under-floor ventilation and to repel white ants. On the evening of Steamer Day – the six weekly arrival from Australia of mail and stores – a larger than usual turn-up could be assured with a determination to obtain a copy of the brown-covered *Times Weekly* or *Punch* while sipping a pink gin or a 'schooner' of Australian lager. These would have been served by the unflappable Ah Sui – doubtless to-day carrying trays of nectar in some choice Chinese valhalla.

The 9-hole golf course played a more important role than in larger communities and the final hole, with one's back to the south-west headland past a row of coconut palms, was done in good time before the sudden sunset. It had proved impossible to have proper greens so rolled laterite 'browns' had to suffice. These were kept in tip-top condition by long-term prisoners (mostly murderers from Malaita) and as the Commissioner of Police was one of the keenest players, a good surface was provided for the first players each evening. Golf balls, if driven more than a very few yards into the rough, were liable to disappear down holes made by land crabs; a cadet who arrived the same year that I went on transfer, writes of fiendish coconut crabs which actually 'bore off one's ball' – but then we all know that the Administrative Service tended to have ways of their own!

It is axiomatic that no capital is representative of the country and I was fortunate in that my work as an entomologist enabled me to do a fair amount of travel thus avoiding what must have been a humdrum life for those tied to their desks. As attempts at descriptive travelogues are clearly not expected here, I shall simply recall some impressions of a few of the larger islands forming a double chain extending for some 600 miles to the south-east of Papua New Guinea. Owing to Guadalcanal being the main island during the Solomon Islands campaign, it changed almost overnight from an unknown place to a household word. Its shape was described by an American scientist as similar to that of *Paramecium* which is helpful if one knows this is popularly known as the slipper animalcule. It measures some 80 miles and has the unusual character of miles of grassy plains along its northern coast, in addition to mountain peaks over 8,000 feet high which is better than anything throughout the continent of Australia. Gold mining was developed in a small way in the thirties which is a matter of historical interest as the first Spanish explorers as early as 1568 made unsuccessful efforts at prospecting in one river.

The most populous island of Malaita, which supplies the bulk of the plantation labour force, has the unusual distinction of one village having persons who are able to call porpoises from their depths to approach the coast. While most people tend to claim that some part of 'their' colony, whether Mauritius, Fiji or Grenada, is unrivalled for some particular piece of scenery, a very good claim can be advanced for the Marovo lagoon on the scattered group known as New Georgia which also includes the conical Kolombangara with its extinct volcanic crater.

The system of government calls for some remarks as the Solomons, as well as the New Hebrides (now Vanuatu) to the south-east, were both administered by a Resident Commissioner responsible to the High Commissioner in Fiji who was also Governor of that Colony. It is easy to see what an impracticable system this was in view of the great distances separating the different dependencies involved, and without air mail it was only to be expected that the RCs played for safety by referring tricky questions to Suva.

A personal experience of this occurred over an isolated island called Rennell whose inhabitants had at this time not been converted and so aroused professional jealousy between some of the more aggressive missionaries. As a result, the island had been officially declared a 'protected' or special area denied any visits from ships. It so happened that its fauna was unknown, thus being of interest to the Natural History Museum, South Kensington. Accordingly, I had been given a letter from the then Director asking if a visit could be arranged sometime in order to secure specimens. The RC quite naturally felt it safer to forbid my going there with the result that I had the mortification of seeing a visiting American yacht being granted a permit on grounds of not being members of the BSIP government. Hence a fine series of new species of birds, fish, reptiles and insects were secured for US museums which normally would have become accessions to the national collections in London. When a British and Danish team went there after the war they were successful in getting a new species of bat.

Some three years before my arrival, there had been a most regrettable murder of a District Officer, his cadet and a dozen native constables. The rising, due to resentment at paying head tax, was soon put down but in certain parts of the same island of Malaita there were standing orders that an escort had to be provided. Shortly after setting out from my quarters came the first of several sudden showers – annual rainfall ranged from 80 to 120 inches – resulting in my escort each time taking shelter under the thickest tree. The reason for this turned out to be a desire to keep the bolt and sling of his rifle dry so as to save him extra work with an oily rag and khaki blanco on his return to barracks. The armed native constabulary was a well-organised force and in those days wore nothing above the waist. The difference between then and now can be seen in the local stamps where the 1d of King George VI shows the pre-war uniform in contrast to the 10/- of 1956 with a rifle-less constable now wearing a long-sleeved tunic.

A good working knowledge of the native language is something which has to be acquired in every colony but, probably uniquely, in the Solomons the official language was so-called 'pidgin English', of which a few examples are provided. Certain words have a restricted meaning: thus 'behind' means later, never to the rear, and similarly 'before' refers to the past as in 'time before'. Harder to get used to is the word 'kill', pidgin for to hurt or injure, while for the real word 'kill' it is necessary to say 'kill die finish'. 'Me look him one fella Mary' means I saw a woman. 'Altogether me no savvy' is I don't understand at all. Lastly 'Shootilight him e bugger up finish' means the torch (battery) is no good – used for a lamp would show that the wick is useless. To those who have had to swot Swahili, Fijian or Malay, it might seem that pidgin was child's play but to speak it well, using only the accepted words in the vocabulary, is much harder than it might be expected by those who have not tried it.

In retrospect, the most significant feature about pre-war life in the BSIP was the permanently acute shortage of cash available both for development and administration. This stemmed from the inflexible Colonial Office rule that every dependency must be self-sufficient financially so that one could have only what one could afford. In our case, we were virtually dependent for revenue on the dues for copra exports, the exceptions being kauri and other timber and a commodity known as ivory nuts from a species of palm. Unfortunately, the price on the world market for copra continued to fall during the thirties so that we were in the position of always having to cut all but essential expenses. Three years before his death, the RC of my time wrote a letter to me containing these words: 'I wonder if any of you fellows . . . realised how difficult it was to work with no money in the kitty . . . However, that is all over and today the Treasury is overflowing with milk and honey.' Never were there truer words as witnessed by current official reports from which it is seen that a training college and a technical institute exist as well as a philatelic section run by the postal authorities. With taxis, cinemas, three clubs and three hotels at Honiara, the present capital is a metropolis compared with Tulagi.

OP 44 (November 1982)

Emergency Days, Malaya 1948-50

by R R H Horsley

In June 1948 I was due to sail for Malaya from King George V Dock and was to be seen off by a man who had been with me at a mine on the Gold Coast. I found him in our appointed bar with an *Evening Standard* spread out. He waited for me to read its banner headline: *TWO BRITONS MURDERED IN MALAYA*, then he smiled, saying, "Are you still going?"

The communists, nearly all Chinese, who as the Malayan Peoples' Anti-Japanese Army had co-operated with our Force 136 as guerrillas throughout the Occupation, had begun their attempt to take over the country which they'd hoped to complete by 3rd August that year.

Posted to Kuala Lumpur for training in the Department of Mines, I followed the fashion by enrolling as a Special Constable (SC), and on evening parades went on patrols by jeep and truck to outlying rubber estates. I suppose we kept the roads open, warned the Communist Terrorists (CT) – also known as bandits – that there was opposition, and gave fleeting encouragement to the planters and their staff and families in their barbed-wire perimeters. But when *we* went back to our secure town, *they* stayed, ensiled in estate and jungle through night and day, answering from time to time the police radio contacts to show that they'd not been over-run.

I showed my rawness one morning when I visited a patch of land some ten miles from town to assess the potential for tin prospecting. I drove off the road along a rough track as far as I could go by car, then walked on. It was wild and deserted, mainly neglected rubber estate that was over-growing with weeds and untapped, because the CTs would hack and ruin the trees if it were operated without payment of protection money. After half an hour without sight or sound of a person, I got back to the road and sat there in my car to make my notes. Traffic was negligible, but a large saloon, ponderous from its armoured lining, its driver peering through the slit in the steel windscreen, passed me and drew up fifty yards ahead. A head observed me from a half-opened door, then a burly planter with pistol on belt and tommy-gun in hand plodded back to me with one of his Malay SCs. He was scowling, When I'd explained who I was and what I'd been doing, he made some rather emphatic remarks, ending with, "You don't stop here! This is bandit country!!" So I set off back to civilization.

After four months of city life, my posting to my first Inspectorate sent me a hundred miles north to Tapah. As I set off from the Lake Club where I'd been staying, a wit asked if there were any special points I'd like mentioned in my obituary. Tapah was a small town astride the Federation's main road, nestling against the jungled range of hills. Through the Occupation, the MPAJA and Force 136 had been very active in the area, as admirably described by Spencer Chapman in *The Jungle is Neutral.* The CTs still thrived there, had recently raided and temporarily occupied the police station at Bidor about four miles south, and one of their main westward tracks, along which they'd shepherded Spencer Chapman to a submarine rendezvous off Pangkor Island, ran through a group of 'my' mines. My work was to include the inspection of mines distributed mainly within a fifteen-mile radius, including five European-owned dredges and some sixty opencast alluvial mines, nearly all Chinese-owned. The handing-over report from my predecessor, who was glad to be going, said that because of the Emergency only half the mines could be visited. I ignored that.

Liaison with the police was easy; we were a small community of government officers in Tapah. I could give them information about the mines and miners of the area; they stored explosives belonging to 'my' miners; they advised and provided escorts for when I wished to visit outlying areas. But such occasions, when my Hillman coupé bristled with the rifles of constables, produced nothing more exciting than the odd pile of steaming elephant-dung or a fresh tiger pug.

Once I was more heavily guarded. Apparently the CTs had sabotaged a water-conduit that brought water for several mines down from the hills behind Bidor. The mines were idle and I had to assess the damage and the potential for repair. The police insisted on an escort, and I was provided with a platoon of the Coldstream Guards who were stationed in Tapah. Their patrol drill was impeccable; we moved through the jungle, climbing alongside the water-conduit silent and alert, for four to five miles, found and inspected the damage, safely returned. We had no alarm except a momentary one during a halt; a rustle of vegetation above us on a bank, we tensed, a monitor lizard apparently four feet from head to tail and about eighteen inches high at the shoulders, a veritable baby dragon, looked us over and with a flick of its head withdrew, disgusted. I thought it a pity that the halt had been for a brew of cha; my Madras Sappers in Burma five years earlier would have gone the five hours on water-bottles.

In my routine visiting of mines, I went alone or with a Malay or Chinese assistant, 9mm pistol at hip, unannounced, where possible returning by an alternative route. Such was easy; but at an opencast mine five miles out of Tapah up a valley towards the hills, the English manager (a rarity at such mines) showed me how far the CTs had got on a night raid at his bungalow before he and his special constables had driven them off; it was into his kitchen.

A new District Officer, perhaps zealously acquainting himself with the duties of his fellows at Tapah, asked if he could do a morning round with me. We drew off the main road near Temoh, three or four miles out of Tapah, to walk the hundred yards to the Chinese-owned and managed gravel-pump mine. It was a shallow dish, a hundred yards across and up to fifty feet deep to irregular limestone bedrock, the far side reaching to the foot of a slope with scrubby jungle. We'd gone only yards, there was a crack, then the whining of a ricochet. We ducked and halted, looked at one another.

"Was that what I thought it was, a shot?" said my companion.

I nodded. But there were no more. We went on and I showed him that representative mine, and he left me to carry on with my morning. He may have got the impression that I lived a risky life! But I shouldn't have remembered that incident without another at that mine a week or two later.

My most distant visits were to a dredge property about thirty miles south of Tapah on the main road and then four miles up the narrow valley of the Slim River that drained off the main range. The company were deviating the river section by section, and dredging the old channel for its wealth of tin ore. Their staff existed in a close assembly of wooden houses with offices and stores enclosed in a high barbed-wire perimeter fence, from which through the eleven hours of darkness lamps blazed from tall poles out to the jungle and anybody who might be watching from it. The track up the valley wound between the river and patches of jungle and stretches of idle rubber estate, to serve for the company vehicles and a small bus to the company's kampong and for a few local Malays.

On my last visit, I was invited for coffee to the manager's house. They were living on the upper floor, with a verandah around the house. Outside each doorway from interior to verandah was a sand-bagged breastwork, in addition to extensive breastworks around the ground-floor that were manned by their Malay guards. Most evenings they endured some sniping, and could never know whether this was merely routine annoyance or the prelude to a major attack on the perimeter. About fortnightly, the manager's wife took a trip in their armoured saloon with escorting constables in jeeps, down the valley and fifty or sixty miles to Kuala Lumpur for her shopping and a hair-do. Perhaps she always had been tall and rather thin, but I felt that the frequent sideways spasm of neck and the tic at a side of the mouth might have recent origins.

OP 63 (April 1992)

Fish Bombs and Copra

by Peter Burbrook

After 4 years in the Indian Army in Persia and Iraq, followed by attendance at the 'First Devonshire Course' in Oxford, I, with my young wife, arrived in January 1948 at Jesselton, capital of North Borneo, otherwise known as *The Land Below the Wind*. We loved it from the moment we first saw it in the early morning light, with Mount Kinabalu's 13,300ft peak as a backdrop. Five months later I was posted as Cadet-in-Charge, Semporna, a tiny isolated mainly fishing community on the south-east coast of the Colony. To the south lay the Celebes Sea, to the east the Sulu Sea and beyond that, the Philippines. I had spent six months in London learning the rudiments of Malay, so as nobody in Semporna except my wife, the Medical Dresser, my clerk and I spoke English, my knowledge of Malay blossomed rapidly.

The township consisted of a couple of dozen Chinese shops, and an 'eating shop' run by a local Moslem. A large number of fish-drying platforms stood out over the water and countless small boats housed the Sea Bajau community. The hinterland was sparsely populated by Bajaus who had 'come ashore'. An old fort with its six inch thick iron-wood walls dominated the scene. It housed the six man police contingent, my office and our only contact with the outer world – an ex-army, two-way radio. Our house, rough-hewn timber with a palm thatch roof, stood by the sea-shore. Its covered verandah faced east, out over the sea. An idyllic setting in a place well-named Semporna, which in Malay means 'beautiful'.

It was at a period when copra (the dried inner flesh of the coconut) was a prohibited export. Coconuts abounded in the Sub-District. Post-war shortages included vegetable oils: copra produces that commodity, hence the prohibition. One day, about six months after our arrival, I had an unexpected visit by the Commissioner of Customs (Martin), the Preventive Officer (Tom), together with his drug-sniffing Alsatian (Cobber), and the new High Court Judge (Sir Ivor). They all arrived on the large sea-going customs launch, the *Malawali*. Our intrepid cook, under my wife's anxious eye, produced a wonderful Malay curry dinner for the occasion. Our kerosene fridge did us proud, with a plentiful supply of ice-cold beer. Martin explained that he and Tom were on a tour of inspection, and Sir Ivor on a familiarisation tour of the

Colony. "Since you've been here you've been very successful collaring several copra smugglers, I hear," he went on.

I, of course, was a jack-of-all-trades; Admin Officer, fledgling Magistrate, Assistant Collector of Land Revenue, Customs Officer – you name it – I only had to reach behind me for the appropriate hat. Embarrassed I stammered, "Nothing much really – "

"Come off it Peter," laughed Tom, "nearly had yourself blown up for your trouble by a fish bomb a few weeks ago".

"What on earth's a fish bomb?" Sir Ivor wanted to know.

"Black powder and small pebbles," I explained, "well wrapped in tough brown paper and bound with rattan cane. A detonator and a short fuse sets it off. Thrown in the water it will stun a shoal of fish – easy fishing, but ecologically devastating."

"Nasty," commented the judge, "obviously it missed its target, though."

I nodded, hoping to change the subject. Martin came to the rescue. "I'd like you to take us out, Peter – catch some smugglers for us. What do you say?"

I pondered that unhappily for a moment then had an inspiration. "Can't guarantee anything, but I suspect Si Amil Island is making hay, so to speak. I can't get there in my little outboard, but the *Malawali* could."

"Right then," said Martin, making up his mind at once, "We sail at dawn. Tom, would you please tell the skipper?" Tom nodded.

"I suggest we take an armed constable also," I suggested.

And so it was. We set off at six. Margaret came with us as well as PC Abdul with his .303 rifle. We sailed past beautiful islands with names like Bohi Duland, Menampilik and Nusatonga before arriving several hours later at Si Amil, 30 miles offshore. As we motored into the lagoon, to my amazement and delight, round behind a headland, lay two Philippine kumpits in the shallows, shored up obviously awaiting the high tide. A quick look through the binoculars confirmed my suspicions. They were loaded to the gunwales with sacks, almost certainly copra. Tons of it. As the launch felt her way cautiously into the lagoon, we saw the villagers running along the beach, still about a mile away. They would stop every now and then, bend over then run on again.

"Curious," commented Martin, "what the hell are they up to?"

None of us could offer any suggestions. The inflatable dinghy was launched and into it piled Martin (handling the motor), Tom and Cobber, Sir Ivor, PC Abdul and his rifle, and myself up in the bows getting very wet. By the time we reached the shore the beach was deserted – something of an anticlimax. I led our party to the shade of the palm trees which lined the beach. A few moments later Ali Yusof, the Village Headman, attracted by all the noise and excitement joined us. After the usual exchange of greetings, I introduced him to the others. We sat smoking and chatting quietly in Malay for a while, before I casually asked the headman about the two foreign craft in the lagoon; and about the extraordinary behaviour of the villagers on the beach earlier. After exchanging a few quiet words with his henchmen he turned to me with a rather bleak smile. "*Al-hamdu-lillah*, my people are happy. We have been doing some trading with our friends from Mindanao, Tuan."

I sat silently puffing at my pipe – waiting for him to go on.

"Nothing much you understand." His lower lip was thrust out to emphasise the triviality of the matter. He drew out his words slowly. "Some dried fish, a few turtle eggs, some trochus shells, in exchange for – um – a few trinkets . . . " he ended lamely.

"Rather a lot of dried fish, turtle eggs and shells for a few trinkets?" I suggested looking pointedly at the overladen kumpits.

Ali Yusof continued to sit there, silent, his eyes down-cast, drawing idle patterns in the sand with his left foot. Meanwhile Tom, accompanied by PC Abdul and Cobber, who had wandered down to the beach, sauntered back towards us, a couple of shining aluminium saucepans in his hand and a bolt of bright red cloth under one arm. "Astonishing what you find beach-combing. Wonder where this lot came from?" he asked, holding up his trophies with a broad smile.

PC Abdul, likewise grinning, was laden with more stuff. Assisted by Cobber they had found all sorts of goods lightly buried under the sand along the beach. This explained the villagers' earlier behaviour. Ali Yusof sighed and told the villagers to dig up all the bartered goods and deliver them to him. Out of the sand came a great selection of goods, iron cooking pots, brightly coloured sarongs, cartons of cigarettes, oil lamps, knives, to name but a few of them. The village children, hesitant at first, soon got the idea and joined in the game. Their bright eyes shone above their delightful smiles as they dumped yet another heap of contraband at Ali Yusof's feet before rushing off excitedly for more. Their parents, gathered glumly in the background, were not quite so amused. Martin, in his capacity as Commissioner of Customs, speaking in Malay, took over. "These are clearly smuggled goods and are therefore seized by Customs. Likewise the copra and the two kumpits. You know what's loaded in the kumpits don't you, Ali Yusof. My colleague here will confirm this shortly," he ended with a nod to Tom standing nearby.

Ali Yusof made no comment but just sighed. I then stepped in wearing my magisterial 'hat', having already quickly discussed the situation with Martin.

"As Village Headman you are aware of the law, are you not, Ali Yusof?" He nodded glumly.

"Well, we have decided seizing the copra and all the goods will be enough punishment. The matter will not be taken any further, but don't get caught again".

"Tuan is generous and we must accept his decision. With Allah's help we shall try to mend our ways," the Headman said, looking rather solemn, which I thought he had every reason to.

"Good." Martin ended the discussion, "Please send for the kumpits' crews and get your people to help load all the contraband goods onto the *Malawali*. We must set off for Semporna on the tide."

Later, with all the contraband stowed away in the *Malawali's* hold, together with seven very surly captive Bugis crewmen, the convoy moved out of the lagoon with the two copra-laden kumpits in tow. Sitting on the raised stern deck of the last vessel PC Abdul looked very pleased with himself, his rifle across his knees and a large torch on the deck beside him. A young Bugis seaman, the eighth member of the smugglers' crews, sat by him quite cheerfully as steersman. The disgruntled villagers lining the beach looked anything but happy. The raiding party, having said their farewells, shook hands with Ali Yusof who managed a bleak smile, as if to say. "*Insha Allah,* you'll not catch me again!"

"No," I thought, interpreting his look, "probably not, *Allah* willing".

On the way back to Semporna well after sunset, we ran into foul weather in the shape of a *Sumatra,* a vicious line squall, feared by small vessels in those waters. It caught us unawares, and, in the confusion the captive crews escaped, fought their way to freedom, leapt onto the leading kumpit and cut the two ropes. Our two prizes, carrying with them PC Abdul, vanished down-wind into the night. These storms are short-lived but the wind remained strong enough for the smugglers to be unable to hoist their sails. With order restored and our fears for PC Abdul's life driving us into hectic action, we set off at full speed in pursuit. In the darkness ahead we suddenly saw a few quick torch flashes and distinctly heard the sound of a .303 rifle being fired. With the launch's search lamp on, it was not long before we spotted a kumpit wallowing in the sea a short distance ahead of us. As we drew alongside it, there, to our intense relief, was PC Abdul on the after-deck. He stood, torch in one hand, rifle in the other, legs astride the tiller, facing an unhappy looking group of Bugis seamen cowering in the bows.

"*Akhbar!* You've arrived only just in time, I have only one round left and they have their parangs out ready to cut me into fish bait," he laughed.

We never saw nor heard of the second boat again, but Martin, like Tom, was delighted with what we had achieved, though the near loss of PC Abdul cost Martin a few white hairs, he had to admit. Had I been older than my 26 years I would probably have ended up with completely white hair. Sir Ivor and Margaret seemed to have thoroughly enjoyed themselves, and my reputation as 'smuggler hunter' was raised.

OP 84 (October 2002)

North Borneo

After North Borneo had become a Crown Colony in 1946, having previously been administered by the British North Borneo Company, the crest of the Company's coat of arms became the badge of the colony. It depicts two human arms, differing in colour and size – representing the people of North Borneo and the British – grasping a flagpole with a small yellow flag flying to the right. The small flag bears a red lion, which had been the badge of the Company since the 1880s.

A New Town Plan for Zuru

by N C McClintock

With only two months experience in Northern Nigeria in 1947, and speaking hardly a word of the language, I had been sent to take charge of Zuru only for want of somebody better. But here I was now, with sergeant-major Bagudu to show me the ropes and to keep me out of trouble with the Zuru Native Authority, a federation of five small chiefdoms, to look after. My first task, I had been told, must be to get on and implement that new town plan for Zuru. For Zuru had grown up over the years at the foot of the hills with no sort of planning whatsoever. It was now an unsightly and insanitary huddle of huts which was fast becoming an African slum, and something would have to be done about it. So the services of the Town Planning Officer had been called upon. Of course the Town Planning Officer was too distant and too busy a man to visit Zuru himself, but a sketch map of the place had been sent to him, and working from this he had produced a new Town Plan for Zuru. It was in front of me now and very fine it looked, with special areas set aside for public buildings, for schools and playing fields, for a new market area and a lorry park, and with wide avenues sweeping boldly up in this direction and in that.

But the more I studied it the more my hesitations grew. For a start it seemed a pity that the finest feature of the present town would have to be destroyed. This was an avenue of noble silk-cotton trees through which the approach road ran, but the new road would cut across it at an angle of thirty degrees. And then there was this borrow pit, an enormous great pit from which the earth had been dug to build the present town, but this had not been shown on the sketch map sent to the Town Planner, and the road to the market would now have to plunge down into it and up the other side again. Nor had our new wells been shown on the sketch map, and these now appeared in the most inconvenient places, in the middle of a playing field for instance, or in a private compound.

And then, as I studied the plan further, the final nonsense appeared; the scale had been wrongly shown on the original sketch map, and so the Town Planner's roads were twice as wide as he had intended and his compounds were four times the size.

I was new to Nigeria and I now made the mistake of reporting these difficulties and asking what I should do. I might have saved myself the trouble, for I was abruptly told simply to make whatever adjustments were necessary and get on with it. So I said goodbye to the Town Planner's plan and made my own. With a hand-held compass and a chain I surveyed the area afresh (a little fudging was necessary, but it looked all right in the end), and then I drew my own town plan upon it.

Now we were back where we had started and I had to implement the thing. And here I struck the next difficulty, for it appeared that only £100 had been provided in the Native Authority's estimates for the work to be done and, even at the prices ruling in those days, this was altogether insufficient. But the five chiefs of Zuru were not at all put out.

"Oh, but we don't need to pay for it", they said, "we can call in the *gwolmo* youths to do the work for us free of charge and then we can spend the money on drummers for them and free beer. The *gwolmo* youths are under contract to work for their fathers-in-law anyway, and it will make no difference if they work for us instead."

It seemed to me that it would make all the difference in the world. This sounded altogether too much like forced labour, and forced labour in Africa was a very hot potato in those days. However, I could see no other way of getting the work done, so after checking up to see that no important visitors who might object were expected to come to Zuru in the next few weeks, I gave my approval.

And so the *gwolmo* youths came in from the district around, hundreds of them at a time and set about the work with a will. After all, they thought, what could be more fun than knocking down the whole of Zuru town, and with free beer and drummers too. For three weeks the noise, the dust and the confusion were indescribable, but in a surprisingly short time a brand new town arose upon the ashes of the old, and everybody seemed pleased. Indeed I found that those who had been loudest in the 'Hands off our lovely town' campaign before the work started, were now the first to exclaim how beautiful the new town looked.

But all this needs explaining. Who were the *gwolmo* youths? Well, the *gwolmo* youths were a feature of the peculiar social system of the Dakakari, a system which ensured that the young men were kept under firm control and were usefully employed until the age of 25 or so, when they were free to marry and settle down.

At the age of 13 a Dakakari boy would join his village wrestling club.

Wrestling was to Zuru what football is in England; it was the national sport and a consuming passion, before which all other interests would fade away. The victories of champion wrestlers were celebrated in song and verse and every young man aspired to be a champion himself. So now for the next five years the growing lad would be a wrestler and one of a very select club, the pampered hopefuls of this village; he was fed like a fighting cock, no farm work was expected of him but, with the other members of the club, he would spend his time travelling around the Zuru area and wrestling there in every village in turn.

In the evenings, after the active business of the market had finished in town or village, a circle would be formed, a circle of loudly enthusiastic and knowledgeable spectators. The boys would seat themselves around the circle, each village in a little group by itself. Then a boy from here would go across and challenge a boy of similar size and weight from another village. and soon there would be four or five pairs wrestling simultaneously in the circle. The dust and the noise would be indescribable as the crowd roared on their favourites, and self-appointed stewards would be holding the ring and keeping the spectators back with whips and curses. After each throw the victor would run across and kneel in front of the principal spectator, one of the chiefs perhaps, or the ADO, to be rewarded with a kola nut or a penny pressed upon his sweating forehead.

This would be the boy's life for five years, but then the word would be given that the class of 1945 had now passed out and he would enter upon the next phase of his life cycle. By this time he had travelled widely throughout the land of Zuru, visiting and wrestling in every village in turn, and by this time he had seen, and had been seen, and admired by every girl there was. By now he had chosen his bride and now he would have to work for her. As Jacob worked seven years for Rachel, so he would work seven years for his beloved.

But this would not be a simple one-to-one contract between him and his father-in law to be; rather he would now become a member of his *gwolmo* club, a club comprising all the young men doing their *gwolmo* service for their fathers-in-law in a given area. Early every morning now in the farming season, the club would parade and the members would be allotted by the sergeant-majors to the farms on which they were to work today.

"Dan Baro needs three men; you three, off you go. Audu has asked for five; you four from here, and yes, Musa, you can go with them today."

And there would be a purpose to this, for Musa was a bumptious young man who needed to be taken down a peg or two, and today he would have to work alongside four men all older and stronger than himself. From the moment they arrived on the farm in mid-morning until the sun went down that evening they would be hard at work without a break. Dressed only in a leather loincloth, alongside each other in line abreast, they would be hoeing between the lines of guinea corn at a furious, frenetic pace, and woe betide the man who could not keep up. Musa would be worked today until, literally, he dropped from fatigue, and everybody would hear of it and would have a good laugh at his expense.

OP 64 (October 1992), OP 65 (April 1993)

Nigeria

This badge was adopted by Sir Frederick (later Lord) Lugard, for the Protectorate of Northern Nigeria, of which he was the first "High Commissioner" in 1900. When the North was amalgamated with Southern Nigeria in 1914 the badge became that of the whole territory. The design is of a six-pointed star formed by two interlaced triangles, with the Crown at the centre, on a round red field, usually shown as a disc. It is claimed that the design stems from a traditional ritual emblem of the Ibo peoples of South-Eastern Nigeria, although Lord Lugard says he came across it on a goblet he found in the North.

Lamu Town

by Peter Lloyd

The ancient Arab town of Lamu is on an island off the north-east coast of Kenya. I first went there some fifty years ago, to serve as District Commissioner. The place was magical. Enchanted, I fell under its spell. It was a full day's drive away from Mombasa. An exhausting drive too, more than two hundred miles of dusty road which became progressively bumpier – when it was passable at all. Floods closed it for about six months each year. To a young bachelor this proved a blessing. Visits by Higher Authority were never inconveniently frequent. Moreover elephant often knocked over the poles which carried the telephone line, cutting off communications. So there was plenty of scope for local initiative. Which of course made the job more interesting.

Nobody really wanted to interfere in any case, provided that Lamu remained a haven of peace at a time when the Mau Mau Emergency was afflicting parts of up-country Kenya. The need was to keep its population happy. That required little effort, for most of them regarded all forms of change with the gravest suspicion. The town itself reflected their attitude, being the epitome of changelessness. As just one example, my palatial residence had been completed in 1892, yet everybody still called it 'the new house'.

And what a house! Despite the absence of both electricity and piped water and the presence of a multitude of bats, it was a palace of delights. So vast that I occupied only a small part of the building. Much of the remainder was used by the station carpenter, or by the launch crew, or by other unidentified individuals, to store supplies. Whole families were established elsewhere in it, claiming to be descendants of slaves of its original owner, with squatters' rights. In return they performed odd jobs, like bringing up water from the cistern. I even discovered, after living there for several months, that someone had started a shop in the back premises and seemed to have a flourishing business.

The district's chief delight was nevertheless the variety and charm of its inhabitants. Foremost amongst them, setting the tone, was the Liwali, who had a name straight out of the Arabian Nights – Sheikh Azan bin Rashid. He looked the part, too, with a spotless *kanzu* of dazzling white, a beautifully embroidered cap, a long grey beard and very impressive dignity.

His was a measured pace as he walked with stately tread along the seafront promenade, pausing to greet each acquaintance. You had to do likewise, for it was the sort of society which believed that 'Manners Makyth Man'. Haste was deprecated as discourteous; and discourtesy could soon have bred discontent.

Besides, you could learn a lot during an evening stroll. Those whom you would be likely to meet included friendly Bajun from the north-east of the district. They might have come in coastal dhows, bringing poles they had cut in the mangrove forests there. Or perhaps they had just been lured for a few days to the big city by its reputation. The town was not really that large, but it reputedly offered pleasures to accommodate every taste.

Next might be visitors from exotic places like Muscat or Oman. Their homelands had not by then become oil-rich, and their graceful ocean-going dhows still had no engines. They, therefore, continued to visit East Africa annually, as their forefathers were reputed to have done from time immemorial, to trade salt and dates and carpets for the mangrove poles which they took back to the Gulf. At one time they had taken slaves too. Perhaps they still hankered to do so, for I learned that during my time at Lamu they were urging leading members of the local community to ask me on their behalf whether they could instead take some Mau Mau prisoners or detainees, of whom many hundreds were then held in various camps around the district.

Or you would recognize some Swahili labourers taking their rest after the exertions of the day. It was well deserved, for they had tough jobs. Neither cranes nor motor vehicles had reached Lamu Island, so all cargo had to be hauled ashore by hand, humped over the sea wall and then loaded onto small donkey carts, or onto the donkeys themselves, ready to be transported round the narrow streets of the town.

A group of handsome Somalis might strut past you, looking pleased with themselves. And no wonder. They had already outwitted the Italian authorities, evading the tax payable when their cattle were exported to Kenya for sale to the Arab dealers who supplied the Mombasa meat market. And they were confident that they would outwit you too, purchasing to take home with them elephant tusks poached by the Boni bushmen. They would later be returned to Kenya stamped 'shot in Somaliland', for sale to the craftsmen who carved ivory.

After strolling, you could obtain liquid refreshment (and hear more gossip) at the local hotel. It was kept by Percy Petley, who looked like a broken-down pirate, with a black patch over one eye, thick spectacles on the other and a hearing aid which was switched off whenever he proposed to tick you off without permitting you any right of reply. He had opened the hotel in the late 1940s, on retiring to Lamu some forty years after he had as a young man first come to Africa from his native Suffolk. Although primitive in many ways, his hotel boasted good food and a well-stocked bar from which guests were expected to help themselves.

Percy once sought an interview with me to discuss what he described as a Matter of Importance. Despite being a stern critic of the Government's bureaucracy, extravagance and other iniquities, he had never called at my office before. His request seemed certain to presage a formidable complaint, and I therefore racked my brain in the hope of recalling some sin of omission or commission which he might have unearthed. When the time came he solemnly explained that he wanted my opinion about a point which was troubling him. Now that the hotel bar had begun to make a profit (its trade having become much brisker) ought he to obtain a liquor licence for it?

I served in Lamu for only a year. But it was a year which I have never forgotten. Nostalgic memories keep flooding back. Something I still remember with special pleasure is the gift which the Bajun people presented to me on my departure. It was a model of an *mtepe,* the fabled craft with planking sewn together and a mat bag sail which had long ago been used for coastal traffic by generations of their ancestors. But the model must have been six feet long. The prospect of trying to transport it with my luggage appalled me. By agreement I therefore left it behind, to be displayed in the house. I was delighted to find it still there, on display, when I revisited my old haunts more than twenty-five years later, though the house had meanwhile become the Lamu Museum.

OP 89 (April 2005)

Malayan Opium Tales

by David Brent

In connection with the account by Mr J S A Lewis of official opium dealing by Government Officers in the Federated Malay States,* I first encountered one of the old opium ration books just near a coastal fishing village, Nanasi, on the South China Sea coast, in the Pekan District where I was the Police Chief in 1953.

I and my team made a *chandu* raid on a chop house, acting on information. On this occasion we found no evidence, but turned up an old opium ration book which belonged to the householder, the first of many I was to come across over the following years. Mr Lewis mentions the packaging of the processed opium, or *chandu* as it was called, in paper packets, or 'decks' as we referred to them. The opium treacle hardened into small, thin flat rectangular portions which were wrapped in red or pink paper. Red is a traditional colour preferred by the Chinese as lucky, and used for festive occasions and for wrapping gifts. It was therefore appropriate for the purpose. However, it did become a 'giveaway' at times. One developed an 'eagle eye' for odd discarded little pieces of rectangular red or pink paper with fold marks which indicated that, somewhere, there was a connection with opium smoking. This often led to a discreet follow-up and a later successful case before the courts. Sadly, though, rarely did we ever catch the 'big fish'.

On raids it was necessary to be very quick to seize the evidence, as the addicts were extremely adept at making utensils, pipes in particular, simply disappear! As a less experienced officer on my first few raids I remember being quite astonished how things just vanished into thin air! I developed the technique of being the first through the door or other opening with a camera and flashlight, and still have some of the shots of astonished addicts and their utensils as I broke in, taking flash shots on the move! In this remote, conservative and languorous locale near the mouth of the great Pahang River where it flows into the South China Sea, with its charming old world ambience of history and romance and the pervasive presence of

---

*See No. 2.5, Page 103

the Sultan, *tengkus* and retinue of the Pahang royal court, such goings-on were considered rather *avant garde!* However, there was testimony to the success ratio of such raids with rows of opium pipes hung on the office wall behind my desk, some crafted with great skill and love, with ivory mouthpieces and elegant, polished brass fittings.

Mr Lewis also touches on the experience of an opium addict 'colliding' with his stationary car. I must say this quite surprised me because I had an almost identical experience in 1956 in the Batu Pahat District in North Johore on the Straits of Malacca. I had just driven off the old ferry pontoon which crossed the river (now replaced by a splendid bridge) and turned left into one of the main streets of the Bandar Penggaram township when I observed an old Chinese cake-seller slowly shuffling along the street towards me straight into the line of traffic. He carried his little cakes in a wide bamboo and rattan tray balanced on his head and, I couldn't believe it, his eyes were closed! He was literally taking a nap while walking along. Fortunately there was no traffic behind me so I stopped my car, a large 1948 silver V8 Ford Custom, and waited. I considered sounding the horn but decided that this might shock the old man too much, and he would drop his tray and cakes all over the road.

A few curious onlookers on the nearby five-foot-way outside the chop-houses watched agog and with heightened expectancy from the outcome of a collision of cakes and car. They were not to be disappointed. I had hoped that something would cause the old cake-seller to open his eyes. But no, he just kept shuffling along until his knees bumped the front of the car. There was immediate consternation as the startled cake-seller felt the shock of contact, and saw a big silver car upon him with the Chief of Police looking at him over the steering wheel! What thoughts flashed through his mind in those split seconds I can't imagine, but I'm sure they remained a highlight with him to his dying day. One arm clawed the empty air for balance, the other flew up to the cake tray on his head as it wobbled and tilted, and miraculously not one cake fell off. In the seconds that followed, as raucous hilarity from the five-foot-way filled the air, the old cake-seller straightened himself up, and with marvellous equanimity, regained his composure to continue on his way, slowly shuffling past my car, hesitating a little as he came abreast of me, to raise a hand to his temple in *tabek* greeting, his gap-toothed smile belying his relief that nothing bad had happened to him.

In swinging, down-town Bandar Penggaram that warm and sultry evening, the talk around town in the coffee shops and eating houses was the story of old Ah Chee, the cake-seller who had tried, single-handed mind you, to run the Police Chief's car off the road. I can only hope that Ah Chee's fame spread far and wide and greatly enhanced the sale of his delicious little cakes.

OP 69 (Spring 1995)

The Day's Work and Odd Jobs : Rescue up the Niger

by Ronald Bird (Dogon Yaro)

We all remember the odd jobs that came out of the blue to relieve the monotony of the usual routine duties of the day's work. Some of those odd jobs are still quite vivid in one's memory. I recall late one Saturday morning in the District Office in Ilorin as I was trying to get rid of a mound of files before the week-end. The Divisional Officer was away on local leave and I was standing in for him. It had been a tiring morning: the usual prison inspection, a long meeting with the NA Tax Assessment Committee, and then even more complainants with lengthy stories than usual. The telephone rang and it was the Resident warning me he had a job for me, something that would get me away from the files, and would I come up to his office right away.

As I entered the Resident's office I saw there was an oldish African in a tattered white gown slumped on the floor. He had a short grey beard and though the face was drawn and haggard there was a gleam in his eye. The Resident showed me a dirty sheet of paper on which a rough note was scribbled. It said 'Hanson and I are held prisoner on an island in the Niger above Jebba. Have been attacked by our labourers. Please send help urgently. Richard Strange, Geologist, Northern Mining Association'. It sounded almost like a joke. Who could imagine in these days of settled administration that two prospecting miners would be held prisoner on an island in the Niger? The tattered figure in the corner was sufficient to dispel any doubts, particularly when his story poured out in clipped Sokoto Hausa. He said his name was Moman Gwadabawa and he was orderly and messenger to the two miners who were prospecting along the Niger a long way above Jebba. He did not know exactly where they were as most of the country was uninhabited bush, except for the odd fishing settlement on the river. They were on an island where there was also a small village; he thought it was a lot south of Bussa but they had come across from the Kontagora side. The work took them and the gang of labourers up and down the river and some of its tributaries. The labourers had been causing trouble for some time, refusing to work although they were well paid, and thefts of property and valuable equipment had taken place. Five days ago the two miners had intended to come down to Jebba to report the thefts, but as they got into their canoe the labourers surrounded them, yelling and shouting, held on to the canoe, dragged them out, and stove in the side of the canoe. The two miners had then retreated to the small mud rest-house where they were living, which the labourers, getting more and more truculent, besieged, yelling abuse and demanding two months extra wages and gratuities so that they could go off home. They threatened him and the miner's boys, and the people of the small hamlet on the other side of the island, and set a guard on the canoes. He said what they were really after was the miner's cash box which contained cash and gold dust. The ringleader was a man called John Umeh, a plausible rogue who they had only discovered too late had served several sentences for theft and robbery. The position had been a stalemate as the miners had a shotgun, but Umeh had openly boasted he would steal it at night and they could make off with the money. All attempts to get a message out had failed until the third night, when the miners had staged a diversion and he had managed to slip out of the back with the note he had brought. He had got away in a small canoe and had then landed at a fishing hamlet and had persuaded them with the money given to him, to take him on down to Jebba. It had taken them most of the day to reach Jebba but he had not been able to get a 'mammy wagon' on to Ilorin until the next morning, and so here he was, *ranka shi dade!* (may your life be long!)

The Resident had no information about any miners prospecting on the Niger, but then they had probably been working mostly on the Niger Province or Kontagora side of the river. On the western side it was all a vast uninhabited stretch of thick trackless bush forming part of the Borgu Division of Ilorin Province. Getting at them from Kaiama across 50 miles of trackless bush in the rains, when one did not know for certain where they were, was quite impossible. The Resident had already made up his mind that he would launch an immediate rescue attempt up the river from Jebba. There was no time to get in touch with Kontagora via Minna, and they would have to be informed later. He had already asked the Superintendent of Police to get ready a small party of Police whom I was to take up river on a rescue attempt. There were few directions the Resident could give me except go and investigate, and do what I thought best, but he was clearly most envious that he could not go himself. No time was to be lost and he wished me luck as I left. We did not know exactly where the miners were, and were dependent on Moman the orderly to lead us, but it might take at least two days from Jebba by canoe as the Niger was already in flood.

I rushed back to my house and not long after, as I was having a hurried lunch, the police truck drew up at the front of the house. I went out to see an old friend who had been out with me before, Sgt Haruna Fakai of the Nigeria Police. He had four constables of the Nigeria Police with their long batons, and four Ilorin NA Police. I was glad to have Sgt Haruna. He was a tough policeman who had served his twelve years in the RWAFF. I told Sgt Haruna as much as I knew of the situation and we decided he would go on ahead in the police truck to Jebba, and organise with the Sarkin Kwata three or four canoes with a sufficient number of strong polers for a long up-river trip. I would follow in my own van as soon as I was ready and my boys had packed up at Jebba waterside.

After heavy rain the road to Jebba seemed even worse than usual, and it took a good 2½ hours to get to Jebba waterside and find Sgt Haruna busy organising the fussy little Sarkin Kwata. Jebba, shut-in beside the river, was always hot and sticky, but it seemed even worse that evening, and clearly a big storm was coming as heavy dark clouds were building up in the NE. It was going to be a long grinding haul against the Niger in flood. I thought we might make a start and stop for shelter from the storm at the first fishing hamlet, but the Sarkin Kwata had not got his canoes and polers ready. At last the canoes were ready, four medium sized canoes with three strong polers each, but just as we were ready to load them, the storm seemed about to burst and it was going be a real heavy end of wet-season storm. The only thing was to shelter and start at the crack of dawn. Sgt Haruna took his men off to shelter at the police post, and I drove back to the little stone rest-house as the first heavy drops clattered on its tin roof before the storm burst with all its savagery in the confined river valley.

The next morning was fresh and clear after the oppressive heat of the previous day, and we embarked in the canoes just as the first light was showing in the east. We struggled slowly upstream against the muddy current, first under the towering steel structure of the great railway bridge, and then past the sinister looking 'juju rock', vegetation and trees rising sheer from the swirling waters to the rocky summit. It was slow and tedious work fighting the current and the canoes crept along in the lee of the banks, the polers pushing against every vantage point with their long *gongolas*. On and on we went through uninhabited country, with just two stops at small fishing hamlets half-hidden in the long grass of the bank, while the canoe men rested and ate a hasty meal. They had been promised double wages and a bonus if they made good time, and they poled away with a will throughout the long hot day, hour after monotonous hour. Progress had been good and, as night came down, we reached a tiny village and rushed for shelter just as another savage evening storm burst. There was no room to lie down and keep dry in the few ramshackle huts, but we rested and then made a start with the first glimmer of dawn. I reckoned that with 11 hours of steady poling we must have covered a good 30 miles or so, and that we should reach the island camp sometime after midday. Late in the morning the river began to narrow between rocky banks with a mass of trees and luxuriant undergrowth and the current ran faster. This was the toughest part of the trip, and the canoe men fought their way up against the current as they poled their canoes from rock to rock. Suddenly the men in the leading canoe dropped their poles and picking up paddles began to paddle the canoe frantically across to the other bank. Yelling encouragement to each other, the canoe men battled their way across and when they reached the lee of the other bank, resumed their poling. We followed into the seething water of the rapid, knowing that our bigger canoe would have a harder struggle to get across. It seemed as if we might be swept back, but suddenly the current relaxed its grip and we crept forward into the lee of the far bank, the canoe men gasping with their frantic efforts. On we went struggling along the bank, clawing our way from rock to rock and branch to branch of overhanging trees. At last the river began to broaden out and we left the rocks and the roar of the rapids behind. After another two hours we called a halt and Moman pointed out a blur of trees some 2 miles ahead which he said was the island camp. Sgt Haruna gave orders to his men about arresting the ringleaders while I, keen to do things in style, hoisted the Union Jack on the makeshift mast of the largest canoe.

With the island in sight all our spirits rose and after a short rest we set off again, the canoe men singing as they paddled across to the heavily wooded island. As we got close I fired a couple of shots with my shot-gun into the air and the police and then the canoe men replied with a mighty cheer. As we rounded a promontory there before us was the landing place with a small mud rest-house above the steep bank. There seemed an unnatural silence as we landed and Sgt Haruna and his men dashed ashore and I saw a crowd of men gathered on the path that led back to the village, their faces blank and expressionless and seemingly resigned. Then I saw the two miners outside their rest-house, quiet too but their faces drawn with the strain of the last few days. Gradually the whole story came out; they had, indeed, been held hostage and besieged in the rest-house until twenty minutes earlier when the police canoes had been seen. At first there had been pandemonium, the labourers rushing about in complete panic, then when they heard the shots all noise had ceased and the men had gathered silently to wait and watch. Sgt Haruna reported they had been unable to find John Umeh, and we soon learnt that he and two of his henchmen had slipped out at the back in the confusion and made off in one of the village canoes. Two squads were sent off in canoes to search for them, while we continued the investigation and took statements from the two miners, Moman the orderly, and others. Substantially the facts as reported by Moman earlier seemed correct and Sgt Haruna took into custody ten of the more violent labourers out of the original gang of about 25, while the rest were given a formal warning. I gained little more from Strange, or the other miner, except that they were having moderate success with their gold prospecting in an area that historically had produced a fair amount of alluvial gold. Next morning all efforts to trace Umeh and the other men having failed, we borrowed an extra canoe and set off back to Jebba with our prisoners. The passage down to Jebba with the current behind us was swift, and sweeping through the rapids without accident we reached Jebba by mid-afternoon, then after paying off our gallant canoe men with a large bonus, we got back to Ilorin by evening. The Resident was delighted to see us back and hear that his prompt rescue decision had resulted in a successful action to uphold the law in the remotest areas of the Niger valley. "I can now report to Resident Niger and tell him that all is quiet along our boundary", he said to me with a twinkle in his eye.

The sequel to this account came not long after, when the District Head of Jebba sent in a report that a burglar had broken into a house in the town, and tried to stab the householder. In the fight that followed, the burglar had been cut down with a machete wound to the head, and had died the next day. The burglar had been identified as John Umeh.

OP 76 (Autumn 1998)

The Day's Work and Odd Jobs :
No Tax? No Bridge!

by Ronald Bird (Dogon Yaro)

The difference between the primitive self-subsistence pagans of the Gwoza Hills, and 800 miles to the south west the Yoruba peoples of Ilorin Emirate with their highly developed trading and cash economy, was immense.

The next tour I was posted on special duties to try and find a solution to the problems of the Oke Odde area of Ilorin. Agitation against Ilorin Emirate was being fomented by politicians from the Western Region of Nigeria who hoped to break up the border Emirate of Ilorin with its mixed peoples. Oke Odde had been the scene of violent demonstrations and my brief was to see if some local government reform could be worked out while retaining the general structure of Ilorin Emirate. It was one of the usual no-win situations where one had to tread very carefully as everything was distorted and blown up in the press in the Western Region and lawyers were ready to pounce on any step beyond the strict letter of the law. Any discussions on possible local government reform had to involve the Emir's Councillor responsible for the area, while trying to win over those demanding change; at the same time the routine administration of the N A (Native Authority) had to be supported.

The first and biggest problem to arise was the annual collection of tax. Normally each Village Area Head received a Tax Demand Notice for his village area stating the number of tax payers, the flexible tax per head, and the total sum the Village Head was expected to collect. Notices were sent out by the District Head in the usual way to all the Village Heads and three days later I went down to attend a meeting in the District Council Hall to find that all the Village Heads had refused to collect tax for Ilorin N A and had stuck their tax notices to the walls of the hall in protest. Individuals refusing to pay their tax could be prosecuted but how was one to deal with a strike of the tax collectors? After thinking about it overnight and consulting the Emir's Councillor I had the beginnings of an idea which with care might force the hands of the Village Heads and get round the lawyers inciting them. Oke Odde had a large weekly market which brought 15 to 18 mammy wagons carrying traders, some

64

from over the regional boundary to trade and purchase produce. There was only one road to Oke Odde from the south and this had 3 or 4 largish all weather bridges over rocky stream beds. Careful examination revealed one about 12 miles from Oke Odde which had cracks in the stone piers and abutments which might be unsafe for heavy vehicles if not repaired. I knew the Provincial Engineer had a legal right to declare a road or parts of it closed to heavy traffic if it was certified as being unsafe. I sounded out the District Officer who thought it risky but worth a try, while the Emir and Council gave their support to the plan. The Provincial Engineer, the key to the whole plan, was a hearty Welshman and prepared to help a fellow Celt in difficulty. After examination of the bridge he declared it unsafe for heavy traffic until repairs could be carried out. One problem was the Resident who had to follow the official politically correct line whatever he might think of it personally. The District Officer agreed to leak the information to the Resident unofficially as an N A plan which had come to his notice. No veto came from the Resident when he heard of this unofficial piece of intelligence so the plan went ahead.

The road was declared closed to heavy traffic at mile 12 from Oke Odde and a barrier with a strong N A police guard set up. The N A let it be known behind the scenes that the N A Works Department would make an effort to get the bridge repaired as soon as the Oke Odde Village Heads had collected the bulk of their tax. The first market day at Oke Odde took place and all mammy wagons had to stop at mile 12 and from there traders had to go on by foot. After 2 market days the people of Oke Odde town and the traders were feeling the economic pinch and peace overtures were made to the Emir's Councillor. He and I agreed that we were prepared to meet the Village Heads in the Council Hall and they were all to recover their Tax Demand Notices and announce publicly that they were starting tax collection immediately. The Councillor and I went down to the Council Hall the next morning and there a most extraordinary sight met our eyes. The Village Heads had been unable to peel their Notices off the plastered walls of the hall and each notice had to be cut out with a chisel with the plaster backing to which it adhered. Each Village Head held as it was a tablet of stone with his Tax Notice on it and solemnly announced the immediate start of tax collection. The N A Works Department by a supreme effort was able to get masons out to start repairs to the bridge at mile 12 within days.

Tax in Oke Odde District came in that year quicker than ever before and the traders were soon back attending the market in increased numbers.

Garbled press reports and threats to the N A appeared in the papers in the Western Region but the lawyers were unable to think up any legal action. In due course Ilorin N A set up a regional council of three eastern districts in the Emirate with power to spend extra development funds on any projects they wanted in the area. This, combined with other local government reforms, seemed to satisfy the rich and vocal trading communities of the area.

OP 96 (October 2008)

"Vive Le Royaume Uni!"

by R E N Smith

In mid-1966 the Joint Administration in the New Hebrides learned, to the mingled delight and horror of the French Residency, and pleasant anticipation in the British one, that we were shortly to have the honour and pleasure of a visit from President de Gaulle. This announcement sent the French Office into a frenzy of planning and all else in the way of work was cast aside. After numerous conferences and heated debate a programme for the visit was produced. As British District Agent in Vila (and therefore the joint administrative officer of the district), I was closely concerned with the visit. I was sent a copy of the English version which I still have. The text is less comprehensive than the French one was, but does contain all the appendices. For a visit that was to last from 10.20 am until 4.00 pm there were no less than eleven detailed diagrams. Starting with the arrival at Bauerfield Airport, there were carefully worked out plans for the ceremony at the Cenotaph, at the Colours, at the French Office, of the routes, of the presentation order of 'notables' at the French Residency and so on, ending with a plan for handshakes on departure.

Having given painful gestation to this *chef d'oeuvre,* our colleagues sat back with sighs of pride and relief. We read this masterpiece carefully and then asked them for the date and time of the rehearsal. They were astonished.

"Rehearsal?" they said, "Why do we need a rehearsal? Is not the plan perfect in every particular?"

To this our reply had to be that it was indeed magnificent, but that in our bumbling and inefficient Anglo-Saxon way we had found, over the years, that a rehearsal for any major state function was essential, if a dog's dinner of a disaster was to be avoided. In an unusual access of good nature, the French gave way and a rehearsal, if only for the procession, was agreed to, though they felt that it was totally unnecessary.

It was a remarkable and unforgettable occasion. Our colleagues did not have enough transport, and had, therefore, been obliged to hire every taxi in Vila, with a motley crew of Frenchmen, Vietnamese, New Hebrideans, Chinese and various permutations of these, gabbling all together and at once in incomprehensible languages. Since by no means all of them understood French, and if they did either failed to take in the instructions or just ignored them, the results were appalling, for the head of the procession was arriving in triumph back at the airfield before the tail had left it, while there were little knots of furiously competing taxis all over the course. It was after all just a demonstration of Murphy's Prime Law, that in any given situation, anything that can go wrong will do so!

Tuesday 6 September 1966 dawned and from then onwards frenzied action was the order of the day. I was only a minor participant, with no executive concerns and what it must have been like for my colleague, the French District Agent, I shuddered to contemplate. All the same all the officials, French, British and Condominial, had to be out at the airfield by 9.30 and in uniform too, in order to witness the arrival of His Excellency and to admire the proceedings. The General's arrival was impressive, but his official entourage was quite modest; there were himself and Madame de Gaulle, and just eight men and two women with him, but the DC4 was stuffed with bodyguards, Secret Service men and a large scurry of press and photographers.

The proceedings started with the usual inspection of the Guard of Honour. Being the Condominium we had two of these, the French Police in one body with their Gendarme officers in front, and the British Police with their officers in full rig with swords; the two forces used their own individual national methods to salute the President. Then the top officials and their wives were presented. We had both the French and British Resident Commissioners, plus our own High Commissioner from Honiara. I do not know why he had got in on the act, unless it was to serve as a counterweight to the French High Commissioner from Noumea, who was escorting the President. Then came the turn of the Co-Presidents of the Joint Court and their wives, followed by another twenty or so notables.

The whole rout then climbed into the assorted transport and sped off to the Cenotaph for a wreath-laying ceremony. Since the Presidential vehicle got there first, proceedings were necessarily delayed until lesser officials had arrived (all panting heavily). The wreath-laying was easy enough for the President, but as everything we did was 'joint', the two Resident Commissioners jointly laid one between them! This only took a few minutes and then the President walked through a large crowd to the forecourt of the French Offices nearby. Here the ceremony of the Colours took place, with assorted and assembled school children wailing the *Marseillaise* and then *The Queen*. Now it was time for the great man to make a speech, with the British on tenterhooks for fear of some monumental but undoubtedly unintentional gaffe from His Excellency. However he was on his best behaviour, and finished his speech with a most unexpected and almost unheard-of clarion call. To a roar of applause, *'Vive la France!,'* he intoned and then, *'Vive le Royaume Uni!'* – perhaps the only time in his life he ever uttered the latter.

We managed to avoid a possibly nasty confrontation on this occasion, for our keen Assistant Superintendent of British Police, assigned from our side to keep an eye on things, had proposed to lurk in the background in mufti, armed with a pistol. We managed to dissuade him, earnestly pointing out that, to the Presidential goon squad, the sight of a strange European, obviously armed, would not only be a cause for the blackest suspicion, but quite probably a target for their bullets.

By now it was well past eleven, and De Gaulle disappeared into the French Resident Commissioner's office for a quiet chat followed by the formal visits of the leading French and British dignitaries. Since it was a joint administration we had plenty of these, and this gave a breathing space to the British officers who were in uniform (starched white, with Wolseley helmet, medals and sword) a few minutes' grace to rush off to the Transit house of the French Residency and change into lounge suits.

We then trooped into the big reception hall of the French Residency and lined up again in order of importance (French style) in readiness to be presented properly to the President. Once again the line was headed by the French and British judges in their Siamese twin capacity of President of the Joint Court, together with their own senior staff, and followed by the Roman Catholic Bishop Juilliard, the (Protestant) Reverend Peak and Father Graafe of the French Reformed Church, all the members of the Advisory Council and then the two distinguished administrators of Vaté (Efate in English). This was where I came in, for while I figured rather low down on the British Office totem pole, on this occasion I had to stand alongside my colleague, the French District Agent, and in French official eyes the district administrators ranked well above mere Secretariat officers, a terrible heresy in British eyes. In rapid succession after us came the Chamber of Commerce, the WHO doctor, the district agents from outside Efate, and then, way down the list the French, British and Condominium senior functionaries, the ex-service luminaries, members of the liberal professions, Boy Scout and Girl Guide leaders, local council dignitaries and anyone else our colleagues could think of.

This presentation did not include any women, unless they achieved status by reason of their personal qualifications; we were terrible politically incorrect in those antediluvian days. Of all the British ladies the only one to be presented was my wife, who as a dental surgeon had to be included in the liberal professions. Once the hour-long reception was over the general rout of British and Condominium officers was free until the departure of the President.

He and his entourage still had an exhausting programme, going on next to an official luncheon. Our colleagues were properly prepared for this, for they had received from Paris advice on His Excellency's preferences, together with a stern warning from Mme de Gaulle NOT to give her husband any bread, for he would eat it and it was BAD for him! No sooner had they eaten than they were off again, for visits to the French Ex-Servicemen's Club and a couple of teaching establishments, before they headed back to Bauerfield. Quite unhurriedly the President walked down the long line of functionaries, firmly shaking hands with us all. He did not look in the least jaded by the day's jollifications, but my colleagues of the French office were thoroughly exhausted. All in all a most interesting day, if not one I would wish to repeat too often. My turn to sweat came many years later in the Gilbert and Ellice Islands, when I found myself heavily involved in a Royal Visit. Only then, as I rushed frantically from point to point, did I really feel any sympathy for my erstwhile colleagues.

OP 72 (Autumn 1996)

Signed, Sealed and Delivered

by John Gullick

In the sixteenth century the Portuguese introduced the written treaty to the statecraft of Southeast Asia. The local rulers took to it with enthusiasm, as they already exchanged elaborate and beautifully written formal letters, each bearing the impression of the state seal, which as a royal heirloom passed from each ruler to his successor.

Malay seals of the old type are superb artefacts and often, like the coins of Roman emperors, make political statements. The traditional seal is metal, sometimes silver, on which the ruler's titles are inscribed by cutting into the surface, so that the text is left white and the background is coloured, when the seal has been blacked in the flame of a lamp and applied to the paper. In modern times however some rulers adopted an embossed seal, with a hand press, to make an impression, or even a rubber stamp to be used with an ink pad. Until, in the 20th century, the rulers were able to sign their names, their 'mark' (a cross) was made on treaties with European powers.

Between 1946 and 1948 HMG retreated from an ill-conceived and highly unpopular Malayan Union constitution and agreed to replace it with a federation of the Malay states. Like all formal engagements with and by Malay rulers, the new regime was to be inaugurated by treaty, ie a treaty with the ruler of each state and a collective federal treaty with them all. As all parties had to be provided with an original of the treaties they had sealed – and there are nine Malay states – they were going to seal a lot of documents.

The ceremony was to take place in the dining room of King's House, Kuala Lumpur (Malay susceptibilities did not permit the governor's residence in a protected Malay state to be designated 'Government House'). I was at the time secretary to the Resident Commissioner of the state of Negri Sembilan, which is itself a federation, so that any treaty to which it is party has to be executed by its six rulers. The royal dynasty and its cadet branch provided two personages who considered themselves a cut above the non-royal ruling chiefs (known as Undang) of four districts, but all six had to play their part.

On all previous occasions of making a treaty to which several Malay states were parties, the treaty had been taken round the royal capitals for each ruler to seal there. But in January 1948 it was decided that Mohamed would come to the mountain, and all the Malay rulers would assemble in Kuala Lumpur for a simultaneous accession to the new arrangement. My job was to get the four Undang 'to the church on time.' A formal letter of invitation to each of them had asked them to bring with them their seals. They all turned up punctually at the rendezvous and we went in to King's House in very good time. The dining room, with the long table, was a scene of chaos. The ceremony was to be filmed and the room was full of cameras and lights. Unless, like Agag in the book of Samuel, you 'came delicately', you would trip over the cables amid the curses of the technicians. However we got the Undang safely to their allotted places at the table. I then asked to see their seals. Three, who were younger men fairly new in office, produced rubber stamps, with ink pads, to replace older seals lost during the Japanese occupation. However the Undang of Johol was an elderly man, long in office in a district that was regarded as a stronghold of ancient custom. He was a real old fashioned type, courteous and most anxious to cooperate in this rather bewildering tamasha. He produced a bundle wrapped in a sheet of a Malay newspaper to reveal a metal, incised seal, and a lamp, filled with coconut oil, for blacking it.

An expert on the TV 'Antiques Road Show' might have been ecstatic but I was in some dismay, and took the old Undang back into the kitchen, where the cooks were preparing bakemeats for the bunfight to follow the ceremony, and we lit his lamp and did a dummy run.

It was awful. Getting the seal blacked, for each impression, was messy, took time and produced a very blurred outline. At the ceremony copies for sealing would be coming down the table at speed, like a game of 'pass the parcel'. In despair I borrowed an ink pad from one of the other Undang, and tried the Johol seal with that. The result was at least no more of a smudge than resulted from the use of lamp black, and it was much more expeditious.

So we went back to the dining room where royal rulers and their attendant dignitaries had now gathered, resplendent in Malay national dress of brightly coloured silk and satin. The sealing began and the Negri Sembilan team did its part without a hitch, or delay. No one commented on the imperfect Johol seal impression. I could not bear to think what the assembled Rulers' reaction would have been if we had set the Johol lamp alight on the table and blacked the seal with it. A plane was waiting to take back to London HMG's copies of the treaties – meeting that deadline was all that mattered. After it was over everyone had his nice cup of tea and a sugary cake, and went his way. So the new federation was born.

Somewhere the Foreign Office presumably keeps all the treaties to which Britain has been a party – in a warehouse in the back of beyond, I suppose. Fortunately no one has any reason to look at the smudge (and of course the signature) that records the accession of the ruling chief of Johol to the Federation of Malaya in 1948.

OP 94 (October 2007)

Africa Past and Present

by Kenneth J Forder

Whether it be famine, hunger, pestilence, tribal wars, destruction of the environment or extinction of species, many members of the former Colonial Service find it frustrating to see so many commentaries in the media (even Government-inspired documentaries) putting over a variety of causes and explanations; anything other than the true cause – the removal from the scene of dedicated officers of the Colonial Administration.

Critics will demand that we justify our view that the rot set in with the phasing out of Colonialism. What indeed were those features of our administration, the absence of which, we might argue, have led to the present (and continuing) desolation of Africa? The only way I can see of answering these critics in a way which is comprehensible without being vague or too generalised, is to give a thumb-nail sketch of how it worked on the ground. Only a few days ago I came across some of my old Northern Rhodesia District Books and what emerges from them will serve the purpose. This is the way we handled three things.

1. Arms *(potentially the most important single heading)*

A visitor to any African village might be intrigued by the display of spears or bows and arrows he might see. I once saw a villager take aim at a Gaboon Viper (one of the most poisonous snakes on earth) with a bow and arrow from a distance of not less than 20 yards. He skewered it straight through the head – a remarkable shot, which I do not for one moment suggest was the norm. Villagers were, even so, remarkably skilful with their spears, on which they relied heavily to obtain the *inyama* (meat, usually from a wild buck) to supplement their diet of maize or cassava.

Guns were virtually unknown among villagers. The procurement of a 12 bore shotgun by one resident of a village made him what would virtually be a television personality in our society. In most villages there would be no firearms at all. This was not for want of asking. District Commissioners operated one of the most rigid regimes imaginable so far as shotgun licence applications were concerned. I did it myself. I remember being posted to a Government outpost and inheriting there a whole pile of box files from my predecessor containing hundreds of shotgun applications going back over 30 years in some cases. Every application was expected to be supported by many testimonials from a variety of directions – and would in any case stand no chance of success without the endorsement of the applicant's tribal chief. Even the District Commissioner did not have the last word. Each year, out of the hundreds submitted, I could forward to the Provincial Commissioner my recommended list of 20 shotgun licences for the year. He would send back the 12 new approved together with the 8 rejects (which would go into the pool for the next year; I have known such applications to be shunted on for 10 years). What a celebration there was for one greybeard who at last received his approved application after waiting since he had been a young man!

Today there is virtually no limitation on the possession of arms of all sorts; not only do those villages have arms, but almost every house has a gun. You don't have to resort to myths about the ivory trade or outside poachers to find out why the numbers of elephants have decreased. Elephant meat is tasty; I know, I have tasted it.

2. Hunting

During the period I was in Africa, far from species being rare, the Government officially offered bounties for shooting them. Anyone who produced a lion's tail to the appropriate Government office received £2 in cash. A similar sum was paid for the head of a wild dog, while a jackal head produced only 50p. In fact, there was considerable correspondence from Government to District Commissioners telling them it was suspected that some villagers were doing a roaring trade in actually breeding wild dogs and then cutting their heads off to claim the bounty.

The picture was slightly different with crocodiles. There were many thousands in every river, but a fact which rendered bounties unnecessary was that the crocodile skin was valuable and could be sold. Not all the skin, mind you, just the soft underbelly, and that was where the problem arose. If crocodile hunters did a night's shoot they would be interested only in the underskins, and this meant that anything up to a dozen fetid corpses would be left to rot in the wild. For this reason we had to issue crocodile hunting licences, making it a condition of each licence that any corpse remains must be disposed of by fire.

And the picture today? No more need be said than that 25 years ago, if you took a Landrover across the Kafue plain you went through massive herds of wildebeest, zebra, eland and kudu. Today I am told you will see nothing apart from a few lechwe.

3. Drought

To judge by all the horror stories, one would imagine that drought was something new in Africa. Western governments pour money into a so-called relief situation, which in fact has always been there and has always been surmounted without any great difficulty so long as the instructions of the local District Commissioners were properly followed. One has always had to cope too with such things as deforestation and overgrazing; increasing urbanisation has not helped.

It has always been a fact of life that the Zambezi river is 50 miles wide in places during the rainy season; 100 yards wide during the dry season. One of the glorious features of life is to see the first rains after the long dry season; we used to go out and stand in it fully clothed and get drenched to the skin. But of course if one does not follow the rules, then disaster may well follow.

One example of such a rule is always to plough on the contour; I wonder how many do it now? But the matter with which I was most directly concerned was keeping cattle alive during those long dry months. Along the Zambezi valley, there grows a type of tall lush reed which is well known for its enduring properties as cattle-food. There is no scarcity – it is in plentiful supply. What has to be done, however, is that cattle owners must cut it in large quantities when it is wet, and stack it rather in the shape of a haystack. It is so rich that it can be used as cattle-food right through the dry season and keep the cattle alive until the rains come again. We used to run propaganda campaigns among owners of some 80,000 cattle in my District telling them to cut this grass for their own use. No expense was involved – just the effort of making the stacks. Never did Nature provide a more accessible solution to a problem. Do you think the locals would cut the grass of their own accord? Instead, after a month or two without rain, they would come to complain that their cattle were dying and that the Government should help them. I suppose today some relief agency will be throwing dollars at them.

Officers of the Colonial Service have so often been vilified (sometimes with justification). The tragedy is that they are not normally given credit where credit is due. In due course the world is going to learn the hard way that famine, pestilence, hunger and extinction of species go to make up the price of dispensing with Colonialism.

OP 65 (April 1993)

Northern Rhodesia
(and Central African Federation)

After the end of the British South Africa Company's administration in 1924 a badge was required for the new British Protectorate. The design adopted in 1927 showed a fish eagle with outspread wings, holding a fish in its talons, above heraldic wavy lines signifying the Victoria Falls on the Zambezi River (and other rivers). The badge was in the form of a shield, not a disc. This badge was used until the creation in 1953 of the Central African Federation. The Federation's badge comprised elements from the three constituent territories, and included the wavy lines but not the fish eagle from the Northern Rhodesia badge.

Signing Off

by B D Wilson

In 1954 I was District Officer and Police Court magistrate on the western side of the New Territories of Hong Kong. In those days, the NT was still rural, largely rice-growing and not yet swamped by the weight of concrete that has since been loaded on to so much of it. On a hot day at the weekend, I was gardening in the DO's quarters when a Police van drove up and a sergeant sought my signature on a warrant to commit a villager to 14 days' observation in a mental hospital. His fellow villagers had asked for Police assistance to get rid of the man because of his disruptive and irrational behaviour. Before signing, I thought I had better have a look at the villager and satisfy myself that he appeared unbalanced. So I walked over to the van from which there came the sound of banging and hammering and looked in through the barred window. A contorted face glared at me and spat. I went off to sign at once.

A few days later, I received a memorandum signed "P M Yap, Psychiatric Specialist", saying in effect "if you are the Mr Wilson who signed the committal warrant, you signed in the wrong place and it appears that you have committed yourself. When do you wish to come in? We will try to have a room ready for you".

OP 94 (October 2007)

HONG KONG

 The design on the Seal for the Colony of Hong Kong was instituted in 1843. It shows a local waterfront scene, with three traders and their goods in the foreground. Beyond them lie two ships – a western type square-rigged vessel and a Chinese style junk. In the background is the conical Peak. This design was used on flags from 1876, with a modification introduced in 1910 that was used until 1959, when it was replaced by a new Coat of Arms.

Two Knights and a Chief in Central Africa

by Brian Reavill

In 1958 I was posted, on secondment from the Federal Public Service, to the Prime Minister of the Federation of Rhodesia and Nyasaland, Sir Roy Welensky.

In my work, I was required to accompany Sir Roy on many of his visits to the cities and towns of Central Africa. There were new businesses to open, mines to tour, conferences and agricultural shows to attend, and fêtes to patronise. Some of the trips were connected with party business and, being a civil servant, I was not asked to take part in that aspect of them. Nevertheless, in the relatively short time I was in the post I flew to Sir Roy's constituency many times. Broken Hill (now Kabwe) had the feel of a frontier town in a Hollywood western. The normal amenities of urban life were so lacking that, at that oppressive time of the year when the thermometer stood well above 40°C and the rains had not yet brought relief, the season was often referred to as the suicide months. After my appointment, the principal private secretary made sure I was always the one chosen to go there.

It was bad driving the hundred-and-sixty-odd kilometres between Broken Hill and the copper-mining town of Ndola: the route passed through a country possessing few landmarks – apart from the inevitable aloes and the hills thrown up by the termites – so that (the story went) after rain, cars spinning off the road in the mud would leave their occupants uncertain whether they were still facing the way they wanted to go.

One memorable experience during this period was the Prime Minister's tour of the north, using the Dakota of the Royal Rhodesian Air Force he invariably flew in. The principal private secretary, Stewart Parker, was ill and so it fell to me to accompany Sir Roy instead. The first stop was Mongu. Barotseland was a separate protectorate within the Protectorate of Northern Rhodesia and Mongu was its official capital, but there had to be two seats of government because the Zambezi plain flooded every year, making it necessary for the inhabitants to fall back, with appropriate ceremony, to the surrounding hills until the waters receded with the coming of the dry season.

It was Lewanika, a paramount chief of Barotseland in the late nineteenth century, who granted the concession to Cecil Rhodes whereby the British South Africa Company enjoyed all the mineral rights in Northern Rhodesia.

Here we attended a session of the *Saa-Sikalo Kuta*, the council of the paramount chief. Before speaking, each *induna* (councillor) would kneel in a form of *kowtow* and clap his hands; when addressing the chief direct he would approach, always on his knees, to within a respectful distance.

A pleasant surprise was to find Hugh Synge, a fellow student at Bristol University who had applied to the Colonial Service at about the same time as I joined the Central African service.

After stops in Lusaka, Kitwe, Fort Rosebery (now Mansa), Abercorn (now Mbala) and Mpika, we made our last overnight stop at Shiwa Ngandu, the home of Sir Stewart Gore-Brown. Sir Roy worked with him in friendly rivalry before World War II when Sir Stewart represented indigenous African interests on the Legislative Council in Lusaka and Sir Roy was serving as a member elected by White voters. At the end of a lengthy drive from Mpika – for the local airstrip had been reconnoitred in advance and found inadequate to take a Dakota although this aircraft would cope with most airfields – and at a height of one thousand five hundred metres, Shiwa House rose out of the surrounding bush like a Disney castle. Erected on ten thousand hectares in the east of Northern Rhodesia, it took ten years to build. It was actually still incomplete, though it boasted a keep, a chapel and battlements, not to mention barns with Gothic windows. We were shown round a hospital in the grounds for TB and leprosy patients. I slept in a mediaeval turret, a surreal experience in the middle of Africa.

At an open-air concert performed by a choir drawn from the people living on Sir Stewart's land, I heard for the first time the hymn *God Bless Africa* which later became a familiar anthem on the continent. The entertainment also included a trip round a nearby stretch of water in a Lake Tanganyika fishing boat fitted with an 8 hp outboard motor. The boat leaked so badly that by the time we returned to dry land we had sunk up to the gunwales and there was nowhere dry to put our feet down.

On his walls Sir Stewart had a collection of macabre prints including two, appropriately captioned, of whites being hanged in Tasmania for murdering aborigines and aborigines being similarly executed for killing whites, which he gleefully brought to the attention of Sir Roy. I cannot say whether this unbiased approach to justice was a novel concept for Australians in the nineteenth century but the point our host was making seemed obscure: the courts of Central Africa were renowned for their even-handedness and in any case they were not a Federal responsibility. However, he appeared to take a malicious delight in having the pictures on display. The two knights were having a friendly joust.

OP 98 (October 2009)

Part 2
PROFESSIONAL & TECHNICAL

Reminiscences of the Leeward Islands, 1931-1934

by Winifred K O'Mahony

"**Y**ou will be posted as Supernumerary Medical Officer in the Leeward Islands – based in the first instance in Antigua." So ran the directive from the Colonial Office to Dr O'Mahony, then my fiancé. That meant a somewhat hurried wedding, and since the ceremony was to be performed by Dr Leighton Williams, Archbishop of Birmingham, no time could be lost. Our wedding took place in the beautiful Oratory Church in Edgbaston and a few days later we left on a small cargo-cum-mail steamer bound for the far away Leeward Islands. Little was known of Antigua in 1931, even the postal authorities in our General Post Office could give us only the vaguest information anent mail. However, we were young, full of good endeavour, and the whole project seemed a tremendous challenge. Money presented a problem, most of our available cash had been expended on medical instruments, tropical kit and so on. The Leeward Islands Government were to pay us a meagre salary of £400 per annum, and anything above this would have to come from problematical private practice.

Two weeks later we were anchored off Antigua and welcomed by the Chief Medical Officer and a tall white uniformed Irish Chief of Police. Once ashore we were taken to what was euphemistically called an Hotel. It turned out to be nothing more than a boarding-house situated over a dock-side warehouse. Here we were quickly informed that water was in very short supply, and that it was an ever-present problem of that particular island. Thus we discovered that no baths were available, and no sewerage system existed. Although septic tanks were installed in many buildings, most of them were constantly out of use. My husband was inducted into the medical organisation and colleagues took him on tours of the various institutions.

A couple of days later we were invited to a formal dinner at Government House, and here came our first social problem. In a temperature of 90° F, how on earth could my husband keep a dress collar stiff for more than 15 minutes, and how on earth could I peel on long white kid gloves over my constantly perspiring skin. Collar studs were lost, buttons came off, we swore and we prayed. But we coped, and with our first milestone passed, we survived crumpled but triumphant.

Antigua is a pretty island measuring some 8 miles by 10, with a few hills, none of which exceed 1,300 feet. Its greatest assets are the beautiful white coral beaches with relatively safe bathing. St John's, the capital, has wide streets lined with two storey shops, warehouses etc, painted a glaring white. The Cathedral, an interesting structure, is a double building, the inside being built of wood, whilst the outer shell is of stone; thus it was hoped to make it earthquake-proof. North of the town lies a big open Savannah around which are built some fine residences, Government House, and the Prison buildings. The General Hospital lies some two miles further north, composed mostly of wooden hutments in a large area of grass and rough gardens.

We had little opportunity of exploring the island as within a week or so we were told to pack our kit and go on to the neighbouring island of St Christopher, locally known as St Kitts. One of their two Medical Officers had died from septicaemia and we were urgently required. We travelled on one of the excellent Canadian 'Lady' boats which called at most of the West Indian islands regularly.

St Kitts is quite lovely. A central range of mountains with Mount Misery, an extinct volcano, dominating the island. Lush tropical vegetation grows well into the mountains whilst cane-fields spread like huge green carpets in the lowlands. Small grey monkeys abound and it is a common sight to see lorries returning from the mountains after week-end 'shoots' with a cross-bar over the back holding a dozen or so of these pathetic little carcases, their heads threaded through slits in their long prehensile tails. Monkey meat is much sought after by the natives and said to be delicious. We did not, repeat *not*, sample it.

But of comfort there was none. Once again we stayed in the only available boarding-house, its bedrooms separated by 8ft partitions. More water was available here, though primitive plumbing, intolerably hard beds, atrocious food, and swarms of mosquitoes and sandflies made for immense discomfort. Cockroaches, some 2 inches long, adorned the walls and floors by night, and when rain came they started flying around and joined up with the other winged horrors.

After a few days in St Kitts we were hurriedly summoned to nearby Nevis. Another Medical Officer had died. By now I was getting distinctly uneasy, wondering what on earth was happening to the doctors in this area.

Gradually I gleaned the truth. These were the days before sulphonamides, penicillin, and other modern antibiotics. In consequence, cross-infections were frequent hazards. In a hot humid climate there was nothing to fight infection, and after operations, for instance, it was only a patient's natural immunity that safeguarded him from sepsis of one kind or another.

A small steam launch plies between St Kitts and its sister island of Nevis, the distance being approximately 11 miles. About a dozen or so passengers are carried on this tiny craft together with produce of every kind. Live chickens, pigs, and even the odd goat or two. Seats at the prow are available to the earliest arrivals, the rest have to scramble on to the hatch of the little engine room or any other available space. Into this medley we climbed and praised Heaven that we were both 'good sailors'.

Hazardous though the journey appeared, we were to find a comparatively comfortable old Hotel, a relic of a more prosperous era. A hundred or so years ago Nevis had been the social Mecca of the nearby islands with a large white population. Now, however, much poverty was apparent and only a handful of white folk remained. Sugar cane and cotton had originally brought great wealth to the island and slaves in their hundreds had worked on the estates. Fame had come through the hot sulphur streams which gushed from open soufrières on Mount Nevis. These had been channelled down the mountain side and into bath houses in the grounds of the Bath Hotel. Their chemical content was said to be a panacea for many ailments, and thus from many miles distant visitors had come to Nevis for their curative value. We ourselves were later to find them of immense benefit after the exertion of climbing in the nearby mountains.

The island boasted two lighting plants, small *Delco* sets. One was installed at Government House where the Warden resided, the other was in the little Hospital. It was not long before my husband had the first of many wretched experiences when the lights failed whilst he was operating for a strangulated hernia. He finished under the doubtful rays of torchlights and hurricane lanterns held by assistant nurses. Small wonder that he stayed at the hospital all night awaiting the outcome of such perilous surgery. However, the patient survived and the operation a complete success.

It was in Nevis that I was first introduced to the practice of *Obeah*. Awaiting my husband at the end of the Magistrate's Court one day I listened whilst Dr O'Mahony gave medical evidence for the prosecution in a vicious stabbing case. I was intrigued to hear the Superintendent of Police ask an already sentenced man to remove his shoes. He had been observed shuffling his feet whilst in the witness box and this was sufficient evidence for the observant police. Inside his shoes was found a filthy piece of paper on which had been written the names of Dr O'Mahony and the other witness for the prosecution. His odd antics had been a warning of dire retribution against anyone who dared to testify against him. The result was a further sentence added to the one already given for the main offence. I soon learned what a hold these practices had on all the negroes and indeed on many white West Indians as well. They were particularly superstitious about corn-meal, fish bones, blue coloured bottles etc. Any of these found on a doorstep or near the entrance to a home would put the owner in a perfect frenzy of fear. Dust from grave-yards and any small bones that were available were considered particularly strong *Juju*. Some months later than this I was invited to sit on the Bench with a visiting Puisne Judge during an *Obeah* trial, and he had before him a vast array of 'Instruments of *Obeah*' which had been seized by police during a raid. Hatred and fear achieve incredible results in those quiet and primitive islands. Servants would put *Obeah* on their masters or mistresses in the hope of inflicting some injury upon them. Years later I was to find a hard substance in one of my own pillows, which, when investigated, turned out to be a tiny muslin cushion filled with small black crystals and an unknown white powder. Obviously this too was the handiwork of a disgruntled house-servant who wished me ill fortune.

Time passed and we gradually got used to the intense heat and many privations. Calls on the doctor were not very onerous and we had time to explore this beautiful island. Many fine old plantation houses remained, though all were in a shocking state of repair. Ruins of the sugar mills with their great sails crumbling away were a sombre echo of the past. Sections of the chains which were used to restrain the more recalcitrant slaves were still to be found in the big archways under the mill structures, but the walls are now encrusted with wild flowers and maiden-hair ferns.

The tiny capital, Charlestown, with its stone-built church and municipal buildings, was clustered around a grass-laden square, giving a delightful English appearance. Unhappily most of these were subsequently destroyed or badly damaged in severe earth tremors of the 1940s. Though there was no eruption from Mount Nevis itself, great columns of steam erupted in the sea offshore. History relates that the original capital – Jamestown – now lies beneath the sea following a severe earthquake very many years previously, when that section of the island subsided into the sea.

A few months passed and we were again transferred, this time to Montserrat, another island in the Leeward group. We now realised from these constant moves exactly what being a Supernumerary Medical Officer meant. Again we were in a beautiful island, lush green, volcanic and exciting. The 'Hotel' was similar to those of Antigua and St Kitts, with bedrooms rather resembling horse-boxes. Our sojourn in this hostelry was short, however, since they charged us to within 10/- per week of our entire salary. Appeals were made to a kindly planter and he put at our disposal a small house up in the hills, partly furnished and long since unoccupied. Oh yes, there *was* a bathroom but we were warned not to make use of it since snakes constantly crawled through the jalousies. This proved to be somewhat of an exaggeration. However, we coped and we managed and invested in our first car, an old Chevrolet for which we paid £25. By now we felt reasonably independent and secure. For my own recreation I was occasionally able to borrow a police horse and enjoy some hacking on the lower mountain paths. There was no bathing, the beaches being covered in black volcanic sand and quite unsuitable for such a pastime. The soil was rich, and abundant flowers and vegetables were available. 'Sea island' cotton was one of the principal crops and together with sugar cane formed the island's main exports. Tomatoes, citrus fruits, and pineapples were prolific, whilst fields of aubergines – known as 'egg-plants' – grew to the size of small footballs.

Time passed slowly and then near disaster came. On a quiet Saturday night a telephone call from the Police Station summoned my husband into Town to look after a woman who had been injured. Just that – no details were given, and I decided to accompany Dr O'Mahony for a cool evening's drive. Once in the little town of Plymouth we realised that the street petrol-lamps were out and indeed smashed, whilst the broken glass started puncturing our tyres. We pressed on at speed to the Police Station and found a screaming mob outside, whilst a Superintendent of Police quickly ushered us within. My husband went straight to the care of his patient and I was sent into the Charge Room where to my surprise I found the Magistrate, his wife, and their small child. It appeared that they had come to the Police Station for sanctuary as the mob had already smashed in the windows of their nearby home. All the trouble had started when a drunken man had resisted arrest. The rum shops were just closing and quickly a crowd had gathered and endeavoured to release the man from police custody. Tempers quickly flared and in no time there was a near riot. The magistrate's house had been the first to be attacked and then the crowd moved on to the Police Station.

Huge stones and pieces of rock were showered on the small wooden building, and soon we heard the smashing of the upper windows which were police dormitories, and as such were unprotected except by jalousies. Fortunately the lower windows at street level were steel barred and so afforded us some protection. Presently several policemen were brought in with severe injuries as the crowd were resorting to broken bottles as weapons. I ventured to offer help to my husband who was overwhelmed with casualties. Within seconds a huge stone came hurtling through the window missing Dr O'Mahony's head by inches and smashing down on his patient's hand. I was summarily dismissed. By dawn tempers had cooled and we prepared to make our way home. Our car, which had been parked outside, was literally smashed to pieces. Tyres, seats and radiator had been literally slashed and it appeared a complete wreck. The other Medical Officer on the island, a coloured man and a delightful person, came to our aid and offered to drive us home, but not before the police had issued us with my husband's revolver, previously deposited with them for safe keeping. In 48 hours or so the whole trouble had died down, and after a handful of arrests the island once more resumed its peaceful existence.

OP 50 (November 1985)

Leeward Islands

This must be the oddest colonial badge of all! It depicts a large pineapple growing unnaturally on the sea shore, with three much smaller pineapples beyond. On the sea behind are two sailing ships of unequal size, both out of scale. Beyond the ships are some low hills. This badge was introduced in 1874, shortly after the Leeward Islands were re-constituted as a Federal colony, of four Presidencies. The most important one was Antigua, where pineapples were a major crop at that time. However, the new Governor who submitted the design to the Admiralty for approval was Sir Benjamin Pine and some believe that he chose to make a punning reference to himself and his family. The badge remained in use until 1956 when the Leeward Islands Federation was dissolved.

The Making of a Colonial Agriculturalist

by Justin Trevor Moon

It came to my notice during my final Summer Term in 1930 that the Colonial Office was embarking on its annual recruiting drive to obtain twenty or so agriculturalists for the colonial territories, and applications were invited. This seemed the opportunity I had been seeking and I sent my name forward. Successful candidates were to be granted a two-year scholarship to cover a post-graduate year at Oxford or Cambridge and a further year at the Imperial College of Tropical Agriculture, Trinidad. I was called for an interview at the Colonial Office along with a hundred or so other applicants, and realised how much depended on this ordeal.

When my time came I was ushered into a room which appeared to be crammed full of the most terrifying old men. I had just sat down and accepted a cigarette when the phone rang and I blessed the caller. It gave me a minute or two to settle down and study the ring of faces. By the time the telephone call was over I had come to the conclusion that the 'terrifying old men' were probably a very decent lot and so they proved to be.

Some weeks later I was informed that, subject to passing my final exams, which I was just about to sit, I had been selected for one of the scholarships. The fact that the job to which these scholarships led was a pensionable one and the salary was about double that of an equivalent Government post in England was to me quite irrelevant. In all probability unless I made a nonsense, I would end up somewhere in Africa, and the prospect was an intriguing one.

I went up to Cambridge for the post-graduate year in October 1930. The post-graduate course placed very great emphasis on field experimentation and the statistical interpretation of agricultural experiments. What it did not tell us was what the wretched Agricultural Officer was to do when elephant or wild pig took a fancy to your experiment, or your own labour force filled its bellies with green corn on the cob from the inner hidden portions of your experimental plots. Many of us on arrival in Africa were thrown in at the deep end on agricultural expansion work and had little or no opportunity to employ our newly-won knowledge of the mysteries of statistical interpretation.

Trinidad

On 21 September 1931, our young party of trainee tropical agriculturists sailed from Avonmouth for Trinidad in an Elder & Fyffes banana boat. Towards the end of the voyage there was a bit of a party on board and I can still remember how painful the white coral sand of the Barbados beaches was the next day. I can imagine no more horrible cure for a hangover than a Barbados beach at midday without dark glasses. At the party, after midnight, some of our students decided that their surplus energy might be usefully employed by stoking the boilers of our coal-burning ship. Still wearing dinner-jackets or, in some cases, white mess jackets, they descended to the stoke-hold where the engineer on watch entered into the spirit of the evening and permitted them to proceed. The regular firemen were only too pleased to hand over their shovels and sit back, have a good laugh and offer useful advice. After a bit the amateur stokers thought coal was pretty poor stuff for steam-raising and foraging parties were sent off to all the lavatories, the 'Ladies' included, to collect toilet rolls. In one of the ladies' lavatories one of the students unfortunately came face to face with the wife of a senior man from the Colonial Office travelling with her husband. The toilet rolls were most effective and in no time we were blowing off surplus steam, and so did the CO man the next morning. After some investigation he found the ring-leader of the whole escapade and said he would be reported to the appropriate branch of the CO. Like so many things in that building, the report must have gone astray, and the culprit subsequently had a particularly brilliant career in the Colonial Agricultural Service.

The world depression, which started with the Wall Street crash in 1929, hit the colonial territories somewhat later. We had been in Trinidad only a very short time when it became only too apparent that competition for the very few vacancies in the Service was likely to be severe. As a consequence, our year soon got the reputation for working a great deal harder than any previous batch of students as a lot would depend on our performance in the final examinations. This did not mean that we did not find time to enjoy ourselves. We soon acquired the art of consuming rum punches, which was an essential part of our agricultural training, for the generosity of the Trinidad planters was quite exceptional.

Readers will wonder why we were sent to Trinidad at great expense to enjoy ourselves. We were young and of course we had a good time. We had all received already a good basic training in temperate agricultural science and the purpose of the Trinidad year was to superimpose tropical agriculture on that knowledge. When we got out there, for most of us it was the first time we had seen sugar cane, bananas, cacao, rice, millet, groundnuts and a host of other crops actually growing. Trinidad was able to show us most tropical crops and, backed up by good and interesting lectures, we felt we learned a lot. It was only later, when we had been working in our own particular territory in Africa, or elsewhere, that we realised how much depended on local experience. Nevertheless, the Trinidad course was a really first-class introduction to the particular problems of tropical agriculture.

In June 1932 we were due to return to England to await appointment. The depression had now hit all countries good and proper and when we landed in England we were told to seek temporary employment but to be prepared to leave at very short notice. I worked for no salary at the Rothamsted Experiment Station in Hertfordshire until my money ran out and then on a poultry farm in Hampshire for twenty six shillings a week, National Insurance being my responsibility. In August 1933, at a tennis party in Wallington, I learnt from the grapevine that I was to be appointed to Kenya. The letter from the Colonial Office confirming this was dated 30th November. I sailed for Kenya in the SS *Llangibby Castle* on the 25th January 1934, and arrived in Mombasa on the 18th February.

Coast Province, Kenya

The journey out was interesting but not particularly eventful. After leaving Europe the ports of call on the East Africa route – Port Said, Port Sudan and Aden – present in general a picture of sandy wastes with little vegetation. Arrival at Mombasa was a marked contrast and the green of that island never ceased to amaze me. After we had docked I received written notification of my posting and it appeared that I would have but a short journey, for I had been posted to the Coast Province. The Agricultural Officer i/c Coast was there to meet me and after lunch with the Provincial Commissioner he drove me the 40 miles to Kilifi, where I was to share his house until he went on leave in June. He had taken his cook to Mombasa with him but the latter failed to turn up and we left him to make his own way out. This created a minor problem about who was to cook dinner but T– was confident that a neighbour, Mollie Lillywhite, would give us a meal. The Lillywhites lived at Sokoki, about seven miles away, and of course there was no telephone. After a bath we set off and I was introduced to the wonderful spirit of hospitality which prevailed everywhere in East Africa. African servants never failed when asked to produce extra food at short notice – in fact, I believe they thrived on such changes to the dull routine of their work.

The road up to Sokoki was little more than a bush track, with tall grass growing between the two wheel tracks. Suddenly a small African child, who had been sleeping in the grass on the road, jumped up in the headlights and dashed into a nearby village. T–, without hesitation, turned the car off the road, over a rudimentary ditch and into the clear area around the huts. He just caught sight of the fleeing child dashing into an open hut and brought his car up tight against the doorway to block it. The village headman was called and told to produce a stick and the child. The stick proved to be only a maize stalk, but it was applied to the child's bottom and he co-operated in the charade by screaming loudly, unhurt by the ineffective instrument but probably badly frightened. Rough justice, but subsequently I don't suppose he persisted with the dangerous habit of sleeping on motor tracks, even bush ones. My first night in Africa seemed eventful to me but, looking back on it later, I feel T–'s actions were more directed at me, the new boy, than to the miserable child, as it was important that I should be educated in the correct way of dealing with such matters.

I took on a head house-boy by the name of Athmani, a Swahili by tribe, who naturally spoke Kiswahili very well, a language I had to learn quickly, and I insisted that he should use it and not English. T–, quite rightly, was determined to push me in at the deep end and the language problem had to be overcome very quickly. I spent a great deal of time getting a reasonable vocabulary and Athmani collaborated marvellously. He was an excellent servant, a real relic of the old days, and had knocked around a bit and seen service as far away as Government House in Uganda. Later, when T– departed on leave, he took over running the house and did it exceedingly well. As part of my training T– sent me on a foot safari well up the Sabaki river in the sub-district of Malindi, which at that time was suffering simultaneously from drought, famine, locusts and smallpox. It was an area which obviously had received very little attention from outside. It was clear that a new boy like myself could achieve little for the benefit of the long-suffering people. Nevertheless, from that safari I learnt a great deal and formed ideas on what an Agricultural Officer should do. In the long term the trip was not a waste of time, but the African cultivators must have regarded the arrival of a youngster as a bit of a bore. However, they poured out their troubles through my Arab clerk, who acted as interpreter, and at least they could feel that they had got something off their chests.

My next safari was in May, to Digo District south of Mombasa, where cotton as a cash crop was being introduced for the first time. I was to travel to Waa, eight miles south of Mombasa, by lorry and thereafter to walk to the Tanganyika border some 50 miles away directly, but considerably more by the zig-zag route I followed to cover the maximum area possible. May is a very wet month on the Coast but I was not prepared for the 25 inches of rain we received in May that year. When I reached Ramisi, 40 miles from Mombasa and the end of the motor road, I had planned to cut across direct to Vanga on the Tanganyika border but before we left the Ramisi Sugar Estate behind it was obvious we were going to experience trouble in crossing the rivers ahead. One bridge taking the estate light railway line over the Ramisi river had lost all the planks laid across the sleepers for the benefit of foot travellers. All of us, including the porters with their head-loads, had to cross on the widely-spaced sleepers with a raging torrent a few inches below.

Further on the whole countryside was flooded and we were up to our knees in water. The porters rather naturally fell much behind and when I reached the chosen camp site I waited on an ant-hill for the main party to turn up. Dark came and so did the mosquitoes. Nine days later, and fortunately at home again, I went down with my first bout of malaria. After an uncomfortable night I learnt that the flooding was much worse ahead and that crocodiles had left the rivers and were everywhere. On advice, I decided we could not get the porters through by the direct route so we should make for Shimoni on the sea by travelling on higher land. The local chief undertook to send a note to Vanga to summon up the Customs boat to rescue us at Shimoni, and the arrival later of the boat at Shimoni indicated that the messenger had survived the crocodiles, at least on the outward journey.

After a night at Shimoni we set off in the Customs boat for Vanga and had a fairly uneventful passage – apart from running on to a sandbank. With all sails set to ease the work, everyone except myself and including the Arab *nahodha* (captain) was on the sandbank pushing us off. I had visions of the boat suddenly freeing herself and sailing away towards India like the *Marie Celeste* without a crew. I was to learn later that all African sailors are used to running aground and are very nimble at climbing aboard at the crucial moment.

The approach to Vanga through a maze of mangrove swamps is most depressing. After many turns in the waterway a low-lying Arab settlement appeared at the end of the creek and we had arrived. During my stay I toured the exceedingly fertile Umba valley which accounts for Vanga's existence. I was very interested to see a coconut plantation which, in 1934, still showed evidence in the form of shell holes through the palm boles of a fierce engagement with the Germans in the Kaiser's war.

My work completed, I returned by the same route to Ramisi and then, for a change, by lorry back to Mombasa. At Ramisi I met Pousse, the French engineer in charge of the sugar factory, who spent any leisure he had with a rifle after game. Once, accompanied by five Luo tribesmen, he had shot a hippo and, turning to his small band of Africans, he suggested they call their friends to join in the feast. They were appalled at the idea and made it quite clear that there was only enough meat for five. The African's craving for meat is understandable but his capacity for eating it is unbelievable. When a beast is shot some tribes cannot resist eating the choicer bits raw on the spot. The rest is carried home in bloody lumps and they gorge themselves sick.

The frenzy for meat is illustrated in the following episode. A Wye friend of mine, shortly after his arrival in Kenya, went on a big game safari. He had shot an elephant, which his African followers rapidly disembowelled. Several of them, stark naked and covered in blood, were inside the carcase hacking off tasty pieces of meat. In the mêlée and semi-darkness one of them, perceiving a very choice piece, seized it and was about to cut it off. It was, however, the particularly personal part of one of his friends, who fortunately yelled just in time.

I reached Kilifi a day or so later and home was very pleasant after a tough, wet and uncomfortable safari. I had learnt a great deal more about another part of the Province and if I was to be of any use to the cultivators that knowledge was essential. Even at that stage of my exuberant youth, I could see that local knowledge of farming methods was vital. What we had all learnt at Wye and Trinidad was useful as a basis, but you had to build on that base with the bits and pieces of local farming methods. Many of these practices were intrinsically bad and slovenly, but others had a reason behind them even if outwardly appearing wrong. One had to discover what it was and whether by a simple change in the system a better result could be achieved with little or no extra effort. At this stage in the development of the country it was useless devising sophisticated plans which were beyond the capabilities of the cultivator.

OP 50 (November 1985), OP 51 (April 1986), OP 52 (October 1986)

Children of Arabia, 1944-46

by Mary Fletcher

In the early part of the famine in the Eastern Aden Protectorate in 1944, many of the sick and starving children were moved from the famine areas of the Wadi Hadhramaut by truck 200 miles to the coast, to Mukalla. This practice was discontinued when all transport was needed for grain movements and when the airlift began to make on-the-spot feeding and treatment possible, but in the meantime, a number of children were being cared for in Mukalla in makeshift hospitals. In time, they were sufficiently recovered to be discharged – but many were orphans, or of unknown identity or parentage.

The boys were easily adopted by the Hadhrami Bedouin Legion (HBL), who were accustomed to training boys from the Wadi as soldiers and who were themselves mostly Wadi Bedouin. The girls were a different matter. At that time there was virtually no female education in Mukalla and certainly no residential possibilities – even in 1946 the only girls education was a Koran class in the house of a leading Sheikh, taken by his daughter as previously instructed by her father. Obviously the girls had to leave the hospital. In this crisis the Bedouin Legion took on the girls as well as the boys, arranged accommodation for them and a 'matron' to look after them, and undertook their care and education. Two years later, when I first met them, there were about thirty girls in the school, age range about six to eleven. As they reached marriageable age, they left to be wives of soldiers or occasionally local citizens.

The Bedouin Legion had, of course, no precedent of female education to go on, so the girls were treated like their male counterparts, as budding soldiers. Apart from having their own quarters with their 'matron' and her woman helper, and learning a little sewing and doing some cooking, they had a soldierly regime of reading, writing, Koran, drill and PT under visiting Legion officers and under military discipline. They were dressed in a sort of female version of the HBL tunic, with a white headdress.

It became my husband's and my habit to visit and also to entertain the girls on such occasions as the 'Ids. On these occasions, they were delivered by HBL lorry, with Matron and her Assistant (duly veiled), and marched neatly into our compound, saluting smartly.

How do you entertain 30 little girls, aged 6-11, without toys, presents, cinema or entertainers? Food, of course, is one way: the luxuries, such as they were, of *Mukalla suq* (market). The children squatted on the ground round the white cloth with its curry puffs, various sweetmeats and fizzy drinks. The children waited politely and silently until invited to begin: thirty seconds later the silence was broken by the noise of thirty pairs of jaws biting smartly into thirty brittle curry puffs. They ate politely, silently, quickly – and extensively.

Before that, there had been games. I dredged my memory for every kind of game, race, team race, team game, playground activity that I could think of. (One thing about parties, it never rained on us.) Perhaps I would say, 'We need three teams'. Up would jump the three eldest girls, salute, pick teams, and salute again. After one halting explanation by me, and a trial run by them, they were hard at it. The trouble was that everything was done at the double, and a game which would take half an hour in the UK would be over in ten minutes. It took a lot of thought and planning to fill the time, and once they had learnt a game, they would play it at school and hope to learn new ones on their next visit.

Games, food, and then a farewell and thank-you speech, learnt and delivered with pre-planned gestures (which went somewhat wrong on one occasion when my husband and I were sitting the wrong way round for the speaker). Often I was presented with a little hand-embroidered cloth. It was all somewhat incongruous but delightful, like so much of life in Arabia to UK eyes.

The establishment of the school had been a triumph of pragmatism, improvisation and commonsense. It ran so contrary to the trend of life in Mukalla at that time that it appeared to be scarcely noticed by the community at large and to have no influence at all on female education. After all, they were only girls.

As so often happens in the Colonial Service, I never saw the end of the story – I suppose the school closed quietly when the last pupil reached the marriageable age of twelve. But somewhere in South Yemen, behind the Iron Curtain, there must be some women aged about fifty who are HBL Old Girls. It would be interesting to know what they are like now – probably very little different from the other women around them, just as I am an ordinary UK suburban grannie. But what a field day the sociologists would have if this could happen (as of course it can't) in the eighties!

OP 54 (October 1987)

A War Effort in Tanganyika

by John H Harris

When the Second World War broke out I was not allowed to enlist and was commissioned to increase the production of gold and other minerals for the war effort and it fell to me to help in the production of rubber and sisal and in other activities unexpectedly related to mineralogical expertise.

Rubber

It so happened that when Tanganyika was a German colony (German East Africa, 1891-1918) an attempt had been made to start rubber planting. Lacking the climate and soil conditions of Malaya the regular rubber tree *(Para)* was not a success, but the knobbly-barked *Ceara* proved hardy in conditions varying seasonally from moist to semi-arid and was a useful source of latex. An extensive stand had been planted south of Morogoro. By 1941 it had all but disappeared in the encroaching bush. Two rubber planters who had escaped from Malaya were brought in to evaluate the trees and they decided that it might be worth attempting production.

The undergrowth was cleared and tapping was tried. The first set of tapping knives was produced by the Tanganyika Railways workshops in Dar es Salaam from old railway wagon springs. The special hook-shaped knife is sharpened on both leading and trailing edges and requires continuous honing in use. In Malaya they used a *Water of Ayr* stone which is a natural fine-grained abrasive, cut into slips four inches long by an inch or so wide, tapered from one long side to the other and used wet. A plea came up to the Geological Survey – could we produce such a honing stone? Yes, we said, but we have no means of cutting it into such slips.

However, it occurred to me that we could fabricate a suitable hone by incorporating grains of abrasive into a ceramic body. Rapid experimentation produced a hone containing corundum as the abrasive bound into a ceramic composed of local kaolin, silt and soda and fired in our own kiln. It proved suitable and within a month we were in production at the rate of hundreds a week. We mined the corundum (which is the hardest natural stone next to diamond and is also the mineralogical constituent of rubies and sapphires) in the Central Province, not far from our headquarters office at Dodoma, and crushed and graded it in our laboratories. The kaolin we mined at Malangali 220 miles away. It was an impure variety on which we had been experimenting pre-war. Its impurities played a part in the formation of our unique ceramic, which was also modified by the addition of the local silt dug out of our water-supply reservoir and of soda from Magadi in Kenya.

All these ingredients were mixed by hand with added water into a dough-like constituency, spatula-fed into wooden moulds to the exact required shape and racked to air-dry. The moulding and racking systems were worked out by my former chief, Frank Oates. I did design an extrusion press and had it made in the Railway workshops but the hand-made system got under way faster, using a crew of ten in a rapidly built extension to our laboratories. We even introduced a hole in the corner of the hone so that the tappers could string it on a cord around their necks. This greatly suited the tribe of Wagogo from the Central Province who proved the most expert rubber-tappers. And so we enabled the production of rubber to get going.

When it became known that we were producing abrasives, new calls arose. The first was for the type of sharpening stone used by carpenters for plane blades and chisels which is relatively coarse on one side and smooth on the other. The problem arose of moulding and firing these two disparate masses together without distortion but we solved that. Several hundred were made and distributed widely, even to Uganda and Kenya.

Rope

The next episode averted a disaster. The loss of Manila to the enemy left sisal as the only fibre available on a large scale for ropes and cordage, in those days before the advent of polypropylene. The prospect of HM ships breaking loose from their moorings as the last rope parted was too awful to envisage, so the great sisal estates in Tanganyika had to maintain and increase production. Critical to the process is the decorticator, a vast machine which separates the pulp from the sisal leaf leaving the fibres long, clean and unbroken. To keep the machine running efficiently in this delicate separation, the beaters on its huge drums have to be honed constantly to fine limits. This is done by an abrasive cup-wheel mounted over the drum and mechanically traversed across the beaters at right angles to their travel and at a rotational speed of 10,000 revolutions per minute.

The industry then broke its last cup-wheel. The prospect of war-time imports was remote so I was set to making cup-wheels. This time, obviously, accurate balance was a priority. Using the facilities of our own workshop (which was designed for servicing heavy drilling equipment) our African foreman turned out from wood the circular forms which were needed for pressing out the cup shapes, which then required special firing procedures to avert distortion. We made the metal bosses of the wheels from the lead of old car batteries and trued them up on the lathe with a tool made of corundum. I took the first one personally to the sisal estate which had approached us and saw that it fitted accurately on to the spindle of the high-speed electric motor. Then I stood back, heart in mouth, as it spun into action, safely, accurately and efficiently. More and more of these wheels were made as requests came in. I think we saved the industry from shut down.

Beef

The next episode was directed towards the acceleration of the production of beef for the armed forces. This demanded the extension of herds of cattle, which in turn demanded control of tsetse fly. This involved cutting swathes through the forests which required regiments of men with pangas and the pangas required sharpening. Scythe stones were the traditional tools, but a supply from home was again out of the question so I started production of sharpening sticks made from my abrasive formula. This time my hand-operated extrusion machine came into use, with a die made from Kisii stone from Kenya, hardened in the kiln to resist the abrasion. The sticks were extruded on to boards provided with grooves on to which the sticks slid and were cut off to size. To facilitate the sliding action the grooves were lubricated with graphite which we also had to mine from local deposits and process in the laboratory. Several thousand of these sticks were fired in our kiln and distributed to the teams in the field. (Some found their way on to the dining tables of Colonial Service colleagues for use as sharpeners for their carving knives.)

Buttons

In between we had a little go at razor-blade sharpeners but the final effort arose from a request from the military for a million trouser buttons. I had already succeeded in making ceramic buttons from Kisii stone so I decided that I could go into production if I could use the pill-press which the Medicals were using to produce anti-malarials from our local growths of cinchona. Our workshop made the dies and we were ready to go when the news arrived that the buttons were no longer required. They were going to use zip-fasteners.

OP 79 (May 2000)

Tanganyika

The Giraffe's head was adopted as the badge of Tanganyika in 1919, shortly before the British Mandate was formally declared in 1920. The head, with a short neck, was supposed to be shown by itself, but was often depicted on a white disc. It is not yet known who suggested having a giraffe, but other British territories in Africa had already chosen badges depicting an elephant, a lion, a leopard, and a kudu, and, in South Africa, a springbok (gazelle) was a national symbol.

How Government Officers Became Official Opium Dealers in the Old Federated Malay States

by J S A Lewis

Before 1874 the Malay Peninsula was comprised of the Straits Settlements, ie Singapore, Penang and Malacca, and nine Native States ruled by their own Sultans. In 1874 three of these Native States, Perak, Selangor and Negri Sembilan, accepted a British Adviser to assist the Sultans in the administration of each State and in 1888 the Sultan of Pahang also accepted a British Adviser. In 1896 all four States became a British Protectorate and were known as the Federated Malay States, whilst the remaining five States continued to be ruled by their Sultans and, in due course, with the assistance of a British Adviser.

Even by 1874 there was a large number of Chinese immigrants in the Federated States working in tin mines and as shopkeepers and many of these had brought with them their opium smoking habit. In order to raise revenue to pay for the administration costs of the Federated States the authorities had, since 1875, imposed a tax on the importation and sale of opium, although their main source of revenue was the export duty on tin and tin ore. The export duty on rubber was not introduced until 1906. For ease of collection, the right to import opium, prepare it for smoking and sell it to their customers was farmed out to the highest bidder in the coastal districts. (This had already been the practice in the Straits Settlements since 1835.) In inland tin mining areas the tin mine owners and large employers of Chinese labour were licensed at a fee to supply the drug to their opium smoking employees.

This state of affairs continued until 1910 when the British Government (which had taken over the control of India and the Straits Settlements from the East India Company in 1867) decided that the Colonial Governments of both the Straits Settlements and the Federation should take over the job of importing and selling the opium themselves. This was due to a growing anti-opium sentiment in Britain at the beginning of this century, which forced the British Government to take some action to reduce opium smoking in its overseas possessions. No doubt this was more profitable to the local treasuries but, of more importance, it enabled the Colonial Governments to exercise proper control over the drug traffic.

In Singapore the Government created the Monopolies Department to implement the new policy and built a factory to convert the raw opium into a form suitable for smoking and to pack it for distribution. The raw opium, which was imported from India, resembled dark brown putty and had to be boiled and otherwise treated to convert it into a thick dark brown treacle (called *chandu* locally) which could be smoked in an opium pipe. This thick treacle was then packed into small paper packets weighing 2 *hoons* (about ¼ gram) but in about 1934 the paper packets were replaced by small aluminium tubes also weighing 2 *hoons*.

In the Federation, the Trade & Customs Department (in which I served at a later date) was called upon to operate the new policy. *Chandu* shops were opened in every town in the Federation, stocks of packed *chandu* were bought from the Singapore Government and sold at the new opium shops to anyone who wished to buy the drug without any restriction. The Government also opened smoking saloons where customers could smoke a pipe in clean and peaceful surroundings and have pleasant dreams.

During the early 1930s the Government decided that more should be done to reduce the extent of opium smoking in the Federation. In order to enforce this new policy every opium smoker had to register with the Customs Department and was given a registration card which enabled him to purchase opium from any Government opium shop on the production of his card. The Government, however, closed its opium dens so as not to appear to encourage the smoking habit. This new policy would mean a big loss of revenue and so an Opium Revenue Reserve Fund was set up to compensate for the loss of revenue when opium smoking was finally eradicated.

As only registered smokers could now buy opium legally and as no one, apart from the Government, was allowed to sell opium, a black market developed in the sale of both Government and smuggled opium to non-registered smokers, but this was on a comparatively small scale. The next step was to reduce the number of new smokers which was done by refusing cards to all young persons under 18 years of age, I believe. Those over 18 years of age could only obtain a registration card after obtaining a doctor's certificate to the effect that they were already opium smokers (new immigrants) and needed the drug for reasons of health. This may appear strange but I was told by a doctor that consumptives were kept alive for several years through smoking opium.

A regular opium smoker usually had blackened teeth and sometimes his front teeth were worn away. I therefore used to observe his teeth when an applicant spoke to me pleading his case for a registration card. On one occasion I told an applicant with good white teeth that he was not a regular smoker and could not be given a card; he quickly realised, however, that I had been observing his teeth and, with a big grin, he pulled out of his mouth a perfect set of white false teeth, which was unusual for an addict. Many of the applicants were Chinese manual labourers who like a smoke after a strenuous day's work. They said it relaxed them and got rid of their aches and pains. They were earning reasonable wages and could afford to smoke. It was the poor labourer who could not afford both to smoke opium and eat who became emaciated and ill, mainly through under-nourishment. Opium smokers are not belligerent or dangerous to other people. They have a feeling of contentment after a smoke and are in a dream world of their own. I remember once when a male Chinese walked into my motor car in broad daylight. Luckily I had seen him 'floating' across the road and had stopped my car before he collided with it, much to his surprise. He was obviously in a dream world after a smoke.

The next step in the campaign to eradicate opium smoking was to limit the quantity of opium a registered smoker could buy at a Government shop. This was done through a rationing system and a smoker's ration was recorded on his registration card. I cannot now remember whether all smokers received the same ration or whether the amount depended on age or other reasons. It was hoped that, as a result of these measures, the smoking of opium in the Federation would be virtually eradicated within a generation when the registered smokers would have died off as they grew old. Unfortunately, the Japanese army interfered with these plans by over-running the country in 1942 and so the policy was never put to the test. The Japanese authorities in charge of Malaya for the next four years permitted the government opium shops to continue business as long as stocks lasted but, as all the opium producing areas were out of their reach, stocks could not have lasted long. The Japanese occupation of Malaya ended in August 1945 and in February 1946 the sale of opium in Malaya was totally banned (I believe at the insistence of the American Government) so that smokers had to seek illegal means of obtaining the drug to satisfy their craving. The result was that opium smuggling into Malaya became big business, but heroin and other hard drugs were not yet a problem. The Customs Department continued as the main force to combat this smuggling, which was mainly by sea and air, and in Singapore a Narcotic Bureau was set up under the control of the Comptroller of Customs. This Narcotic Bureau kept in touch with Customs and Police forces in Hong Kong, Bombay, Calcutta, Rangoon and Mombasa and sent a quarterly report on the local drug situation to the United Nations Narcotic Bureau. An Opium Treatment Centre was set up by the Singapore Government on St John's Island to help convicted opium smokers break the habit and to teach them a useful trade.

In 1957 the old Federated Malay States and the rest of Malaya became independent of British rule and the control of drug smuggling became the responsibility of the local Governments. The smuggling of opium and other narcotics into Malaya has now been overcome by the effective deterrent of the death penalty for those in illegal possession of any forbidden drug. This is a deterrent which the Colonial Government could not have imposed without wide criticism.

OP 68 (Autumn 1994)

Season of Green Leaves

by *Kuldip Rai Moman*

Music of the morse – Rustle in the mango tree –
Lord Baden Powell's grave – In the domain of the dead –
Wanderlust – Kingdom of the NFD – A lament.

Only stay quiet while my mind remembers
The beauty of fire from the beauty of embers
John Masefield

There was freshness in the sunshine. A waft of breeze blew from the lake shore. The place was Kisumu, earlier known as Port Florence. It was January 1938 and I had completed my nineteenth year. After an interview, the head of the Post Office, P G Carmichael, a marvellous fellow, got me tested in Morse Telegraphy and Typewriting. His was a fascinating way of assessment. After calling a senior telegraphist, Mbalire, he placed 5 one cent pieces on the palm of his left hand and gave a go-ahead nod to signal. At the end of every 60 seconds he would transfer one of the five one cent coins to the right hand pocket of his jacket. When the last cent got into his pocket my receiving test in telegraphy was over. And then the trial in reverse, that is, I was the signaller, and Mbalire, the transcriber.

I can still listen to the music of the Morse, *gat gat gar, gat gat gat* of that bright morning. From the Telegraph Office window I can see the vast expanse of Lake Victoria Nyanza. Thus I set out on my career as a Postal Clerk and Telegraphist (Learner) at a kingly wage of 50 shillings a month in the Posts and Telegraphs Department, which covered His Majesty King George Sixth's territories of Kenya, Uganda and Tanganyika.

We used to have an All Up Air Mail service and you could send a letter, *Par Avion*, throughout the British Empire, including Australia and New Zealand and the tiny isles of Pitcairn, Tonga and Samoa in the Pacific by affixing a 20 cent postage stamp. Amrik Singh with driver Umari and two office messengers would go to the airport to fetch the Air Mails. On return around seven in the evening, mail bags from all over the universe were counted and ticked in. Their seals were thoroughly examined to make certain they were not tampered with. Thereafter, the opening process would ensue. The bundles of letters were passed to various racks for sorting. I recall we had a rack destined for Tanganyika. The sorting at this work-station was considered difficult and therefore important.

I would like to mention that the Postmaster was an exceptionally conscientious, very efficient and meticulous person. After his daytime normal working hours as chief of the station, when the dusk fell, he would come to the sorting office. In those days of yore, there was no electricity. He had taken it on himself to light the petromax lamps. I can visualise him pumping these lamps vigorously. He would then go home, which was next to the Post Office, across the green fence. He would come back after having his dinner and would go straight to sort mails for Tanganyika. Later, when he proceeded on home leave to UK, I took over from him the sorting on this rack which had 48 pigeon holes. I felt I was a cut above others! It may be of interest that I was allocated his government house as well. The reason was that it was a so-called European house in an Asian housing area. Imagine a 50 shillings-a-month clerk occupying a four bedroom house, with a garage and a garden on the verge of a city park. By any stretch of imagination, I did not need accommodation of this dimension. I shut the whole house but one bedroom for my use.

For some time, I was assistant to Amrik Singh in despatch of airmails. Some of the staff would do sorting of letters in the post office boxes. After a space of over half a century I remember certain boxes, eg number 47 was District Commissioner, Central Kavirondo and number 40 was John Riddoch Motors. Most of the box renters of my days in Kisumu have vanished into oblivion. It may be they no longer exist any more on this planet. Due to prolonged working hours, my overtime used to amount to one hundred hours monthly. Calculated at 30 cents an hour, I was paid 30 shillings which was a colossal addition to my salary.

During the Christmas period we dealt with heavy mails. On Christmas Eve a desire took hold of me that we continue sorting the mails throughout the night till daybreak, so that I could hail the sun on 25 December, rising from the East. It was a warm tropical night. There was a mango tree outside the office. At times I would go to the door to feel the swish and rustle of the leaves, and inhale the fragrance in the wind. The staff felt weary and we left before dawn. My yearning to see the Christmas sunrise did not materialise. All those who handled His Majesty's Royal Mail that night have departed to their sojourn in the sky.

I was keen to move to pastures afresh and applied for a transfer to anywhere in Kenya or Tanganyika. Instructions came from Nairobi asking me to proceed to Rumuruti. I had packed my bags when a telegraph message was received cancelling the move. So it happened I never got a chance to see Rumuruti. Eventually, I was transferred to Nyeri as an assistant to the Postmaster. Nyeri, as is known, is a pleasant and beautiful spot. The wind whispers a melody in your ears, the whole day.

Lord Baden Powell, the founder of the Boy Scouts Movement, is buried there. The graveyard was 500 yards from my octagonal shaped residence. After the day's work, I would go to the cemetery which had enchanting surroundings and looked like a park. You could watch the hills and dales and, on a clear day, gaze at the glistening, snow-clad peaks of Mount Kenya and the white clouds floating in the sky. I would sit, or rather squat, at the foot of his grave and provide company to the great man who has his eternal abode there – away from his native land. One evening I dozed off and fell asleep. When I awoke, a dark night had descended and I found myself in the silent domain of the dead.

I had a built-in wanderlust and invariably thought as to how I could have a career whereby I could travel to varied places. In sickness or annual leave whenever a replacement was required, Nairobi Head Office was supposed to provide a relief to the post offices under its control. An idea struck me that Nyeri was ninety miles from Nairobi and mid-way between Nairobi and many of the post offices in Central Province and further afield in the Northern Frontier District. It would therefore be expedient and economical if a relief hand was stationed at Nyeri. Accordingly a communication was sent to Nairobi. I had never expected the scheme would work, but, as luck would have it, the Head Office commended the proposal. An additional member of staff was posted at Nyeri and I was ear-marked as relief Postmaster. I must say my heart leapt up.

A new post office was lately opened at Kiganjo where there were some complications. I was asked to inspect that office and submit a report to Nairobi. On receipt of my account, I was told to take over Kiganjo temporarily. Subsequently, the arrangement was made permanent. I was flabbergasted. It meant that I was once again stuck to a particular office. All my dreams of journeying to different post offices were shattered and came to nought. I was back to square one. I thought I had lost the Kingdom of the NFD.

We had twenty thousand Italian evacuees at Kiganjo who were brought there from Eritrea, Somaliland, Ethiopia and Libya. They left long years ago; the grass has overgrown their camps. I remember an episode when three prisoners of war escaped from their camp and hoisted the Italian flag on Mount Kenya. At our telephone exchange, we had overheard Major Ridgeway, the Commandant of the Italian Evacuee Camp, who had a commanding voice, exchanging information about the getaway. One of the escapees, Felice Benuzzi, subsequently wrote the tale of their escapade and adventure in *No Picnic on Mount Kenya* which is an interesting classic.

After a year's stay there, I was transferred to Nairobi where I was asked to act as relief Postmaster for outstations. At times I would reach a new place at an odd hour. Arriving somewhere unknown in the darkness after midnight added to my excitement. There was rapture in those safaris.

I look back to days of long-drop lavatories, light from petromax and hurricane dietz lamps and rain water pouring down from heaven into the tanks as elixir. A longing comes over me to see once again long-forgotten faces and places from the dim, hazy past. The smells, sounds and sights from far away, agitate me in slumber.

> *Oh call back yesterday, Bid time return*
> Shakespeare

A few keys of my former dwellings, for no reason whatsoever, have been lying around. With the passage of time I do not remember which doors they opened. They seem familiar. I try to fit them to the gates of an era which has fled.

> *A rainbow and a cuckoo's song,*
> *May never come together again*
> W H Davies

OP 72 (Autumn 1996)

A Woman Education Officer on the Niger

by Joan Russell

It was February 1947 that I, who was a quite a new recruit to the Colonial Education Service, set off on an inspection tour of schools which were accessible only by river. I kept a diary of this safari by canoe, and now, nearly 50 years later, my diary still has the power to excite me.

Friday 28th February

6.45 am. Alison (a friend from Lagos who was spending local leave with me) and I left Bida by NA (Native Authority) lorry for Dakomba, a village on the bank of the river Kaduna (Kaduna means crocodiles). We were delayed enroute by an unsafe 'ridge' over a culvert, which had to be filled in with grass, earth, stones etc to make it safe. We walked from Dakomba to the riverside, with some twenty carriers to carry our loads (on their heads). We took with us all our requirements for the next eight days. By 'all our requirements' I mean all, since these included table, chairs, beds, bedding, mosquito nets, bath (canvas), washbasin, lavatory seat, lamps, kerosene, all cooking and eating utensils etc.

Two canoes were ready for us, one for Alison, me and our personal loads, and the other for Mallam Anike, Garba and Momman. We were astonished at the size of the dugouts which were about 60 feet long. We left the river bank at 8.45 am, by which time the sun was already fairly high in the sky and it was very hot. Alison and I both felt a thrill of excitement of a new and exciting adventure, albeit in the course of duty. The centre part of the canoe was roofed with matting made of split palm fronds. We made ourselves comfortable under the canopy and proceeded to have our breakfast, putting up the table in the approved manner.

Below our starting point the River Kaduna widened out considerably, and the vegetation along the banks varied from open grassland to mixed grassland and forest. At 3.30 pm we caught our first glimpse of the lordly Niger, the appearance of which reminded us of Kipling's 'great, grey-green, greasy Limpopo'. It seemed enormously wide. At 5.00 pm we reached Mureggi. As we were approaching the village we heard the sound of drums, and suddenly, from round the bend of a creek, the sight which met our eyes made us both gasp.

We saw a huge dug-out canoe, with brilliantly coloured canopy and trappings. It appeared to be full of war-like Africans, brandishing what looked very much like dangerous and menacing spears. With their paddles (for such they were) waving in the air, they let out an ear-splitting yell of welcome and the drummers redoubled their efforts. As this State Canoe came nearer we saw Sarkin Ruwa, the local headman, standing beneath a very beautiful, gold tasselled canopy, surrounded by his councillors. They drew slowly alongside, and as we came face to face with Sarkin Ruwa, the drums suddenly ceased and every one in the canoe went down 'noses to the ground' in salute. When Sarkin Ruwa rose he greeted us, and I replied in what I hoped was a suitable speech (not very easy when one's knowledge of the language is as limited as mine). The royal canoe then preceded us into the tiny creek at the head of which stands the village of Mureggi.

Mureggi is built on a number of small knolls and, as we approached, it seemed to us that the landing beach and the rise immediately behind it were seething with people. The whole village had turned out to greet us. We learned from Sarkin Ruwa that few of the inhabitants of the village had ever seen a white woman before. We were informed that the rest house was not in a fit state to house us, and that some of the rooms in the Palace compound had been prepared for us. We were made to feel extremely welcome, and we were presented with an enormous *giwan ruwa* (a huge river fish) for our supper.

I went to the school which, being so inaccessible, laboured under great difficulties, not the least of which is the fact that during the wet season, ie for about 5-6 months of the year, the knolls on which the village stands are surrounded by water and the children paddle their own canoes to school. As the chief occupation of the people is fishing, the main craft of the boys is the making of nets, the raw materials of which is obtained from a particular kind of palm tree which grows in the vicinity. The girls spin and weave cotton, which is also grown locally. We are trying to encourage and preserve these local crafts in the school.

Saturday 1st March

I spent the morning at the school, and we left Mureggi at 11.30 am amid the cheers of the people. We spent the rest of the day on the canoe, and it was midnight when we reached our next port of call, Katcha. Being paddled down the vast expanse of the Niger, in the rather ghostly light of a pale moon, was a never-to-be-forgotten experience. The swish of the paddles in the water, the rhythmical singing of the paddlers, and the various animal, bird and insect sounds which occasionally reached us from the banks made a delightful sound background to the scene.

Arrived at Katcha, which lies some distance up the Katcha River from its junction with the Niger, we had to walk 1½ miles uphill to the rest house and by the time our carriers arrived with the loads and our beds were unpacked and made up it was 2.00 am. We were much too thrilled and excited to feel tired. We were warned that there were many hyenas around and that we should not let my dog wander during the night.

Sunday 2nd March
Up at 6.30 am for school at 7.00 am. During our afternoon siesta we received a message to the effect that traders travelling by canoe had been chased by hippos. And then our carriers reported that they had seen several hippos, and advised us that it would be dangerous for us to continue towards Baro. We ascertained that there was a train from Katcha to Baro next day (there were only two a week), so we decided to make use of it. 4.30 pm saw me pedalling along the road to Loguma on the village scribe's bicycle to visit the school there. After our very late night we retired to bed early.

Monday 3rd March
I cycled to Loguma again to finish my inspection, visited the Baptist school at Katcha, and then we entrained in Baro. The shade temperature at Baro at 5.00 pm was 97.7°, but having had little exercise recently we braved the heat and climbed the hill behind the town. Our efforts were rewarded by magnificent views up and down the Niger. As the hippos had delayed us a day, I tried to find some means of making up time, and to our great joy we found that the SS *Mungo Park* was leaving for Muye the next day. The Captain agreed to take us aboard and to tow the canoes.

Tuesday 4th March
The carriers who had been instructed to come for our loads at 4.45 am arrived at 3.00 am. My dog greeted their arrival with loud barking and there was noise and commotion until the blast of the *Mungo Park's* hooter, blown specially for us, sounded at 5.00 am. It was pitch dark as we made our way down the very uneven path to the jetty. We had to walk the plank

by the light of a bush lamp, and climb the vertical ladders to the top deck of the *Mungo Park* in semi-darkness.

There we found a bedroom at our disposal and a bathroom! Watching the dawn and sunrise on the Niger was breath-taking. The *Mungo Park* is a paddle steamer, and we chugged merrily downstream at a much faster rate than we should have done by canoe.

We bade farewell to the Captain at 10.30 am and boarded our canoe to take us into Muye Creek, a somewhat precarious operation in mid-stream. Sarkin Muye had planned to meet us in his canoe as Sarkin Ruwa had done, but as we arrived earlier than scheduled, he was somewhat disappointed. Mallam Anike went in by a back entrance to give warning of our approach and by the time we reached the landing stage the village was ready to welcome us.

Sarkin Muye and all his councillors, the whole school and nearly all the villagers were on parade. We were most amused to see that many of the schoolboys wore brightly coloured cricket caps (Muslim men are not properly dressed without some sort of head covering). Once again we were told that a place had been prepared for us, Sarkin Muye proceeded to lead us to it, followed by the whole village. Our abode for the night turned out to be a half-finished mud house, with a grass veranda built on to it especially for our benefit. It was one of the most primitive that I had yet stayed in, but as we were sleeping out all the time, it didn't matter.

I inspected the school that morning, and in the evening I was taken to see the new school building which was started only a month previously, and was almost finished. The difference between the rough and ready methods which apply here and the elaborate plans drawn up for a new school building in Britain astounds me.

Thursday 6th March

We were given a great send-off by Sarkin Muye who accompanied us for a short way in his canopied canoe, complete with drums and queer, long, thin sort of trumpets. Before leaving, however, we held a meeting of the parents of the schoolchildren, with Sarkin Muye and all the local village heads and councillors, some of whom had travelled as much as 12 or 18 miles by canoe to attend this meeting. They were very keen and interested in the school. Sarkin Muye told me that some of them, who as a result of their trading had drifted to towns such as Lokoja and Onitsha, had returned to Muye when they knew that a school had opened there. During the year that the school had been in existence only four absences had been recorded.

More hippos had been reported as having been seen on the river but we saw none of them. In any case, we simply had to travel by canoe as there is no other means of transport from Muye, except trekking along bush paths. We arrived at Rigido, a tiny village right on the river bank at 5.30 pm, and again found ourselves in an odd-shaped, half-finished hut, this time without grass verandah. The path along the river bank is Rigido's main street. Our hut faced directly on to this and as we pitched our beds outside the hut it was like sleeping in the High Street.

OP 73 (Spring 1997)

Magnet Brand

by J D Kelsall

It was in 1951, when I was serving as a Fisheries Officer of the Lake Victoria Fisheries Service and was stationed at Mwanza, Tanganyika (as it then was), that I first became acquainted with gill nets made from nylon twine – then a very new and high-tech material so far as nets were concerned. My boss, Lt Cdr George Cole in Kisumu, sent me a couple of these nets with instructions to try them out and report on them. This I did and found that they not only caught more fish than conventional cotton and flax nets set alongside them in the same 'fleet', but also that they appeared to have a very long life by comparison with the other nets. I reported to my boss in these terms.

A few weeks later, George came to Mwanza on one of his periodic visits, bringing with him a bulging sack. This, he told me, contained 50 nylon gill nets, and I was to take these on safari with me and to sell them to any interested fisherman who would like to try them. I asked how much I was to charge for a net.

"Seventy-five shillings," said George. "And that's cost price."

Apparently the nets had been made by hand by African Explosives & Chemical Industries, the South African subsidiary of ICI.

To say that I was staggered would be an understatement. At that time, most of the African fishermen in my area used home-made cotton nets which they made from sewing-twine produced by the well-known firm of J & P Coates of Paisley. A fully mounted net cost about Shs 7.50 to produce – the fisherman's time counted for nothing and a man would walk down the road with his netting wound on a forked stick over his shoulder, knotting away at it as he went. That being so, who was likely to be interested in paying ten times as much for a kind of net with which he was totally unfamiliar? African fishermen might be simple folk, but they are definitely not daft! However, I knew that they set great store by the actual strength of net twine and by their ability to break it with their bare hands – not too difficult in the case of cotton or even flax twine. I therefore devised a 'publicity' scheme, based on a small spool of nylon twine which had come with the nets. Arriving at a fishing camp on the Lake shore, I would assemble the fishermen under a convenient shady tree and extol the virtues of this new twine. I would go through an act of really exerting myself in an effort to break a length of twine and finally, using that dodge one employs to break parcel string by winding it round one hand, and then looping it over itself and giving a smart tug, I would finally succeed in breaking the twine. I would then cut off a length and hand it to the nearest fisherman, inviting him to try to break it himself. The man would carefully wind the twine round a finger of one hand and then round a finger of the other hand and would then give a hearty tug, expecting the twine to part easily – as it eventually had with me. Of course it did not, and usually cut his fingers to the bone, evoking much merriment from his mates as the blood dripped from his wounded fingers. I would then suggest that he must be a weakling and, taking the twine from him, I would break it easily (using the parcel string dodge). Brutal maybe, but it certainly kindled keen interest and quite a ready sale for my nets – even at Shs 75.00 a time.

I noted the names of the fishermen who bought nets and asked them to keep a record of the catches made in them. In the course of a safari a couple of months later, I visited the fishing camps where I had sold nets and asked the owners how they had found them in service. In every case there were beaming smiles, and expressions of astonishment at the performance of these nets. As I had known would be the case, they had caught as much as five times as many fish as the old-style nets, set adjacent to them. One man summed them up by telling me:

"These nets have magic like a magnet. They draw fish into them."

From then on, my nylon nets sold like hot cakes and my stock of fifty was soon gone. The fishermen who had them named them *Chapa sumaku* (Magnet brand) and clamoured for more – which, in due course, were forthcoming. As time showed, not only did they catch many more fish than cotton or flax nets, but they were virtually indestructible, whereas the other types of net seldom lasted for longer than a month or so.

Having off-loaded my fifty nets at ten times the cost of a cotton net, I occasionally wondered whether perhaps I had made a mistake in choosing a career as a Fisheries Officer. Maybe I should have been a salesman . . . ?

OP 72 (Autumn 1996)

Dura Camp

by James Lang Brown

As a young Assistant Conservator of Forests in Uganda in the 1950s I was protected from the more unconstitutional aspects of my job by my very understanding boss, George Leggatt. He would tactfully cope with a tea planter who appeared to have encroached on forest land, or a member of the African Royal Family who inadvertently caused a valuable tree to be felled. However, when I had been in the District Forest Office, Toro, for a year, a situation arose which could scarcely be ignored and in any case involved some of George's closest friends.

The background was this. The Uganda Development Corporation had in its wisdom started a cement works in Tororo, 350 miles to the east, based on the impure limey rock of a long extinct volcano. Only after the factory was in production did they realise that the cement was so weak, the concrete would wash away in the rains. You could make very smart mud huts with it, but definitely not a new Legislative Council building. Enter the Collins family. Many years before, this enterprising band – brothers Beetle and Jack and their sister Spadge – had come out to the neighbouring district of Ankole to farm, to hunt and to prospect for gold, titanium, wolfram or anything that could make their fortunes. Alas little was found, and nobody made any money except perhaps the Indian traders who supported the miners in hard times, and sold them a great deal of gin. The Collins did, however, come across a phenomenal deposit of calcium carbonate so pure that the crystals were fully 9 inches long, of a wonderful translucent pink. They registered a claim and waited. Their first stroke of luck was the failure of the cement works. The second was that the Uganda Railway was being extended west from Kampala to the copper mines in the Ruwenzori Mountains. It naturally served the cement works, but it also passed the Dura River deposit. The brothers offered to ship pure lime to Tororo. They were in the money for the first time in their lives.

The Dura River is one of the remotest spots in Western Uganda. Although it was in Toro (my district) there were no roads, and the Collins had cut a track to it from the neighbouring district of Ankole. In the normal way I or my staff would have inspected our forest boundaries on foot, but we knew there was no settlement and no cultivation within many miles. George, on a shooting weekend as a guest of the Collins family, had been told of their run of luck and thought that it sounded as if the mine might be within Kibale Forest. This would never do. Africans found growing a banana tree in a forest would be unceremoniously bundled out. On the other hand George could hardly turn up the following week with a warrant for the arrest of his hosts on a charge of illegal activities in a forest. Round 1 to the Collins family. His only course was to send me. I was to take no forest staff, as George was still stumped as to which way to play this – he just wanted a verbal report.

My houseboy loaded camping gear and food for several days into the Land Rover and we set off for the Deep South. The way to Dura is tortuous. First 60 miles of dirt road following the eastern foothills of Ruwenzori and then through the Queen Elizabeth National Park across the Kazinga Channel into Ankole. We then followed another 60 miles of very minor roads winding through the hills of northern Ankole and back into Toro at Ibanda, and then another 30 miles of bush road to the new railway where we picked up a railway construction track which led us to the camp. Operations were substantial. They were not only mining the limestone, they were felling a large area of forest and were burning it in kilns to produce the pure white lime needed in Tororo. My problem was that while the forest boundary was clear on the map, it had vanished entirely on the ground. George had suggested that I might measure the firewood being cut and agree a licence to legalise it – not a practical proposition.

The camp itself was a village of grass huts – enough for a formidable labour force. The largest was a lovely banda – dark and cool, with very thick thatch. On the stoop were Jack and a new character, Ack-Ack Price. He was an old Etonian, down on his luck, acting as cook and general camp superintendent. They were engaged in the very important pastime of downing pink gin and warm dirty water ('the gin sterilises it') to ward off malaria. They were immensely hospitable. We drank and we drank. The stories of prospecting, mining and big game hunting were enthralling. Eight o'clock came, nine o'clock, ten o'clock and still Ack-Ack made no move towards the kitchen quarters. I believe we ate sometime before midnight, but memory is dim. I think we had a kipper and a fiendish hot curry. And more gin. They gave me a bed for the night and my boy had lodging in their boys' quarters.

In the morning the camp was quiet; no miner would be up before the sun. I had plenty of time and in spite of my hangover and lack of breakfast

I could look round. While the workings were outside the forest, the fuel cutting was definitely illegal. We slipped away unseen.

I was determined to salvage my expedition and as I drove back towards the railway workings, I saw a construction train and wondered whether they might take passengers. They had a loading ramp for machinery so I was bold enough to ask if I could drive the Land Rover onto a train. To my surprise they agreed and they even sold me a ticket – for a very nominal sum. After a few hours wait an engine was connected and we proceeded at a snail's pace over lines laid over very rough ground through the hills and then over the game-filled plains to Kasese. This was probably the smallest railway terminus in the world – one shed, one siding, two pairs of buffers. We had become the first paying passengers on the Western Uganda Extension. How George solved the problem and salved his conscience I never discovered.

OP 91 (April 2006)

Resettlement of Suspected
Mau Mau Sympathisers in Tanganyika

by J M Ainley

During the Kenya Mau Mau emergency, the Administration in Tanganyika were concerned that the troubles would spread southwards, their concern being mainly centred on the Arusha, Moshi, Meru areas where there were considerable numbers of Kikuyu, some having perhaps inter-married with the WaChagga (Kilimanjaro) and WaMeru. It was felt that those who might foment unrest should be rounded up and confined for the duration of the Kenya emergency, or until such time that the Tanganyika Government was satisfied that no possible danger remained. My background was as an agriculturalist, joining the Colonial Service in 1948 and serving as an Agricultural Officer in Tanganyika until I resigned in 1964, some three years after Independence. It was in this capacity that I became involved in the settlement of the Kikuyu. In 1954 I was stationed in Handeni, a 5,000 square mile District, some 100 miles SW of Tanga, with the *Boma* situated on the old road from Korogwe to Morogoro. It was mainly *miombo* country with an erratic rainfall of some 28 inches per annum, and a sorghum, maize and cotton economy.

In the centre of the District there was a much more fertile area, hilly and with a higher rainfall and only sparsely populated. Here there was an old German estate of some 500 hectares, now reverted to bush, with the only signs of pre-First World War usage being a fairly substantial stone-built house, some derelict outbuildings, old quinine trees, some overgrown coffee bushes and old plantain (banana) stands.

Such estates were not unusual in parts of Tanga and Southern Highlands Provinces. Farmed by German settlers before the First World War, they were confiscated by the British and held by a Government body, the 'Custodian of Enemy Property'. Between the two world wars and into the mid-fifties, many of these estates were let out on 99 year, or longer, leases to settlers of several nationalities, Greek, Turkish, British and some East African Asians. Others were not let, nor settled by local inhabitants, and the one called Tamota in Handeni District was one of those.

Before the detention of the Kikuyu, some effort had been made to grade them into categories of high, medium and low risk of Mau Mau sympathies.

The term used at that time was Black, Grey and White (somewhat politically incorrect these days!). The former were detained in the Tengeru area of Arusha and were strictly confined within a secure camp. The latter were sent to the Central Province and allowed free access to that area. At Tamota we had the medium risk category, but it was stressed there could well be dangerous persons among the 200 or so families sent for settlement.

In early 1954 I was informed by my Provincial Agricultural Officer at Tanga that I would be required to assist in the settlement of the Kikuyu who were currently being rounded up at their homes, and who would be sent to Tamota shortly. I was to place myself at the disposal of a District Officer who had been selected to administer the resettlement. This was Mr Bill Helean, a New Zealander, who had been selected with some care as he was a 'no nonsense' District Officer who could be relied on to undertake this very difficult task. The other European was a Police Superintendent whose name escapes me. We each had our African staff, the District Officers with clerks and messengers, the Police with six policemen (Askaris) and myself with four Agricultural Instructors who I brought with me from my staff at Handeni.

We arrived at Tamota some days before the detainees were due so that clearing round the old German house and surrounds could be done, and temporary accommodation in some of the old buildings, roughly constructed huts and tentage could be made for the 200 approximate families, who would arrive in lorries with some food and their household and agricultural effects. Labour was recruited from the local tribe, the WaNguu, to assist us. Recruitment was not without its difficulty as the area was sparsely populated and the African 'bush telegraph' had spread many rumours that 'dangerous' people were due to arrive. Nevertheless preparations in the form of temporary accommodation, food supplies and a plan of action were completed before their arrival, a considerable task considering that Tamota was a remote area some 60 miles away from the small station of Handeni, with the added difficulty of some eight miles of unkept and overgrown dirt track.

Our task was to select suitable sites for the Kikuyu to build their houses and have access to suitable land for cultivation within reasonable distance from the 'village' sites. Whilst there were not detailed maps of the area, the task was made easier by the nature of the topography and the availability of water which was plentiful. Basically we had valleys and ridges, the former full of napier grass (and some buffalo!) and the ridges fairly clear with some light timber. The topography was not dissimilar to the Kikuyu area north of Nairobi and suitable for their preference of building their homes on ridge tops.

Nobody knew how long the Kikuyu would be held at Tamota, but a time- scale of at least a year, probably longer, was a reasonable supposition. Using this as a yardstick, I drew up a settlement plan to provide sufficient land for each family to become self-supporting and remain so over a long period. What we could not know was the attitude that the detainees would adopt. To be uprooted from home and sent miles away to detention could have resulted in complete non-cooperation, despite our efforts to make the resettlement as easy as possible by providing facilities, albeit basic. I think their attitude really hinged on the number of people within their midst that had been indoctrinated by the Mau Mau oath taken against Europeans, and their standing within the community. Fortunately it turned out that the great majority of the settlers were prepared to make the best of their circumstances, and those few who, it later transpired, had taken the oath, had little influence in the community. Arrangements were made later, when confidence had been gained, to arrange for them to be 'de-oathed'.

Jointly with the Administration and Police we agreed that I would select ten ridge-top building sites with enough room for twenty families and, within reasonable distance of the homesteads, enough land based on approximately two acres per family, giving a total of about 40 acres. Such a plan would be flexible and could be adjusted as circumstances might warrant once the detainees arrived and discussions held. It was hoped that the Kikuyu themselves would select ten headmen who should act as spokesmen for the village groups, and with whom we could liaise and in the event, with good cooperation, this is broadly how the settlement evolved.

Choosing the sites was not without its difficulties, as with no maps and fairly heavy undergrowth in the valleys it was hard work. As a starting point we climbed one of the higher hills to establish our bearings, and with the aid of a compass drew a rough map of where we should plan the villages. Each Agricultural Instructor, together with some local labour to clear paths, then followed a route to the proposed sites bearing in mind that they should not be too far away, half an hour's walk at the most, from the central administrative camp, within easy reach of water and adjacent to sufficient land. By the time the first people arrived we had earmarked five sites so that they could be shown to the headmen who would make their comments, and we could alter our plans if necessary.

Arrangements had been wisely made for the detainees to arrive at intervals which enabled us to proceed with caution and try and reassure them that we were trying to do the best in arduous circumstances. They were very tired on arrival having been transported in lorries from many miles away, quite apart from the trauma of being removed from their homes. It was explained on arrival that temporary housing was available at the administrative site, food was to be issued initially and as they had brought their cooking utensils with them few problems should arise in that respect. It was further explained that on the following day, after a general baraza, they should select headmen and village sites would be shown to them. There was no language barrier as many spoke Swahili and for those that did not others were able to interpret.

From those first few days a pattern was established and the settlement, much to everybody's relief, went well. Snags there were, but generally these were ironed out with the cooperation of the Kikuyu themselves. For those of us used to the somewhat 'laidback' attitude of many of the Tanganyika tribes, and in particular the WaBena and WaNguru, the industry of the Kikuyu was a revelation. Clearing of sites and the erection of huts went on apace, the latter assisted by the availability of large stands of giant bamboo, some twenty feet in height with a girth as thick as a man's arm, presumably planted by the Germans all those years ago, as this type of bamboo was not indigenous to the area. It certainly made for the easy building of huts and, with ample supplies of napier grass in the valleys, roof covering was to hand.

It was not long before cultivation started, mainly with the initial planting of beans, followed by maize and some sorghum. I had made no actual plans of what crops had to be planted, but I arranged for a supply of the basic seed staples, beans, maize and cassava cuttings as a start. Not knowing how long the detainees would be at Tamota, a comprehensive agricultural plan could be drawn up later to cover food crops and the provision of cash crops, should the settlement be of long standing or perhaps even permanent; the criteria of adequate land had been arranged in the initial village layout.

Writing this some forty years after the event, I recall how much better the settlement went than we thought possible at the time. There were problems, but in general and considering the enormity of the task, and perhaps the dangers of an assault, there were few major difficulties over the (from memory) year and a half before the Kikuyu were allowed to return to their homes, when the Government decided that there was no longer a risk to security in Tanganyika, and indeed, when the situation had improved in Kenya. There were amongst the families at Tamota some uncertain persons, but when these were identified they were sent to the secure camp and others, as previously mentioned, had the oath removed.

I remained under canvas at Tamota for several weeks, but then returned to Handeni to carry on with the normal agricultural extension work, calling in at Tamota once a month to see how things were going and if any assistance was required. Bill Helean later went on leave and his place was taken by a Mr Ferguson who also brought his wife with him to live at Tamota, an indication of how settled the community had become. My wife and I have a happy recollection of spending New Year's Eve at Tamota having been invited by the Fergusons to celebrate the onset of 1956; the Fergusons, true Scots, he in full dress kilt and she with the appropriate clan sash, all of us sipping *atholl brose* to see the New Year in!

Memories fade and there are, I am sure, other matters and facts that could be added, or corrected, but this episode does give a broad account of what, in those days, was an important aspect of the way Tanganyika handled what could have become a serious disturbance in pre-Independence days. It is also for the record that our approach was one of firm but sympathetic consideration to those involved, and was in no way the autocratic approach sometimes depicted by those apologists for the Colonial period. Perhaps there is a lesson here for some independent African governments in the way that their dissident and unpopular minorities have been, and perhaps still are, treated.

OP 72 (Autumn 1996)

Rain Stimulation in East Africa

by B W Thompson

If you're throwing a party in the garden some day, and conversation begins to flag, look up at the sky and pop the question: "What's a cloud made of?"

People will look at you as if you're mad. Most have probably never thought about it and if some have they are likely to answer, 'water vapour'. Water vapour is a gas and you can't see it: it's mixed in the air with the oxygen and nitrogen, all invisible. No, a cloud is made of tiny water droplets, too small and light to fall under gravity. In the late 1940s an American meteorologist theorised that if a means could be found to convert the small droplets of a cloud into large drops, they might become heavy enough to fall to the earth as rain. Thus a means might be available to alleviate periods of dry weather or even more serious long-term droughts. The problem was how to convert the small droplets into large drops. It was suggested that spraying dry ice (super-cooled particles of solid carbon dioxide) into the cloud at very high levels might do the trick and experiments were undertaken to test the theory. The main trouble is that even after spraying you can never be absolutely certain that the rain, if any, was due to the spraying and had not occurred naturally. Lengthy trials lasting many years were undertaken in America and elsewhere and it was eventually decided that, in general, artificial rain stimulation was unpredictable in both location and amount, and was also uneconomic in relation to the high costs of the seeding and little has been heard of the proposal since.

In the early 1950s I was a meteorologist in East Africa, and in one of those years a serious drought occurred. Crops failed, game died and the Masai tribe and others that lived mainly on their cattle were in serious difficulties. Drawing on exaggerated newspaper reports of the American experiments, our political masters insisted that the Meteorological Department do something about it – make some rain and solve the country's problems. Naturally enough, no extra money was provided to support the work, and we were therefore left with only our own very limited resources, ensuring that any manufactured rain really would be produced as the cheapest of the cheap.

We believed that rainfall in the tropics occurs under different conditions and for different reasons from that in high latitudes, and the dry ice technique was unlikely to be successful. We had, therefore, to dream up our own operating method. Following a good deal of thought and lengthy after-hours arguments, we hit on a possible method that seemed, at least theoretically, to offer a degree of hope. Everybody used to know that salt is hygroscopic even if they didn't know what 'hygroscopic' meant. I use the past tense because modern salt has additives to prevent it happening, so the effect is not often seen nowadays. Hygroscopic means 'to absorb water'. Salt in salt-cellars used to absorb water and become damp. That's why salt-cellars used to clog up, to the annoyance of diners struggling to season their eggs. We thought that if we could introduce dry salt into a cloud, large water drops might accumulate around the salt grains and, if we were lucky, become heavy enough to fall as rain. We crossed our fingers.

Getting the salt into the cloud was a problem debated at length and then somebody said that if salt in the shops was impregnated with stuff to stop it absorbing water, there didn't seem much point in the whole idea and we could all go home. Since going home wasn't on, we decided to make our own salt by boiling some seawater and precipitating out the salt. Good idea except that as soon as the salt appeared, it absorbed all the water it could and became useless for going up into the sky. We decided we'd have to dry it immediately before scattering it in the cloud, if we ever could scatter it in the cloud.

How were we going to get the dried salt into the cloud so that it could be scattered? We couldn't throw it out of an aeroplane because we didn't have one, nor could we afford one, and even if we could have done, it would have had to be a little one, and little aeroplanes didn't like going into big clouds, and for us the bigger the cloud the better. So was there an alternative? Now in those days all meteorological departments had small balloons (and hydrogen to fill them) to send up into the sky to find out which way the wind aloft was blowing because aircraft were always wanting to know. Debate produced the answer: fill the balloon with hydrogen and attach a film canister to it with a length of string. Film came in little aluminium cylinders about two inches long. We punched holes in the bottom of several cylinders and, to act as wicks, lengths of string that had previously been soaked in a gunpowder solution were stuck through the holes, the lengths depending on various anticipated heights of clouds. Next in the cylinders was about half an inch of gunpowder and above that to the top of the cylinder came the sea-salt, held in with a thin rubber cap. The salt was dried and ground to a fine powder before being put into the cylinder and the rubber cap served to keep it dry before release. When the burning wick reached the gunpowder, the cylinder would explode, the salt would be blown out and distribute itself into the cloud. Rain would eventually fall, the drought would be over, and we would have earned our keep. That was our theory. All fine and dandy. The next step was to try it out.

The Masai plains provided a perfect location for the experiment. In the early part of the year beautiful cauliflower-topped cumulus clouds drift over the area looking as though they'd love to provide showers of rain if only the process could somehow be kick-started. We hoped our aluminium cylinders would do just that. On the savannahs new green shoots soon follow any small fall of rain and it didn't matter where the rain fell because cattle could easily be driven to the new foliage. Of course one had first to find a suitable cloud and get into a position, not underneath it, but from a point where the wind would drift the balloon and cylinder into it. This involved perilous, and bumpy, journeys across the savannah, circumnavigating anthills, prides of lions, dry streambeds, occasional grumpy rhinos, patches of thorn trees and other impedimenta designed by nature to frustrate budding rain stimulators. Often by the time all this had been done, the cloud would have died out or drifted away, so we'd have to start again. However, an objective having eventually been attained, it remained only to guess, some would say 'calculate', the necessary length of fuse (string), apply a match, then sit down, have a drink and hope to hear an explosion in the cloud and see some rain 10 to 30 minutes afterwards. Or, of course, look for another cloud, preferably in the direction from which one had just come, and repeat the performance.

Don't get the idea that the savannahs were ever inundated with rain. They weren't, but at least some rain fell after occasions of seeding, whether due to us or not, and the Masai certainly came to believe in the great white rain-giving gods. So much so that when some real seasonal rain eventually arrived and alleviated the drought, a party was held to which folk came from miles around. Local eminences were invited, the politicians amongst them claimed all the credit, and the Meteorological Department was a guest of honour. Sitting under thorn trees, we dined in style on goat meat and cattle blood, with fermented milk to taste, sang Masai songs, watched the young bloods dance and hoped it would soon be over.

That party did eventually end, but not the rain-making. Too many people heard about it, and East Africa being a dry country, we soon had demands and invitations to alleviate droughts from southern Tanganyika to the Northern Frontier Province of Kenya, and from the coast to western

Uganda. Perforce the methods and techniques changed, became far more menacing and hilarious and perhaps improved. But that is another story.

OP 91 (April 2006)

Kenya

Kenya's badge, from the creation of the Colony in 1920 until Independence in 1963, was a poorly-drawn red heraldic lion "rampant guardant", (i.e. upright, standing on hind legs, facing towards the viewer). When used on the Blue Ensign it did not have the white disc, but on the Red Ensign it had to have the disc in order to be seen.

First Foot *Ulendo*

by *Ted Wilmot*

Shortly after I had arrived at Chiromo (Nyasaland) upon my first posting, my predecessor left on holiday and I saw him off on the train. As it had not been practicable to organise a walking *ulendo* (tour) while he was still around, it was agreed that the ADC for Port Herald would let me come with him on a joint *ulendo* to the Chief Mlolo, whose area included Chiromo, but whose headquarters was about 15 miles north of it at the foot of the escarpment. Carriers were required for tents and loads, and I was advised to request them from a large village, Jiwaki, about one mile from Chikonje where I was housed. These duly arrived and under the supervision of my messenger, who knew the drill, we all moved to Mlolo's headquarters. I am not sure whether the ADC used his car, and gave me a lift, or whether he had come up on the train with a bicycle and we both cycled. In any case he introduced me to the Chief, the camp was set up and a meeting held. I remember particularly that the "gifts" of the Chief included two fat *chambo* fish on a plate. The ADC did his bit, which was to give a short exhortatory talk, listen to any comments or complaints, and then look into the Court books and the record of tax payers, including the granting of waivers to the old and infirm. Then I was turned on. At that stage, although I had a smattering of the language from my studies in England, I was in no position to make a comprehensive address to the polite village elders! The technical policy which I was supposed to impart was "Ridging for Soil Conservation". The local Agricultural Instructor was an old timer, but did not speak English. So I had either to go through the ADC or use signs. That first day he helped. The following morning he announced that much as he would have liked to continue the *ulendo,* he had been recalled urgently to Port Herald, and that I was to carry on for the next 7 days. He gave me a list of the villages to which I was expected to go, and explained that they had been warned, got on his bicycle (or was it car) and was off.

At that point it came to me that here I was for the next seven days, entirely dependent on my rudimentary knowledge of the language, expected to communicate with those around me, and also to try and get technical ideas across to the local population, while at the same time making my mark as an individual presence in the district and with my staff.

(I learnt subsequently that this was an established technique for getting new officers to get to grips with the language quickly.) Also, for this was very important, I had to learn as soon as possible the pattern of agriculture and life in the areas where I was assigned. I had been briefed earlier that I should not try and advise the locals on the growing of food crops, as they knew infinitely more about it than I did. I was there to observe, and to facilitate economic production. It was only by travelling around, seeing the villagers in their gardens and discussing with them that I would he able to understand their way of life, what were their needs and what could be used to influence them. I had already reached an understanding with the messenger and the houseboy over the more domestic items, but I had to learn the technical terms. I had some inklings as I had tried to read the vernacular monthly reports of the staff for the previous month. I fell back on rehearsal. During the mornings as we travelled, we would accost some villager. Taking a hoe, I would endeavour to show a sample of what we were talking about, then I would get the Instructor to repeat the spiel, but with the proper Chinyanja explanations. I could then see if he did not get it quite as I wanted it, and could get him to correct it. After three or four of these performances, the Instructor had got pretty well what I wanted to demonstrate. So at the afternoon meeting, where I was introduced, I would say a few words in bad Chinyanja, that I was glad to be there, to thank the chief and people for coming to the meeting. and then saying that I would ask the Instructor, Jailosi, to explain the message as he would do it much better than I could.

This area lay between the escarpment and the River Shire, and in fact included much of the Elephant (Ndindi) marsh. On the upper side the gardens could be quite hilly, and here rudimentary soil conservation could be valuable. However, below the line of the main villages there were extensive alluvial flats *(madimba)* where, even to my inexperienced eye, I could not detect any great signs of erosion! In one of these the department had a small rice variety trial which I found I was supposed to supervise. One of the villages we camped in I remember because it was known as *Cimbuzi*, which is the word used locally for "latrine". It was so called on account of the quality of its well water, which was in fact exceptionally saline. This was awful to drink or in tea, but made quite passable coffee. In fact the word *Cimbuzi* (literally "the goat-thing") was correctly the term for the little tuft on the top of a thatched roof, where the thatch was fastened together. Its application to "latrines" was a transfer carried out by the early settlers, as latrines were an unknown matter before the settlers came. We finished up on the last day, in the village where the carriers had come from, so on the final morning it was an easy descent to the office and to open the cash chest to pay the carriers, extracting the requisite thumb prints!

I might add as a corollary, that as a result of this shock treatment (which at the time I regarded as inhumane) I was able to pass my Lower Chinyanja examination within my first year.

OP 88 (October 2004)

Nyasaland
(and Central African Federation)

Nyasaland was granted a Coat of Arms in May 1914, with the striking design of a leopard standing on a rock, with the rising sun above. These arms in the shape of a shield were used as the badge of the Protectorate until 1953, when Nyasaland became part of the Central African Federation. The Federation's badge comprised elements from the three constituent territories, and included the rising sun but not the leopard from the Nyasaland badge.

Train to Iganga

by Kuldip Rai Moman

When time who steals our years away,
Shall steal our pleasures too,
The memory of the past will stay
And half our joys renew.
Thomas Moore

My first vacation leave in India was coming to a close. I set out to say farewell to my village Moron, literally, abode of the peacock. The day I alighted on Mother Earth, these birds of paradise descended on the roof-tops and danced. The dance continues with their rainbow plumage fluttering in the aromatic air. It is a spectacle to be witnessed to be believed. I returned to Sunetra where I grew up. Its history goes back 5,000 years. The original place is now ruins. The Greeks, Scythians, Parthians, Kushans and Yodheyas once held sway and had their mint sites here. There is a mound where I have often sat. In the seclusion, silence and emptiness, I have tried to listen to the rattle of swords and footsteps of the ancients. It may be I inhabited the neighbourhood in a former incarnation!

A 1,000 miles long train trek from the vast plains of Punjab brought me to Bombay; and then drifting for ten blue days on the bosom of the great and wide Indian Ocean, the ship cast anchor at Mombasa. It was the 6th day of May, 1946.

I was on my familiar terrain, amongst smiling faces and was glad to feel the tossing sea breeze. Alas, the analogous days of sailing ships are no more. A representative from the Crown Agents boarded the ship and handed me instructions of my posting to Kabale in Uganda.

My wife Kaushalya, whom I had met and married during my holidays, was hesitant to accompany me to the dark continent. Uganda, specially, was considered an arena of mosquitoes, malaria and blackwater fever. She had belonged to Lahore, the most beautiful city of the Orient. It is said that who has not seen Lahore, is not born. As I had spent my first tour of service in Kenya, cruising from office to office, almost all over the country, I was not pleased with the transfer and felt distressed.

We took the train to Kampala. When it halted at Nairobi, Mr Sethi from the Postmaster-General's office delivered me another communication, telling me to proceed to lganga instead of Kabale. We went to the General Post Office to try to have the transfer altered to Kenya. Unfortunately, the officer concerned was not available. We therefore returned to the railway station and proceeded to Nsinze, the railhead for lganga.

To my surprise, at Nsinze I saw Shankerbhai Patel, the station master, whom I had known during my tenure at Miwani in Kenya, greeting me at the platform. He telephoned his friend Dayabhai, the owner of a cotton ginnery at lganga, to put us up with him till we could move to the Postmaster's house. I took over from Yusafali, who sadly left this world years back. The Post Office was in the wilderness, away from the township, next to the small Police Post. As usual, the Postmaster's house was attached to it. The accommodation had one bedroom, a drawing or an all purpose room, a verandah and a large compound. Our long-drop lavatory was some 200 feet from the house. During the night, if my wife needed to visit the loo, I would stand with a Tilley lamp in my hand. In the pitch dark, the mango trees sighed and swayed. The wind wept, wailed, shuddered and shrieked. The twigs and leaves would fall from the trees over the roof of the latrine with a clatter.

The staff comprised of the Postmaster, a telegraphist-cum-telephonist and an office boy named Rajabu. Rajabu was a cheerful fellow in his late forties but looked far older than his age. Besides all the services generally offered at a Post Office, as it was the post-war period, we had to deal with an abnormally large number of Savings Bank withdrawals. Hundreds of men who went to different battle fronts in various capacities were due their lump sum gratuities. The authorities had seen to it that the money paid to them should last for a reasonable period. They were thus issued with Savings Bank pass books with the amount due to them, duly entered. It varied from person to person but as far as I can recall, was in the region of 2000 shillings.

In the early morning the King's warriors, after walking long distances from their villages, would begin converging at the Post Office. They would sit, squat or lie down on a patch of green grass, some smoking a pipe. They had tales to narrate about their exploits from distant war zones. As the day advanced, a hawker with a giant teapot would appear and take it around and sell them a cup of hot tea. The combatants' comings and goings went on. The assembly reminded you of a scene from a Persian bazaar.

No sooner had we opened at 8.00 am, these tall, hefty soldiers would make a sprint at the counter window which measured 18 inches high and

15 inches wide, the money book issued by the *Serikali* in hand. There was glare in their eyes and alacrity in their stride. Their fortnightly withdrawals usually amounted to twenty shillings. At this pace, their savings could last for some four years. To be honest, to attend to some 40 persons a day for one specific class of transaction and satisfy yourself about proof of their identity which was not easy to establish, I must say, was a tough and exhausting task. However, it was part of the game. I would have missed their company if and when they had exhausted their deposits. By the time we were shut, they had turned their backs on us and trickled homewards, walking majestically, with the wage packet or *mshahara* in their pockets. Their big day and excursion were over.

Wherever I saw service in East Africa, I had a habit of rummaging to find old and obsolete records in a forgotten corner or a tiny forsaken store. During my quest at Iganga, besides other interesting material, I came across an old Post Office guide. It bore the name: Churariji Lal Phakey – 1927. I leapt up at the discovery as the writer was my maternal uncle. When I met him in his village Katani in the Punjab, he related to me the saga of his days at Iganga. He had manned the Post Office from a tent. It was not an uncommon sight to spot a leopard skulking, or hear a lion roaring in the vicinity. Incidentally, three of my uncles worked for the Posts and Telegraph Department. A number of my relatives were employees of Kenya Uganda Railways and Harbours. Their ashes, in some cases, have become part of the African soil without name, slab or stone.

When the shadows of darkness fell, we were left on our own in isolation. Occasionally someone would enter the premises to clear his Post Office letter box. Otherwise there was nothing to disturb the stillness and solitude. There were times it rained throughout the night. In the morning, the environment was pellucid, fresh and fragrant. The smell of crisp, wet African earth and the foliage is a bliss to experience. A peculiar sensation passes through your veins.

We had twenty mango trees and two gulab jambu* trees. The latter bears greenish-white fruit about two inches square and is thought to help in heart-related ailments. At lunch hour, our house boy would climb the highest branch and pick the sweetest, orange-red, ripe mangoes. In a fairy tale it is said that if you pluck a pomegranate or a mango from the top branch and,

---

*gulab jamun = *syzigium jambos*, or rose apple tree

135

of course, if the luck is with you, a princess would emerge from the fruit, kiss you and wed you! In real life or stretch of your illusion, if you travel to Iganga, remember the royalty is looking forward to kiss her Prince Charming!

At certain Post Offices there was a custom of minor local perks. At Iganga, the Postmaster was eligible for a full lorry load of *kuni* or firewood which was delivered as and when required, and any quantity of cotton from the local ginnery for mattresses, quilts and pillows. There used not to be tapped water in the town or at the Post Office. A month before my arrival, a hand pump was installed by the town committee, where a four-gallon *debe* was sold for 20 cents. The Postmaster was allowed 20 complimentary gallons daily.

I remember my young servant fetching water from half a mile away. He would balance the tin on his head on a roundish cushion, made of grass, in such a fashion that both his hands remained free. His whole structure would swing and fly in the crunchy, invigorating, unpolluted surroundings. There was elasticity in his gait and he would hum a song of wild Africa in his native Busoga. The ecstasy of the music from the days glided away comes back to me from afar and I feel glum for the passage of two score and ten years.

There were about 100 Indian shops or commercial establishments which met your needs. They included three provision stores, a garage, a photographer, carpenter, and a barber. Lalji Jutha's was the best well-stocked shop. The off-licence was owned by a Goan, Mr Cota, who was a real gentleman. There was a cotton ginnery and a mission.

Some 15 miles away is Bugiri, a hamlet where you could buy sweet, juicy superior quality tangerines. Another place is Kalaki, 22 miles from Soroti. In subsequent years, I used to make a deviation from the main road to call there. An Arab who knew me from my Postmastership at Soroti would make an exceptional endeavour with his long bamboo pole to get for me the best fruit.

The Education Department appointed my wife as a teacher. I handed over the office to Mr Swami and we prepared to go to Kampala. It was a sparkling morning. The ex-troopers had begun gathering. I had a last, lingering look at their camp and the mango grove. I was leaving magical moments of dawn of spring in my life. With all our worldly possessions at the back of the vehicle, the lorry started with a jerk. A bird hovered overhead to say goodbye.

OP 75 (Spring 1998)

A Learning Experience

by Eric Cunningham

It was late 1953, and the second year of my service as an Education Officer in the Gold Coast. I was one of a band of six officers who were the last to be appointed to pensionable service there. It was also the second year of internal self-government in the Gold Coast. This had come in February 1952, while the six of us were Cadet Education Officers pursuing the Post-Graduate Certificate in Education course at the University of London Institute of Education. Shortly before we sailed from Liverpool in August 1952 to take up our appointments a letter from the Colonial Office had told us that because of internal self-government we should expect changes in the Gold Coast, and that a new salary scale had been introduced, details of which would be given after arrival. There were also gubernatorial assurances that our careers as Colonial Service officers were in no way a cause for concern by us.

I had been posted to the District Education Office, Kumasi. Kumasi was the chief town of Ashanti, a traditional tribal kingdom with a famous reputation for its own authority and independence, and the education district was a large and busy one, with over 500 primary and middle schools. One of the first acts of internal self-government had been to promote fee-free primary education, as promised by the *Accelerated Development Plan for Education*. The District Education Officer was an experienced and highly regarded African, an ex-Government teacher promoted on merit. He was one of a select band who were in the vanguard of what was known as the Africanisation of the Civil Service, and the six of us, in our various postings, were among the first expatriates to have African superordinates. I found him fair, positive, hard working, and genuinely concerned that I should learn both fully and fast what the job of an Education Officer in his district involved. I had great respect for him.

Much of my work involved visiting schools throughout the district to make inspections and write reports, and assisting with the in-service training of a rapidly increasing number of African Assistant Education Officers. The expansion of primary schools required a rapidly increasing number of pupil teachers too, and the setting up of in-service short courses for them. One day I was asked to do something different: to attend the

Board of Governors' meeting of the Methodist Girls Boarding School in Juaben, some twenty miles from Kumasi. I welcomed the change.

The meeting went well. The chairman of the Board of Governors was the Juabenhene, the Paramount Chief of the area. He was clear about what he wanted, and took us purposefully through the agenda. As the meeting closed the Juabenhene thanked us for attending, and in an expansive moment invited us all to visit him in his palace (his own description) for refreshments. It would have been grossly discourteous for me to decline his invitation, and besides I was curious, never before having visited a paramount chief's abode. In due course we were all given chairs on the verandah, servants brought a bowl of water for washing hands, and refreshments were served: sweet biscuits and tepid beer, as was the local custom. As we ate and drank, conversation became quite animated, but I could contribute little, so I listened and watched with interest.

Time passed and the Juabenhene's expansiveness increased. He announced that he would have a photograph taken to mark the occasion; a messenger was despatched. During the wait more refreshments were served, and eventually the photographer arrived, his equipment a large glass-plate camera and tripod, and black velvet cloth. Chairs were arranged in a row, and we began to group around them. As a Government officer I was not a member of the Board of Governors, but merely in attendance, representing the Director of Education, and had been at the meeting only to provide, when appropriate, an official perspective and guidance on policy if required. I therefore stood behind the chair at the edge of the row, giving precedence to the school governors.

The Juabenhene eyed the group, and quickly commanded me to come and sit on the vacant chair beside him, in the middle of the row. I protested gently, saying that I was not formally on the Board of Governors but merely represented the Education Department. The Juabenhene would have none of this. "No, no," he said firmly, "you come and sit here. You are the only coloured man here!"

It was a salutary experience, never to be forgotten. Colour, like beauty, is in the eye of the beholder.

OP 93 (April 2007)

A Matter of Understanding

by Simon Templer

The young Customs Officer sat at his office desk within the Custom House in Kampala, Uganda. He was ploughing systematically through the paper work which had come in for his attention. It was all very orderly. From time to time an office messenger came in with a pile of correspondence which he deposited in the officer's 'In Tray' and at the same time collected up all the paperwork which had accumulated in the 'Out Tray' for distribution to various other offices within the building. Routine stuff, the product of a long established and efficient colonial governmental system. Once or twice a week the officer would get ahead and find that he had some time on his hands before the next round of the messenger, in which event he was able to spend time studying the Laws and Departmental Procedures in anticipation of his promotion bar examination later on in the year. There were three distinct advantages to such practice; firstly, if anyone came into the office he was seen to be busy, secondly, actually gaining useful knowledge and thirdly he was not having to use up his own precious after-hours time in the study work.

The afternoon was typically hot and sticky and the collar of his white uniform tunic was stiff and uncomfortable as usual. Oh for half past four when he could go home. There was a knock on the door. The office messengers did not knock so this had to be someone else, probably one of the clerks from the outer office. The officer called out the usual invitation and indeed, there was one of the clerks together with a European man standing behind him. They shuffled in and the clerk explained that the accompanying 'gentleman' had a problem which was too difficult for the public counter outside to deal with and with that smartly withdrew.

The Customs Officer sat the visitor down in the chair opposite and invited him to explain his problem. It appeared that the newcomer was a Belgian but normally a resident of the former Belgian Congo. That country had achieved its independence from Belgium not long before and had very rapidly degenerated into civil war and general anarchy. Those Europeans who had stayed on in the country were obliged to flee for their lives and a considerable number were unsuccessful. Now here was one more who had managed to get away and made his way into Uganda, then still under

British Administration, and so 'safe'. Over the last few weeks there had been a steady trickle of such refugees and they would travel on through Uganda and Kenya until they reached Mombasa where they would take a ship for Europe with what little they had with them.

So far as the Customs Officer was concerned, it was merely a matter of regularizing the man's entry into Uganda because he had had to use unauthorised back roads and tracks to enter Uganda, thereby bypassing the official frontier post where all formalities were normally conducted. These were exceptional times so a blind eye had to be turned upon the illegal journeying of the refugee. In any case, it was good of the man to report in at all; many had not, only to fall foul of the Customs people further on, including the Immigration Department, who were a quite separate authority. Those were intolerant colonial days when penalties were handed out without hesitation to the defaulters.

The Belgian refugee rambled on with his dramatic story of how he had only just managed to escape from the Congo in his pickup truck with guerillas just behind him all the time and practically no personal possessions except for a very few, also in the truck. His command of the English language was very poor and his accent was dreadful. In fact so bad that it was not at all easy to understand him. He was asked to make a formal declaration of what he had with him and it appeared from what he said that there was only the pickup truck itself and a very few personal and household possessions for he had had to abandon almost everything else he had over there in the Congo, such had been the urgency of leaving alive. The guerillas had been close behind him all the time.

The Customs Officer felt that despite the communication problem he had managed to absorb the gist of the refugee's story; it was not so different to that of many similar stories told by such refugees who had appeared recently with a few basic personal possessions to show. Fairly routine stuff. The refugee would have to be issued with a fourteen-day entry permit for his motor vehicle, assuming it was registered in the Congo, and the rest of his personal possessions would be free of any restrictions anyway. They would have to be checked for firearms and any other restricted imports, but the chance of finding anything of that sort was extraordinarily unlikely for the refugees well knew that they must not antagonize the British Administrations in East Africa if they were to enjoy safe passage through to the sea port of Mombasa.

The form-filling and rubber-stamping was concluded and all that remained was to go outside and examine the refugee's truck and personal effects. There it was, a thoroughly muddy but quite good truck with some large wooden crates on the back. The Customs Officer had half expected to find the odd bullet-hole, but there were none. Presumably the Belgian had managed to stay well enough ahead of the guerillas to be out of range or, more likely, they were just appallingly bad shots anyway. He thought that the refugee had nevertheless managed to pack up quite a lot of his household stuff, presumably the valuables, before he fled so had managed better than many. He peered into the driving cab and made a note of the indicated mileage run up so far (it was an American left-hand drive vehicle). Then he asked the Belgian to open the bonnet so that he could record the engine number and chassis number. All correct. The front number plate conformed to the registration papers as expected.

Now the crates in the back had to be inspected and possibly opened. The Officer hoped that the man had tools for it was his responsibility to do the opening if required. In that way if anything got broken or lost the owner could not lay blame upon the Department; in the ordinary course of events the Customs could look but not touch. The refugee had not suggested that there was anything of interest other than his personal possessions which he had just managed to load, with all those guerillas close behind him.

The Officer moved round to the rear of the truck and gazed up at the three or four large crates. Then he stood staring in amazement. Each crate contained a young live gorilla.

No false declaration had been made and suddenly the Uganda Game Department needed to know.

OP 92 (October 2006)

Part 3
TOURING, TRAVEL & TRANSPORT

Journey to Yola, 1929

by B A Babb

On 11th September 1929 I found myself walking up the gangway of Elder Dempster's MV *Accra*, bound for Lagos. This was the start of a journey which was to end in Zanzibar 25 years later.

It had come about almost by chance. In the spring of 1929 I was doing a term's teaching at Christ's Hospital, as part of the course for the Cambridge University's Diploma of Education. During that time *The Times* published a West African Supplement and while having a fairly casual look at this I noticed a report on careers opportunities in the Colonial Education Service – the one that appealed to me most being in Northern Nigeria – the main reason being that shooting was good and horses cheap, both of which I loved and saw no prospect of ever being able to afford as a schoolmaster in England. Lest it should be thought that these reasons were unworthy, it must be remembered that I had already decided to become a schoolmaster! I also recognised the fact that the starting salary of a schoolmaster in England was about £180 pa, while Nigeria was offering £480! Without much delay I applied for Northern Nigeria and was called for interview by the Colonial Office Selection Board, whose Chairman was the famous Major Ralph Furze, a keen devotee of cricket. I have often wondered if the fact that I had played county cricket (albeit Minor) added some weight to my extremely modest academic attainments! I was duly appointed and with my £60 outfit allowance I felt passing rich. Visits were paid to Griffiths McAlister to get my kit together, and a Banker's Order of £10 per month arranged to pay for it. This remained in force for several years and it was often said that 'Griffmacs' were almost as much our masters as the Colonial Office!

Before sailing I had received a letter from Randall Ellison, at that time Education Officer in the Assistant Director's Office, Kaduna, telling me that I was to be posted to Yola, Adamawa Province, and to report to Kaduna to be told how to get there. The fourteen day voyage passed very pleasantly, with the added interest of first sights and sounds of Africa at Sierra Leone, Takoradi and Accra. Naturally a few 'old coasters' did their best to terrify us beginners with lurid tales of life (and more usually death!) in the 'White Man's Grave'.

On arrival at Lagos I was bidden to lunch with the Director of Education, E R J Hussey, father of the present Chairman of the BBC. Later I picked up the night boat train for the two day trip to Kaduna, where Randall Ellison met me and put me up. Next day I met the Assistant Director, G A J Bieneman, whose widow remains a dear friend to this day. He told me I was being posted to Yola since I had read Modern Languages at Cambridge, and Fulani, spoken in Adamawa Province, was considered a more difficult language than the more usual Hausa. Next day, Ellison produced a cook, Kadim, and a steward, Musa, the former a useful cook who remained with me for many years and the latter a very short time indeed! I then boarded the evening train for Makurdi and was told to take the first available Niger Company Steamer for Yola. These boats were stern-wheelers, their main function being the transport of stores and trade goods to trading stations on the upper reaches of the Benue River, returning with the annual groundnut crop, loaded into barges and lashed alongside. They had the wonderfully evocative air of boys' adventure stories, which I was still young enough to appreciate. They provided no food and only basic accommodation for two to three Europeans, ie unfurnished cabins and communal galley. One used one's own camp equipment. The lower deck provided seemingly unlimited space for Africans – men, women and children and their assorted livestock, including cattle and the odd horse. Kadim, I found, had the extraordinary talent, possessed by so many African cooks, of producing good meals from often poor materials, under very difficult conditions. The basics, flour, sugar, tea, etc, came from 'Griffmacs' chop boxes; meat, chickens, eggs and fish from the riverside markets when we anchored for the night.

It was not possible to steam in darkness as all navigation was done by the African skipper, clad in pyjamas and sitting in a deck chair in the bows of the ship. He had an unerring eye for sandbanks and too shallow water and gave all navigational directions by shouting to the man at the wheel. Some days later we arrived at Lau, to be greeted with the news that the boat would not be going on to Yola since the river was too low, and would not be navigable again until the next shipping season. This left me a six-day trek to Yola. The District Officer, Captain L C Schlotel, MC, had been sent a telegram which asked him to provide carriers and point me in the direction of Yola. Thus a lorry was waiting at Lau to transport me and my loads the short distance to the Muri District HQ at Jalingo. On reaching there I was delighted to find that the Cadet there was Jack Gill, an old Cambridge friend, who had already been in the country a couple of months. Jack put me up and then took me to pay my respects to Schlotel. We found him trying out the effects of an arrow on a home-made shield, made of corrugated iron (or 'pan', as I soon learned to call it). Apparently, on his last visit to the pagan Mummuze country, some bright young spark had had the temerity to flick off an arrow at him and he wished to be well-prepared for his next tax-collecting visit! At this time, Mummuze country was 'closed territory' and I had a nasty shock when told that part of my trek to Yola would be through it, but that I would be given an escort. I began to ask myself if I had made a mistake in not sticking to schoolmastering in England!

Next morning I awoke to the sound of clanking chains to find a gang of prisoners in leg-irons from the Native Administration gaol cutting the Station grass – all singing very cheerfully! A horse, carriers and escort were ready and we set off on the first day's trek of about 17 miles – the average, for which carriers were paid 9d for carrying a 60 lb load and 6d for returning 'empty'. My natural apprehension (windiness would be the more appropriate word!) was in no way diminished by finding on arrival at the first rest camp in Mummuze country, that the pagan chief of the village and most of his subjects were very drunk indeed and were carrying bows and arrows! However, eggs and chickens were forthcoming and everything passed off quietly (apart from the drunken belching!). It cannot be denied, however, that I was happy a few days later to see the thatched roofs of Yola in the distance and a little later to be having breakfast with my new master, Captain Jeremy Taylor, the author of Fulani and Hausa Grammars and the Fulani Dictionary.

This 'breaking-in' trek taught me the joys of trekking on horse-back, once a daily routine had been established. In my case this meant picking four of the heftiest carriers overnight to start off at 5.00 am with the cook and his equipment, and for him to set up camp and table under a shady tree at about 8.30 am. I would set off with the rest of the carriers about 6.00 am and have breakfast about 2½-3 hours later. Having reached camp about mid-day, it was pleasant to take a gun out in the evening to shoot a guinea fowl for the pot. A very enjoyable first tour followed, which included much trekking in distant parts of Adamawa Province, since during the heavy locust invasion of 1930 many departmental officers were seconded to the Administration for locust control duty. Having passed my Fulani exams, I was looking forward to a second tour in Yola, but was posted to Bauchi, not to return to Yola for six years.

Incidentally, a bonus of the three tours in Bauchi was the privilege of having Mallam (later Sir) Abubakar Tafawa Balewa, the first Nigerian Prime Minister, on my staff for that whole period.

OP 57 (April 1989)

First Footsteps

by John Cooke

Biharamulo was my first station as a District Officer in Tanganyika. On arrival in Mwanza, the headquarters of the Lake Province, in late September 1951, as a very green DO (Cadet), I was informed by the Provincial Commissioner that he was sending me to one of the last lingering corners of ancient Africa, as he put it. So off I went by the lake steamer *Sybil* to Bukoba on the west side of the lake. There I was met by my District Commissioner, Ronald Smith, and we travelled for four hours in his landrover the 113 miles of rugged earth road to my new place of work. I noticed that a single line of telegraph wire bordered the road, and was informed that this was the sole means of communication to the world outside, apart from the road we were on, and that there was a morse key and receiver at each end. Apparently elephant frequently put the line out of action.

Biharamulo was a fairly large district of 4500 sq miles, at the south-west corner of Lake Victoria, but with a population of only about 50,000 people, and these were concentrated into sleeping sickness-free enclaves. It had only merited a single Administrative Officer, the DC himself, but Smith reckoned he needed an assistant, and I was the fruit of persistent badgering of the PC. My first task was to supervise the building of my house. This was built of raw local rock, held together by mud mortar and with a thatched grass roof. It was entirely innocent of any form of plumbing. While this was being built I enjoyed Smith's generous hospitality. I quickly got down to my work as a DO, functioning as a Magistrate of the Third Class, and as the coroner, supervising the Accounts Office and answering Treasury and Audit queries, overseeing our small prison and Police Force, out in the district visiting Native Authority offices and Local Courts, checking case records and Local Treasury accounts, and visiting schools and clinics. As my Swahili improved I began to deal with a host of petitioners of one sort or another, both in the office and out in the district. Social life was limited by the fact that the station was so small. We were the DC and myself, a District Assistant, a Settlement Officer, an Agricultural Field Officer, and an African Police Inspector, none of whom were married, and also the McGregors, man and wife. They had gone out to Nyasaland pre-1914 to grow cotton. They were as tough as old boots, and his task was to try to teach the Bazinza to grow fire-cured tobacco. Most of the subordinate staff were Bahaya from Bukoba. Incidentally, our Police Inspector, Saidi Maswanya, eventually became Minister of Home Affairs in Nyerere's first government after independence in 1961. I met him again in Dar es Salaam at the tenth Independence Anniversary celebrations in 1971.

I began to get just a little bit restless, and pestered Smith to let me out on some foot safaris. He was very understanding and so I was able to get out quite a lot. I was particularly eager to see some of the huge wilderness areas of the district at first hand. So one weekend I got a lift to Nyakahura, and the next day, a Sunday, walked back to Biharamulo cross country with Daudi, a District Office messenger (*tarishi* in Swahili), a very competent and cheerful companion. It was a trip of about 35 miles and I was thrilled by this magnificent country. But the elephant we met at close quarters I found rather intimidating, especially as we were quite unarmed!

My first longer working safari was to the neighbouring district of Ngara. Here I went with the DC, George Gordon, by bicycle to a new road he was building northward towards western Biharamulo. I was greatly impressed by what could be achieved by hand labour. New lands were being opened up and it pleases me greatly to see on modern maps that that track has now become a main road going north.

A rather unusual safari was occasioned by a request from the War Graves Commission that someone should visit and inspect some Belgian 1914-18 war graves out in the bush in the east of the district towards the lake. I took five porters and we did the round trip in four days. It had been raining and we walked for miles through water about one foot deep, viciously assaulted by tsetse and mosquitoes. We found the graves and cleaned up the site. Over the four Belgian graves there had been erected grave stones on which were engraved the name, rank, and birthplace of each officer and the words *MORT AU CHAMP D'HONNEUR.* The askaris were buried under a large pyramidal cairn. The Belgians and their askaris had been wiped out by a German ambush, and buried on the spot. I made a note of the names and we left in a rather sombre mood.

A longer ten-day foot safari took me into the western parts of the district. The area was remote and seldom visited, and at each camp large numbers of people had gathered to meet me and discuss their affairs. Eventually I reached the very impressive Rusumo Falls on the Kagera river. Here we crossed the river and marched from there up to Ngara. Crossing the river in dugout canoes with the roar of the falls close by was a trifle disconcerting! At the present day there is a bridge there.

A safari of a different sort was with Smith in the government launch from Mwanza. We visited the islands in Emin Pasha gulf which lay within Biharamulo district. The people seldom saw visitors, least of all from Government, and they were very pleased to see us. Each night we anchored off an island and we slept on board while the two crew men went ashore.

Apart from work in the office, in court, and on safari out in the district there were other things to do. There were lots of guinea-fowl and partridge close by and so we had plenty of good shooting. I borrowed an ancient single-barrel twelve bore from the Native Authority for the purpose. I also went hunting after buffalo with a Husqvarna 9.3 mm rifle I had bought from Smith. This was an exciting if chastening experience!

The rock known as the Bukoba Sandstone outcrops in a long escarpment south of Biharamulo, and I found that it was similar in many ways to the gritstone of my native Pennines, on which I had learned the arts of rock climbing. I used to take the long suffering Daudi with me to do some interesting climbing. He must have thought me quite mad but was far too polite to say anything, and was content to watch.

Eventually, with a government loan I was able to acquire a Landrover, which gave me greater scope for travel. Apart from getting about my work in the district more easily, it enabled me to spend a couple of weekends enjoying the flesh-pots of Bukoba. I was also able to go down quite often to Nyamirembe on the lakeshore, only twenty six miles away, to visit Bryan Cooper, the Game Ranger for the region. He taught me a great deal about wildlife and its habitats.

Biharamulo was giving me much satisfaction. The work, the people, the opportunity to do things I had always dreamed of doing in a fascinating environment were wonderful. But young District Officers were not left for long in one place, and sure enough after eighteen months I got my orders to cross the lake to Musoma. That turned out to be an equally absorbing place in which to live and work.

As a postscript, many years later and after our retirement from Africa in 1991, my wife and I found ourselves living near the Smiths. He gave us a superb leopard skin, which came from a leopard that had been terrorising the Katoke area of Biharamulo when I was there. Eventually it had been trapped and shot, and Smith had had the skin cured and mounted in Nairobi. It is a priceless memento of a very happy time spent in Biharamulo, and of my DC, Ronald Smith, now alas deceased.

OP 86 (October 2003)

Ulendo

by R E N Smith

*U*lendo, safari, bush-bashing, on tour – all romantic words redolent of
the immaculately turned out Bwana, with his faithful gun-bearer just
behind him, followed by a retinue of *kanzu*-clad servants, messengers and
askaris, the tassels on their crested bright red fezzes swinging free, and a
long line of happy carriers, each bearing the Bwana's essentials, as they head
for a palaver at the Chief's picturesque thatched-hut kraal. This was the
popular image of the majesty of District Administration, or for that matter
of any of the other services that brought the benefits of Western civilisation
to the forlorn and friendless in their darkness. If the scene is more watery,
then there is the DC on his river steamer, majestic with its polished brass
work and disciplined Hausa soldiery, moving steadily upstream to subdue
a recalcitrant Old King. Well if you were brought up on Edgar Wallace's
'*Sanders*' stories, or the reminiscences of early administrators, perhaps there
was a smidgen of truth in all this, but in my time, at the end of the era, we
were not quite up to this grand view.

I must preface my remarks by noting that judged by some standards
Nyasaland was somewhat scruffy in dress. I well remember the arrival of an
officer on transfer from Uganda who appeared for work, to the stupefaction
of all beholders, refulgent in all the glory of a pith helmet, khaki drill bush
shirt and shorts, with the shirt sporting polished brass crested buttons.
The usual dress for officers in our Boma was a short-sleeved sports shirt
and khaki shorts, plus long stockings. In the cities and in cold weather
you might wear a tie with this gear, but not in the average district. On
ulendo the same dress would suffice, but you would probably replace the
long socks with short ones – they did not collect quite as many prickles
and burrs. I remember one forest officer (not noted for excessive energy)
who kept a matchbox full of burrs, and sprinkled them on his stockings
when visiting his masters in Zomba! On one's feet would be a battered
pair of Bata crépe-soled shoes – lineal descendants of the 'brothel creepers'
of wartime. I usually owned three pairs of these most comfortable princes
of footwear, which cost only 25/- a pair, one for best, one for *ulendo*,
and, in a descending scale of serviceability, one for gardening. I do not
think many of us ever wore a pith helmet, or a cork helmet except for the

pipe-clayed white horror that crowned us when in civil uniform. On the officer's head would be a soft Australian felt bush hat. My own was slightly unusual in that it was two hats sewn together and had once been part of my uniform in the army; now stripped of the distinctive insignia of the Third Ghurkhas, it served me well in Africa for many years.

One's retinue varied according to choice. There were usually a house boy and a cook, a clerk plus a messenger or two. I have remarked on these latter stalwarts before, but they were the essential part of one's tail. They organised the carriers, put up the tent, saw that a toilet had been prepared, and on top of that they would round up any miscreants one wanted, would form the 'complainants' (the villagers with any sort of request) into a little line, and generally serve one's dignity and comfort with zeal. Their uniform was modest enough – shirt (with brass buttons) and shorts, a leather belt and the brass-crested and tasselled fez. You could distinguish between Boma messengers and Native Authority messengers by these tassels – red for the Boma men and black for the NA ones. On top of that, the level of smartness was always in favour of the Boma messengers, almost always ex-*askari* of the King's African Rifles, and as loyal and dependable as one could wish. They usually went barefoot and carried no weapons; the only firearm visible on *ulendo* was my 12 bore shotgun, with which I chased guinea fowl in the early mornings and evenings – with only minor success, for I was never a Great White Hunter.

My first *ulendo* was not on foot at all, but by canoe. I did not rate a river gunboat, a launch or even a rowing boat, for the Lower River District did not boast any such luxury. I was honoured all the same, for Chief Nyachikadza had sent his personal flagship for me, and it was a grand enough canoe, dug out from a remarkably large tree to hold me, my clerk, a messenger and a couple of servants. From Port Herald to Nyachikadza's capital was no great distance, and going downstream was quick and easy, while out in the middle of the Shiré River there were neither flies nor mosquitoes. This was luxury indeed, but the return voyage was rather different. Because the canoe was so large, it made much poorer progress than the usual two-man affair. We crept slowly and with difficulty up against the current and hugging the marshy bank, so that the pests we had foiled on the way down had their revenge, while the heat was horrid; well, at least I personally did not have to do the paddling or poling.

The number of carriers you were permitted to take at Government expense was laid down in General Orders. You could have twenty two, with extra if you were traversing waterless areas. This may sound a lot, and certainly you did not always take that number, but you needed six for the clumsy and heavy tents that were standard issue – double fly, verandah, bathroom apse, plus poles and pegs. For my gear I had had several petrol boxes adapted. For those who have not met these humble but essential items, they were sturdy wooden boxes, each holding two flimsy four-gallon cans of petrol or kerosene; used in the War they had been grossly wasteful of petrol, but for my purposes they were perfect. The Boma carpenter put a hinged lid on each, and they then held food, pots and pans, clothing, crockery, and all the other essential impedimenta of travel. One held the pressure lamp and its attendant paraffin tin. These lamps gave excellent light but were subject to constant failure of their little burned-cloth mantle or 'bulb' – and the replacements were not cheap. This brilliant light also attracted the multitudinous aerial creatures of the night, all intent and often succeeding in self-immolation – the flying 'sausages' were particularly annoying and as they burned they cooked with a horrid stench.

Another petrol box I had cunningly adapted as a luxury box, with two doors on the side and folding legs at each end. Inside lived a couple of shelves of paper-backs and my Saucepan Radio, a fore-runner of the little transistor sets, and yes, its cover was a saucepan. On arrival in camp the legs were folded down, an aerial wire thrown on top of the tent, and contentment settled on me. This happy state was aided by a demi-john of Portuguese wine; Port Herald was close to the Mozambique border where a few unhappy trading stores nudged the frontier at Marka Nyathando, and one could buy a demi-john of quite passable wine cheaply indeed. With a glass of red wine to accompany one's dinner, a book, the radio and a quiet pipe of tobacco, what else could one want? Other carriers had the gear of the staff and servants, and any other unconsidered trifles we acquired on the way. In another district an officer of an unusually sensitive nature had a personal carrier-borne toilet seat that was fitted over the usual hole in the ground inside a grass walled surround, but he was the only such sybarite that I heard of.

There were two exceptions to the 'twenty-two carriers' rule, one legal, the other highly incorrect. There was a dispensation in General Orders for an officer who was physically disabled that permitted him to be carried by 'machila' men. A machila was no more than a hammock slung on a long pole, and had been a common mode of transport for the more idle of Europeans in the earlier years of the century. I only knew of one officer who could legitimately have used machila men, an ex-Indian Army officer who had lost a leg on the North-West Frontier, but I do not think that he ever availed himself of the privilege. All the same, by a process of immutable habit so dear to officials, it was usual for there to be a couple of machila men on the roll of each Boma (I do not know how one machila man could have performed his duties) and they were the indispensable performers of odd jobs that every station needed. Efforts to have them abolished were thwarted by renaming them 'station hands'.

The other exception to the rule was the Department of Agriculture. The Director, a highly experienced, able and forceful officer, had spent all his career in Nyasaland and had, I suspect, imbibed deeply of the 'Cinderella of Central Africa' belief that was often thrust upon us. In a praiseworthy attempt to get the maximum of *ulendo* consonant with the least damage to his touring vote, he laid it down that his officers were not permitted more than sixteen carriers. Such was his *manu* that no one questioned his contemptuous infraction of General Orders, for he had no authority to override them. He just did it, and his department fell into line.

The Lower River was not a large district, and the distances between camps and villages quite modest, so one recruited carriers at each halt and paid them off on arrival at the next. It was not highly paid work – I think that the rate in 1950 was nine pence a day, though it did improve later. The scene each morning was animated, as the clerk and messengers tried to get the milling mass of young men into some sort of order. Once all the gear had been packed, and the tent taken down, the loads were allotted. By a worldwide phenomenon among organised manual labour, it was invariably the biggest and strongest man who picked the smallest load, but my trips were usually enlivened by the downfall of this little quirk of human laziness. My clerk, the servants and messengers would smile in anticipation as some great hulk of a man rushed for and seized the little padlocked wooden box that stood all on its own. Unaccountably he had much difficulty in lifting it, and there was laughter all round when it was revealed that this small box was lined in metal and packed with 12-bore cartridges. In later years portering became most unpopular and in a commendable spirit of national pride, young men were reluctant to carry, even for the princely sum of 2/6d. At Visanza in the Central Province in 1960 I made no attempt to recruit men, for it became much easier to find women to do the work. From their point of view, they were paid to carry comparatively easy loads for a few miles to a village where they would be able to visit their friends, and be paid handsomely for it – for I doubt if the men would ever have handed over their pay to their wives!

In the interests of taking government to the people, whether they wanted it or not, the Governor of my day had laid down minimum *ulendo* standards. Every District Commissioner had to do seven nights touring each month and every Assistant District Commissioner fourteen nights – and no excuses were acceptable. This sounds reasonable enough and was generally not too wearing, though *ulendo* in the wet weather could be extremely unpleasant for all concerned. In my first tour I was a bachelor, and so constant touring was no problem. Its effect on some officers however, could be odd. My first District Commissioner in the Lower River District formed the habit of having his tent erected at the Boma itself, some four miles from his house, and camping there, thus obeying the strict letter of the directive, if not its spirit.

OP 87 (April 2004)

Jungle Trip from Grik to Temengor

by Mrs M C Barkway

Temengor in 1939 was a fairly large Malay village of some 200 inhabitants, surrounded by extensive padi (rice) fields. It is situated on the very attractive Temengor River, a tributary of the upper Perak River, and about 30 miles from Grik.

There is a mixed boys and girls Malay school at Temengor, and it was in order to visit (and inspect) this school that I, as Domestic Science Supervisor, was asked by the Education Department to arrange an expedition, starting over the Easter weekend when it was easier to find a few friends to accompany me. Plenty of men were anxious to do the trip, but I had a difficult job to find a married woman to come as chaperone!

The party eventually consisted of Phyllis, whose husband was an Education Officer in Teluk Anson, Kenneth and Bill, both masters at the Malay College in Kuala Kangsar, and therefore very anxious, as I was, to further our knowledge of Malay, and Tony from a commercial firm in Taiping and a neighbour of mine. The Malay Visiting Teacher from Grik, whose job covered the Upper Perak District came with us. His name was Jabit and he brought along a friend called Mat Wi (always complete with umbrella), the husband of the headmistress of the Malay Girls School and an old friend of mine.

Our transport consisted of two elephants provided by Government, which carried all the baggage, and a third smaller elephant which we hired at the rate of $2.50 a day (about 5/-) to carry any surplus baggage and any of the party who wanted to ride. The elephant drivers, or *gembalas*, were called Mahmud, Mat and Sam. Mat was a most cheerful character with a face always wreathed in smiles and almost invariably a cheroot between his teeth. Mahmud was also a cheerful old rogue, but suffered from a dreadful hacking cough which frequently kept us awake at night! Sam who drove the little elephant, was my favourite with a most amusing face. He possessed no teeth and very sunken cheeks with a kind of squashed look that made his chin and forehead almost meet when he laughed, which he did often and kept us all in fits. One other Malay called Omah did nothing but follow the elephants and carry a gun. The only other gun was carried by Jabit, but neither weapon was ever used, though it was well to take precautions as we were going through tiger country.

Last but by no means least, we were accompanied by three members of the hill/jungle tribes of Malaya known as Sakais. Their leader, Herring, by curious name, was a most intelligent chap, with a knowledge of Malay, Chinese and even some English. Their clothing consisted of a string round the waist, and they carried blowpipes with a sheaf of poisoned arrows which they demonstrated on several occasions. They also had a blanket or sack as protection against cold. As well as being highly entertaining and instructive in jungle lore, they proved a tremendous help in numerous ways, fetching water, opening and closing boxes, carrying our lunch each day and erecting our mosquito nets in a most professional way at night.

Grik is situated at a fairly high altitude and the Monday morning was distinctly chilly with a dense white mist which cleared later. We all went up early to the DO's house to make sure the loading of the elephants was started in good time and then returned for breakfast. Before we had finished they turned up packed and ready to start, so we followed them up to the end of the village where at least half the inhabitants turned out to see us off! The first two miles followed a good hard track, and watching our elephants swinging along at a good pace on the level made me realise how sick one might feel riding on their backs. As it happened that was the only level or smooth part of our trek, and our last sight of civilisation was a tiny Chinese shop, where Herring demanded a few cents to buy tobacco. It was about 10.00 am when we left this track and turned off into the jungle. For a while we followed the elephants, taking numerous photographs, mainly of their rears. We crossed numerous small streams on rickety bridges and in each case the elephants had to make a detour into quite deep gullies and then climb the other side, often using their front knees on a particularly steep bank. The bridges, of course, were unable to support their weight, but this was very slow going and we soon realised why it would be impossible to cover more than the allotted 10 miles each day.

We reached Basir, our first halting place, at about 3.00 pm and called on the headmaster of the small and rather attractive Malay school which was surrounded by a bamboo fence and well kept vegetable garden. There were about 40 pupils with one master but there were no children present, as Malay schools only open from 8.00 am to 1.00 pm. Basir was a small village with a population of about 80, and lies close to the bank of the upper waters of the Perak River which we roughly followed for the first two days. A walk of about ¼ mile from the school brought us to our 'halting bungalow' or 'hotel' as Jabit called it, in a tiny clearing on the bank of the river. There were three of these huts built by Berkeley (a British pioneer)* on the route to Temengor many years ago, and all were of the same pattern. They consisted of two separate wooden-walled rooms with corrugated iron roof, two windows and a door, and connected to one another by a wooden or bamboo platform 10 to 12ft wide. The whole was raised 12 to 15ft from the ground on strong wooden piles, thus enabling the elephants to be loaded or unloaded straight from the platform. There were of course no bathrooms and no furniture except a large sand tray and some bricks on the platform on which we did all our cooking in true Malay style. The huts were terribly hot in the afternoon but pleasantly cool in the evening and night, and really cold in the early morning. We waited, panting with thirst, until our elephants arrived and almost as soon as they were unloaded we had our saucepan boiling merrily on our fire and were assuaging our thirst with what we unanimously agreed was the best drink of the day – a cup of tea. After that, into our bathing gear and down a steep sandy bank and into the river, where we had a good scrub and a lot of fun with an old bamboo raft. Shortly afterwards the elephants joined us for a dip, and how they enjoyed it after their long trek! They lay on their sides in the water while their *gembalas* clambered over them and scrubbed them with brushes made from coconut fibre.

Our beds and mosquito nets were put up by the men folk, aided by the Sakais, and we all turned in early. Phyllis and I occupied one room and the three men the other one, sharing the two mosquito nets. Our room also acted as a store for all surplus *barang* (a useful Malay term covering luggage, stores, possessions etc). We also made our room the dining room, where the floor at least was fairly level to accommodate our folding table and whatever we could find to sit on. The *gembalas* slept on the platform outside our door, having tethered each of their charges to a long chain attached to a tree or post a short distance from the hut. The chains were the exact length to allow the elephant to crop or graze a measured amount of vegetation and no more – strictly rationed in fact.

Our second day's march was very much more difficult than the first, the track was bad and more overgrown and for the most part through really dense jungle. Though there was little direct sunlight, the atmosphere was hot and humid and we were nearly driven mad by leeches. They were waiting

*See No. 7.2, Page 303

in their thousands, poised on every leaf and blade of grass. If you stopped to remove one, four more climbed onto your foot or leg, so we tried not to stop until we came to any sort of stream where we each found a different rock and proceeded to de-leech. Some of the men with shorts or slacks fared badly and the water ran red with blood. The best way to remove a leech that has already taken hold is with a lighted match or cigarette applied to its tail. They must never be pulled off by force as that can leave a sore which can later fester. They are almost as thin as a hair and only ½ to ¾ inch in length before attacking, but can swell to the most disgusting size of a man's thumb after a good feed, when they eventually drop off of their own accord. The great thing was to try to catch them before they climbed over the edge of one's shoe or crawled through an eyelet hole, because once inside shoes or slacks one felt nothing until they had been feeding for some time. The Sakais, who wore nothing on their feet, never seemed to be worried by them.

We climbed to a good height on Tuesday, always in dense jungle, then skirted round some hills and eventually dropped pretty steeply to the river again. For the first part of the way the elephants followed another route, but they caught up with us when we were eating an early lunch in one of our little de-leeching streams. After that Phyllis and I decided to ride as we were fed up with the leeches and because we were looking forward to a unique experience. It certainly turned out to be the most interesting and, at times, exciting journey that I have ever made. The path was so uneven and our steed had to move so slowly and carefully that there was none of the rather unpleasant swaying motion that I had heard about. We sat side by side on a kind of basket seat facing forward with our legs hanging down on each side of the elephant's neck, while the *gembala* sat right on his neck with his feet tucked up behind the elephant's ears like a tiny jockey. Of course there was quite a lot of luggage piled up behind us, but we were assured that our extra weight made little or no difference, especially as the other elephants were carrying a much greater load. The cleverness and surefootedness of those beautiful creatures is quite amazing. Sam, like all the *gembalas*, had his own special language for talking to the elephants who understood and obeyed every word. This language was originally brought over from India, when Indian mahouts were borrowed to teach the Malays in training the Malayan elephants to work, so none of us understood a word. Sam carried a short rattan cane, with which he would tap a tree trunk, etc if we seemed to be passing too close and the elephant would automatically sway in the opposite direction to give the load on his back a wider berth. We had to make frequent stops while Sam cut away roots, or lianas, or fallen bamboos so that we could pass underneath. Often we had to cross fallen tree trunks, sometimes two trunks lying athwart one another, but the elephants never slipped or made a false step. We traversed deep gullies where they would test the depth of each pothole with their trunks before risking the next step, and the mud might be over 5ft deep. Being on the third elephant we could watch the two ahead making a path for themselves and watch their huge feet coming out of the mud with a sucking squelching sound. We noticed that they always put their back feet into the holes made by their larger front feet. At almost every step they would wash the mud off each foot with their trunks. Sometimes the path, just wide enough for one foot, wound along the side of a hill with a steep drop to the river below. One slip and we would have crashed down the hillside. Sometimes we had to cross streams or gullies where a bridge would not bear us and going down an almost perpendicular bank I was sure I would shoot over the elephant's head! We only rode for 4 or 5 miles but it took all of 3 hours, the last bit being a long slippery drop down a rocky and muddy ravine to the edge of a river which had to be crossed. The river was wide with three quite deep channels separated by shoals and sandbanks. We had to tuck up our feet to prevent getting wet, but the elephants must have loved the refreshing paddle, as they douched themselves constantly. Fortunately they were well trained and only sprayed the water underneath, but the water shot out between their back legs and we got much of it in our faces.

We spent that night, Tuesday, at Kuala Temengor (Kuala means mouth) where the much narrower River Temengor joins the Perak River. We were now surrounded mainly by bamboo forest, and the very small village consisted of 3 or 4 Malay houses built entirely of beautifully clean bamboo, so we did not have many visitors that evening. It was there for the first time we saw our Sakais carrying water in long hollow sections of bamboo. Partitions are removed except at one end and a 15ft section would hold nearly 2 gallons. They were carried at a slope over their shoulders and were much easier to carry or empty than buckets. Malays use bamboos for piping water from, say, a waterfall, or storage tank, to lower levels.

Our 'hotel' was similar to the first one, except that the slatted platform was extremely dangerous, half the bamboos of which it was constructed being rounded were slippery and either missing or too widely spaced. Many of our possessions, especially soap, cutlery etc, were constantly dropping through and had to be retrieved by endless climbs down and up a very rickety single bamboo ladder. We enjoyed another delightful bathe in the clear sparkling river in company with our elephants, but there was much first aid to be carried out on the many leech bites from which the poor men were suffering. Riding on the elephants was a tremendous relief from the leeches. The only thing that worried us were the elephant flies, rather like horse flies and with a nasty bite. Phyl, wearing shorts, fared worse than I did; in fact my riding breeches were a boon throughout.

We rose early on Wednesday and after a hurried breakfast of tinned salmon, Jabit and Mat Wi, one of the Sakais and a young Malay guide who had joined us at Basir and knew the route well, and I, set forth after 7.00 am, leaving the rest of the party to pack up and follow at their leisure. Our previous day's walk had made us realise why ten miles a day is the limit for a loaded elephant. It was quite enough, too, for a man on foot through jungle, climbing and dropping incessantly. We had been extraordinarily lucky in having 2 days without rain (unusual in Malaya) for the paths could have turned very slippery and the going slower.

The path on Wednesday was wider and not so overgrown, hence there were fewer leeches and we made better time. As we were in a hurry we set a steady pace only stopping 2 or 3 minutes at a time at a few streams for a drink, a refreshing wash or a de-leech. Our route followed the Temengor River without crossing it, sometimes dropping to the water's edge, sometimes high above it with just a glimpse of sparkling water through dense green foliage. The sound of running water all day was very pleasant.

I had just begun to feel that I could not go another step when to my surprise we reached Temengor at 12 noon having done a good 10 miles in just under 5 hours. Our now familiar hut was a very welcome sight. The *Penghulu* of the District was away, but the *Ketua* (Headman of the Kampong) was there to greet us, and he sent a message to the school a couple of miles further on, to tell the children to return after their lunch. I had brought a change with me, and for the first time that week I donned a dress, as trousers were certainly not the garb of a woman teacher, especially among Mohammedans. Poor Mat Wi was completely worn out and disappeared for a well earned rest, but Jabit and I squatted in the shade under the hut in a spot we hoped might remain free of ants (a great hazard of picnicking in Malaya) and ate our lunch, mine consisting chiefly of tomato juice and an orange. Slightly refreshed, Jabit and I then set off for an unbearably hot walk to the school across 2 miles of unshaded padi fields on a narrow, very muddy path. We passed several very attractive clean-looking bamboo houses on stilts, some having gaily-woven red, black and white walls, and each surrounded by its own little cluster of banana and other fruit trees. We later managed to procure some delicious pomeloes which are rather like very large grapefruit and usually sweeter and very juicy.

Children appeared from the houses and *kampong* (village) and followed us in a long line across the padi fields. When we came near to the school they dived into the trees and reached the school before us and were already in their desks. I was very tired and hot and glad to sink into a chair and accept a fan, but not until the children had risen as one with the habitual greeting of "*Tabek Missi*" (to me), "*Tabek Enche*" (to the men). After that you could have heard a pin drop, as they sat wide-eyed in their shorts and white shirts (the boys) or brightly coloured sarongs and *bajus* (the girls). The school was tiny with approximately 80 pupils, run by a man and his wife who had only been there a few months. I think they had not yet really got used to living so far from civilisation, and I found from the visitors' book that no European had visited the school since 1930. The Visiting Teacher from Grik (at present Che Jabit) goes up once a year, and the Malay ADO pays an occasional visit, but to most of the children I was the first *orang puteh* (white person) they had seen. After a hygiene inspection and looking at some of the work, we sent the children home, and concentrated on stocktaking and inspection of furniture, buildings, school garden, compound and toilet facilities, most of which I left to Jabit and the head master. I spent a long time giving the woman teacher a needlework lesson and making a list of materials she would require. Sewing is an important part of the girls' curriculum, while the boys do mainly basket weaving, carpentry, etc, and all do gardening. We finished our work at about 5.45 (Kenneth and Bill having spent a very profitable couple of hours repairing the school clock with a pocket knife and machine oil!) and after taking a few snaps and inviting the Headmaster and his wife to pay us a visit at our 'hotel', we started our trek back to the river. The path was even more muddy and slippery by this time, but I just managed without sitting down. We found Phyllis and Tony busily preparing tea, while the Sakais were erecting beds and nets. Meanwhile beside the bank, four stalwart Malays who had come up from Grik some days ahead of us were putting the finishing touches to our craft for the return journey the next day – a magnificent raft on which we hoped to reach Grik in one day (travelling downstream).

OP 58 (October 1989)

Lake Victoria Passage

by J D Kelsall

It was on an occasion in the early 1950s that my wife and I were on passage on Lake Victoria from Mwanza, Tanganyika, to Kisumu, Kenya, in the Lake Victoria Fisheries Service's motor fishing vessel *Heron* for an overhaul at the Department's headquarters. This was a comfortable three-day voyage and, on the evening of the second day, we anchored for the night in a bay on the mainland south-east of Mfwanganu Island near the mouth of the Kavirondo Gulf, some 55 miles from Kisumu.

The following morning we were all set for an early start. From the wheelhouse I called down to Omari the engineer (always known, in accordance with nautical custom, as *Bwana Chifu*), telling him to start up the engine, a big Widdop diesel. His cheerful shout of acknowledgment and the whirr of the electric starter were followed by a resounding crash. Clearly, something serious was wrong. It did not take long to discover that the heavy bronze rod driving the piston-type cooling water pump had fractured. This was something far beyond the possibility of an on-board repair. The immediate question was what should we do? For mobility while at Kisumu, I had with me on board my Triumph Speed Twin motorcycle. My first thought was to get this ashore and to make my way through the bush and over the nearby mountains to the nearest road, and thence to Kisumu to summon assistance. However, a brief reconnaissance ashore ruled this action out. The terrain near the shore was simply not conducive to motorcycling – and that was without going anywhere near the mountains.

It was at this point that Sadiki, the Cox'n, came up with a suggestion. "Bwana", he said, "we have that old tarpaulin in the hold and the big bamboo we use for punting the boat in shallow water. I think that we could perhaps make up a sail and sail *Heron* to Kisumu." We examined these limited resources and discussed the technical problems associated with their use. In the end, we decided to give Sadiki's idea a try. From the outset, however, it was clear that sailing a heavy 45ft vessel without a proper keel would only be possible with the wind dead astern, or, at worst, fine on either quarter. With the only rig we could set up, there could be no question of working across the wind. Fortunately, at that time of year, a strong south-west wind blew straight up the Kavirondo Gulf every day from around midday until evening. The immediate problem would be to get into the Kavirondo Gulf from where we were. With the limitations imposed by our anticipated sailing capabilities, there was no way that we could get out northwards to the west of Rusinga Island, and round the northern tip of that island into the Gulf. The only possible route was through the Mbita Passage between Rusinga Island and the mainland. This was a narrow, shallow and rather twisty channel, normally used only by native craft, though I had heard that SS *Nyanza*, the EAR & H's cargo vessel, did occasionally use the Passage.

We worked all morning to set up the somewhat tattered tarpaulin on the big bamboo as a yard, with guy ropes from the bottom corners of the tarpaulin. Hoisted on our short mast this did, however, bear some resemblance to a square rig, and we lowered it again to await the afternoon wind. Once it began to blow, it was obvious that we should not be able, under sail, to get *Heron* out of the bay where she was anchored. The pump drive having been disconnected, we decided that if the engine's cooling system could be filled manually with water, we might be able to run the engine for long enough before it heated up to get the vessel offshore to a position where we could turn before the wind. Working with a bucket and a tin mug, Omari managed to fill the engine's water jacket. Starting the engine at the last possible moment, we weighed anchor and headed out offshore. We just managed to get a reasonable offing before Omari called up to me that the engine was getting too hot. At that point Sadiki, assisted by Shabani and Juma, the other two crew members, hauled up our tarpaulin sail and guyed down the bottom corners. At the wheel, I turned *Heron* before the wind, the sail flapped and filled and, rather to my surprise, she began to move slowly through the water, even answering the helm, if somewhat reluctantly, the rudder being designed to steer a boat driven by power.

During the afternoon, we crept up towards the narrows of the Mbita Passage and we were still a mile or so short of it when the wind began to die away. This was no time for choosing the most sheltered anchorage and we dropped anchor where we were, to await a fair wind on the morrow which would enable us to tackle the tricky part through the Passage. We could only hope that no fierce squall would blow up during the night and blow us ashore!

Next morning, we went out in the dinghy taking our sounding line with us, in order to assess the safest route through Mbita Passage and to discover where the bends were. The chart showed that the narrow channel shoaled to only 8 feet in one place. While this was twice *Heron's* draft, the channel shallowed quickly at its edges, and if we were to run aground under sail, we might have great difficulty in getting off again. By the time we had completed our survey of the channel and I had made some notes to guide me, it was nearly time for the afternoon wind to get up, and we hastened back to *Heron* to get everything ready for departure. The wind, when it arrived, blew more strongly than on the previous day and we set off in great style.

In the event, our transit of Mbita Passage was almost an anti-climax. Shabani was in the bows with the lead-line and his soundings, combined with my notes, enabling me to cut the corners slightly when we came to the bends, thus avoiding having to alter course to steer round the bends and to bring the wind forward of the quarter. Almost before we realised it we were clear of the narrow channel and in the mouth of the Kavirondo Gulf. It was only when I looked at my watch that I realised that the short transit of some three miles had taken us an hour and a half. We were able to carry on for a further five or six miles before the wind began to die away and we had to anchor, fortunately a little to the south of the fairway used by the Lake steamers. Nevertheless we took the precaution of hoisting a hurricane lamp on the mast that night to make sure that we were not run down by a passing ship.

We were now in a position where we could set a direct course for Kisumu and, at the same time, keep the wind almost directly astern, *Heron's* best point of sailing. Next day, the wind arrived rather later than usual, but we made good going. At times I could even hear the propeller being rotated by the movement of the vessel. During the afternoon, my wife came up with a suggestion for improving progress. Her idea was that if we could manage to hoist our hessian cabin carpet above the tarpaulin, we should be increasing our sail area by an appreciable amount. With Sadiki and Shabani I investigated the possibility of doing this and by using our boathook as a further yard we managed to achieve a somewhat disreputable-looking 'topsail'. It must have done some good because I estimated our day's run at about 11 miles.

The day after that, we had a punctual and strong wind and did some magnificent sailing, the day's run being an estimated 12 miles. However, both my wife and Omari (who did most of the cooking for the crew) made it known to me that provisions were running out. We ourselves had budgeted for four days at sea and we always had a small reserve of tinned stuff on board. The crew, relying on fresh provisions, had no such reserve. However, we had a few gill nets on board and we decided to set these when we anchored for the night in the hope of getting some fish. My wife had a basket of beautiful mangoes which she was taking as a present for a friend in Kisumu and we decided that it might become necessary to use these to eke out our supplies.

By now, we were reaching a point where it would have been possible to get my motorcycle ashore in the dinghy at Homa Bay or some point near there, whence I should have been able to reach the main Kisii/Kisumu road and thus have been able to summon assistance from Kisumu. However, it had now become a matter of pride to try to get *Heron* to Kisumu under sail, without calling in outside help. The following afternoon provided a moderate breeze and we held on as long as possible, finally anchoring at dusk some 4 miles short of Kisumu. Our only worry now was that someone might have seen us and raised an alarm with our Headquarters. However, nobody seemed to be looking our way and we had an undisturbed night, making some inroads into the mangoes for supper!

Next day, the morning seemed to be unbearably long and we expected to see, at any moment, a boat putting out to salvage us. Nothing came before the afternoon wind arrived, blowing very strongly here at the head of the Gulf. I had decided that it would be impossible to sail right in to the old flying boat dock at our office and that we should have to repeat the exercise carried out on the first day of filling up the engine's water jacket by hand, so as to give us a few minutes' running to enable us to dock. This Omari did and when we arrived off the dock, he started up the engine and, running at a tick-over, we were able to creep in and tie up, eight days out from Mwanza! My boss was on the dockside, anxious to know what had been happening and (being an RNR Lieutenant-Commander) looking askance at our motley rig! No matter, we had made it under our own sail and honour was satisfied.

(After this demonstration of sailing capability, the Department's three MFVs were all equipped with big bamboo yards and proper lateen sails, for use in an emergency. In a good breeze, *Heron*, under this rig, could make about 4 knots – provided that the wind was from astern!)

OP 63 (April 1992)

Karamoja Journey

by S Nicholl

The dry season in the Karamoja District of north-eastern Uganda should have ended. It was late April and the rains should have come in March. Fields which had been planted in anticipation were withered and scorched. By the roadsides and in the bush, borehole pumps were working all day and, in many cases, through the night. These crude clanking contrivances, which pump water from Karamoja's two hundred and seventy odd boreholes, are often all that save from death the pitiful stock that water at them. Cattle are the basis of Karamojong tribal economy. They are sacrificed in tribal religious ceremonies; their possession is the cause of most inter-tribal conflict and they can buy a wife.

A safari north from Moroto to inspect sites of rural water supplies seemed indicated. The Jie County HQ were in Kotido, about sixty miles away. Most important to my crew and me was the fact that at Kotido there is a rest-camp. One of the pleasant things in the job of maintaining rural water supplies in Karamoja is to come back to a rest-camp after a day of bone-shaking scrambles in a Land Rover, of thorns scratching paintwork, of rocks chewing into tyres, until one wants to get out and carry the car. And then the rest-camp. What a pleasure to sit back in a camp chair and relax in the wonderful stillness. We left Moroto early next morning and arrived at Kotido in the late afternoon. On the way we had checked and repaired boreholes and had been annoyed by thousands of flies. The flies of Karamoja have a unique persistence that keeps a person on the brink of going berserk, but never seem to have that little bit extra needed to tip the balance. A couple of mornings and many borehole pumps later, the horizon all around had taken on a dark threatening look. Lightning flashed in the distance, although its thunder was still faint. There was no doubt about it this time, the rains were coming at last and, what was more, were going to fall that day. Only one job remained for the crew to complete our work in the area. I, in my Land Rover, had completed the inspection of boreholes pumps and dams in the area.

In pouring rain I returned to the rest-camp in Kotido. With visions of roaring rivers and gooey mud, I feverishly threw my safari kit into the Land Rover. The rain was now a steady heavy roaring downpour. Earth that was yesterday scorched and dry had now taken on a glistening voracious look. Large puddles had formed and rivulets were starting to run. A panicky getaway from the rest-camp in four-wheel drive and the journey home to Moroto had commenced. Toror mountain, a few miles away, which had stood proud and aloof throughout the dry season, was now hidden in a humiliating blanket of grey. Water hissed and mud sloshed and spattered underneath the car. But what about the lorry! The lorry and crew were about five miles along a bush track in the Panyangara area. "They'll be all right", I reasoned. "There are five men on the lorry and they have chains for the wheels. I will probably meet them along the road."

Before I realised it, the access track to Panyangara loomed up through the rain. Still undecided what to do I turned into it. From now on it was low gear work. The pump where the crew were working was in a low-lying stretch near a river. If only they had packed up in time and were on higher ground the situation would not be too serious. I got the answer fifteen minutes later in a pathetic picture. Poor struggling mortals. Lorry bogged to the axles with engine roaring and a bedraggled crew straining and pushing in a vain attempt to shift it.

"Why didn't you get out of here, Josefu, when you saw the rains coming?"

"We had nearly finished, Sir, and it seemed such a pity to leave the work uncompleted."

How could I be angry?

Now for the lorry. A rope fixed to the back of the Land Rover, the strain taken and off we go. But no, Land Rover wheels and lorry wheels all spin ineffectually. The rain still lashes down. Perhaps jerking the lorry with the Land Rover might help. It works! In a long series of jerks, taking over four hours to earn us one and a half miles of progress, we eventually reach higher ground. From there, we slosh our way to the main road. Main road? By now it looks like a river but, from the wide smiles and looks of the crew, it could have been the Great North Road. The crew were by now fagged out. It was now late afternoon and, besides having done a morning's work, they had pushed and heaved at the lorry in the pouring rain. Wearily they climbed aboard the lorry. It was up to the driver now. He would have to drive fast enough in order to have sufficient momentum to overcome deep clutching muddy patches and yet be slow enough to control skidding. "Safari, Musa, let's go home."

We convoy a few hundred yards apart with my Land Rover in front. If only the Kalotharich River isn't too high. We should be near it now.

Another Land Rover looms out of the rain. It is stopped by the Kalotharich River. Only one answer, the river is up. And how! The second Land Rover belongs to the District Agricultural Officer. Together we huddle in his car and eye the torrent that is now the Kalotharich. It was hard to believe that the day before it had been a harmless dry river bed. The rain lashing on the bonnet, seems scornful and omnipotent.

Musa, in his oilskins, appears at the window. "Musa."

"Yes Sir."

"Musa, we are going to cross this river now. If we wait conditions will probably get worse. You take the lorry through first. If you get stuck, our two Land Rovers will pull you out. Everybody out except you and the turnboy."

"Yes Sir."

No hesitation about Musa. A few moments later the lorry moves towards the river. At once my confidence deserts me. What if it overturns? What if the driver and turnboy are drowned? Too late, the front wheels dip and the lorry is in. A cloud of spray, a few lurches in the swirling waters and the bonnet starts to climb the opposite bank. They've made it! My heart, still palpitating, sinks slowly back into place. My turn now. The remainder of the lorry crew pile into the two Land Rovers. Into bottom gear and creep to the bank. In go the front wheels, full accelerator, water comes through the floor, and then we are up the other bank. Amen to that. Now the Agricultural Officer. "What's it like?"

Apprehensively. "Piece of cake. No trouble at all. You'll make it all right." Funny the reaction hysteria has.

We are on the way again with the Agricultural Officer in the lead. I take the number two position where I can keep an eye on the lorry with the rest of the crew. Further on the Agricultural Officer slows and stops. Puncture perhaps? No, just a culvert washed away. Only one thing to do, back up a couple of hundred yards and detour. A stroll in the drenching rain finds us a suitable detour and, after a bit of pushing and pulling, we are soon on the way again. The accelerator feels odd with a one inch layer of mud between it and the sole of my shoe. Another culvert with an approach causeway looms up. Must be okay as the Agricultural Officer is out of sight. Over we go and on. Five minutes later on a straight stretch, a quick look back shows no lorry. Stop and wait. Another five minutes and no lorry engine sounding in the distance. Trouble. Probably at the last culvert. A careful turn around and then back towards Kotido. A few minutes later the lorry is revealed athwart the causeway before the culvert.

"Not your fault, Musa. Too much camber on a muddy road." Rope out again and hook on the back of the Land Rover, Alas, jerking and pulling avail nothing this time. The lorry is fast athwart the causeway and resting on its chassis. "Right chaps, shovels out and dig. You other two collect branches for putting below the wheels. The bigger the better." Poor chaps, by now their meagre clothing has reached saturation point and water, quite literally, is running out of them.

It is dusk when the causeway is eventually persuaded to release the lorry. Only another thirty miles to Moroto, and the only sizeable obstacle in between is the Lokichar River. That should not present too much of a problem, however, as it is bridged. My headlights pick up the Agricultural Officer's car again. It is stopped. What was the Lokichar River is now revealed as a sea of water a quarter of a mile across. Defeat on the last lap? Mud, Kalotharich and culverts all crossed for nothing. Why didn't we just stay in Kotido? At least we would have enjoyed some degree of comfort. As we stared in frustration at the water, we noticed that our headlights showed most of the bridge rails showing above the water. What if we drive our cars on a line between the bridge rails? The depth of water over the causeway and above the bridge might be shallow enough to allow us to cross. Get out and test it first. If a piece of the causeway or of the bridge were missing, we dare not attempt a crossing. A cautious and frightening wade across the causeway and bridge reveals that a crossing by car is possible. I secretly hoped that the lorry crew or the Agricultural Officer would raise some objection. No hope, those chaps were Moroto bound, come what may.

My turn to cross this time. Dark water all around. Slowly does it. Once on the other side I looked back to give the thumbs up sign, but neither the Agricultural Officer or Musa had waited. They were already half way over and their easy confident manner destroyed completely the dare-devil grin I was trying to manufacture just for their benefit. On again and I began to feel a bit tired. Should be striking the main Moroto-Soroti Road soon. Yep, here is the main road at last. Only twelve miles to Moroto now. The main road is a sea of mud in places, but somehow it has a warm friendly look about it. I work the Land Rover up to twenty mph and it appears to be flying. Then the township and then we go our three separate ways. But before we split, I stop the lorry for a moment to congratulate and thank the crew. They had been magnificent.

Home at last. My wife meets me on the verandah with a torch. It is 11 pm.

"Had a good safari? I would have thought that with the rains you would have tried to get home a bit earlier. Were you shooting guinea-fowl or something?"

OP 88 (October 2004)

Massa Gets Transport

by R R Yearley

On the evening of my first day on the Gold Coast in January 1948 a colleague and his wife invited me to dinner, along with two other married couples from the Department of Posts & Telegraphs. Much of the conversation was about the UK, but it was mainly advice for the newcomer. The question was "What car are you thinking of?"

"I've no idea", I replied, "I can't drive."

"Don't worry about that. Buy the car and you'll soon get the hang of it."

They told me that I should be staying in the Rest House for a few weeks until a bungalow was allocated to me. It was only a mile or two from GPO Headquarters so I could walk or get a lift to work. There was a local bus service but it was not reliable and overcrowded – and in any event by long custom, Europeans did not use public transport. I should take every opportunity of 'getting behind a wheel' and this is what I did.

People were very willing to let me 'have a go'. My first experience was in a huge kitcar – it seemed as big as a London bus – which an admin man staying in the Rest House had just bought. He explained the rudiments and with great trepidation I let in my first clutch, with the usual succession of kangaroo hops. The Public Works Department had the week before laid tons of gravel and I made a terrible mess of their beautifully rolled parking area, much to the annoyance of the other residents. After a few improving starts and stops John said "Right! Let's go to Achimota, there's a cricket match there and I've arranged to meet a girlfriend."

"But I don't have a driving licence."

"Not to worry. No one will bother." So I drove the ten miles, mainly in low gear and with my heart in my mouth. It was Saturday with little traffic but the occasional mammy-wagon seemed to come perilously close. I drove back too, and began to feel quite confident.

In the next two months I drove all kinds of cars and no one refused me to 'have a go'. The only mishap was in Bill's Ford Prefect. I was travelling at a steady 30 mph on a straight road. About half a mile ahead a cow was standing across the road.

"Don't worry", said Bill, "she'll move when we get near." But she didn't and frantic emergency braking ended in our gently probing her in the ribs.

It frightened me horribly but it did give me confidence that I could cope in an emergency.

Meanwhile I had begun negotiations to buy a car. A loan was available from Government sources. The largest amount which I could afford to repay would cover the smallest car on sale, a Standard. Although only eight horse-power it carried four people, and would reach 60 mph if coaxed – I would never go at that speed, I thought – and I arranged to purchase AR 721. When I went to the dealers to take delivery, I explained that I had not obtained a driving licence, but they said it was all right and they would let me have a mechanic to sit with me to get the car home. The poor chap selected must have 'feared too much'! It was early evening and the rush hour in Accra was at its height. But we covered the five miles to the bungalow where I was then housed without any major alarms, and only a few stallings of the engine – I forgot to push the choke in! I thought the car was beautiful. It was dove grey and had an enamelled Union Jack on the nose. I spent hours reading the handbook, looking at the engine and polishing the chrome. Colleagues were very kind and volunteered to be passengers-cum-instructors while I practised emergency stops and reversing.

There was the great day when I found myself alone on the Nsawam road, travelling at 40 mph! I felt I really was ready for the Monte Carlo rally! I applied to the Government Transport Office to take the driving test. I went to the GTO in the middle of the afternoon and picked up the examiner. He asked me how long I had been driving, and then told me the route to follow around the town. The test seemed to go without incident. At one point the examiner said "Let's see you stop", and when we got back to base he added "Always keep well to the left. Don't stop if you hit an animal or bird – too much palaver. You'll be all right. Here's your licence". I was glad he didn't ask me to do a three-point turn!

The roads in Accra were full of pot-holes and there was the hazard of the open drainage ditches which lined the main roads. Outside the town the roads were sometimes tarmacadam, but in a poor state in spite of the devoted maintenance by the Public Works Department. Villagers thought nothing of digging a channel across a road if it helped to disperse flood water; drivers had to be on the alert for broken culverts. Even main trunk roads were simply compressed laterite which was corrugated by the motion of wheels and sent up clouds of red dust. There was a theory that you should keep up a regular speed whatever the surface conditions, and that this would balance the corrugations, but most drivers found that the suspension and shock absorbers wore out even more quickly.

Mammy-wagons, the local all-purpose transport, were notorious for travelling in the middle of the road, especially coming over the brow of a hill. This was another hazard for the newly qualified driver to get used to as well as the universal parking without lights in the most unexpected places. Another confusing practice was the 'Pavlova' or 'Dying Swan' signal. Drivers intending to turn left put their right arm out of the window palm down on the roof and raised and lowered the hand. I found myself adopting it as a clearer intention than the official vague circular movement of the hand pointing to the ground.

It is not surprising that before long I had my first accident. I had taken a nurse friend to the cinema. When I drove out on to the main road and had covered a hundred yards or so through crowds of people, a mammy-wagon hurtled along at break-neck speed scattering the walkers and ripping the off-side of AR 72I. I chased after it, jumped on the running-board and shouted at the driver to stop. He was in a state of panic and took no notice. I was in peril of my life so I pulled out the ignition key. When the wagon came to a halt the driver 'went for bush'. By this time the police had arrived. I gave them the key and told them what had happened. Then I ran back – I had travelled more than a quarter of a mile – and found poor Marjorie still sitting in the car, very self-possessed considering that she was surrounded by a great crowd of very noisy and excited but friendly Africans. Luckily the car was still driveable. In the court case which followed months later, I gave evidence but the driver got off with a caution. My Errol Flynn-like exertions went for nothing, except that Marjorie was impressed. What it was to be young!

Another accident was when I was driving in the Usher Fort area of town at night. With no street lights or illuminated road signs, the flares of market stalls and the throng of people it was difficult to drive safely. I failed to stop at a crossroads and collided with another car. No great damage was caused and no one was hurt. I found myself surrounded by hundreds of Africans, instant supporters of the taxi driver whose car I had hit. Then a friendly voice said "Why, it's Mr Yearley of the Post Office. Good evening, Sah." The crowd changed allegiance and started to abuse the taxi driver for driving too fast. The police arrived and in the subsequent hearing at the Magistrates Court I got off with a warning, mainly because the charge papers had wrongly given the time of the accident as 'am'.

Then there was the time I was sharing a bungalow with Charles. He also was a newcomer and he had just bought an Austin A40. He had parked it outside the front door behind my car. When I came out in the evening my mind must have gone blank because although I saw his car, I very carefully and gently backed into it, smashing the headlights. Charles was not pleased. Another day when I was closely parked at the beach, the owner of the car alongside mine kindly guided me out. But when he said "left hand down" I responded too promptly and scarred his nearside wing! Another learning opportunity.

On my first UK leave I hoped to hire a car. I took my International Driving Licence to a firm in Kensington. The agent seemed doubtful when I told him how long I'd been driving and where. After being taken through the London traffic for ten minutes with me at the wheel, he looked very pale and said he didn't think I was quite ready to be entrusted with any of his cars.

In later tours of duty on the Coast I became more competent. I progressed through a Hillman Minx, a Ford Consul (home delivered on my third leave), a Standard Vanguard and, after my marriage, a Morris Minor Traveller. During my second tour I drove my Standard Eight the 150 miles on corrugated roads to Kumasi in Ashanti to join a colleague to go on trek in his kit-car around the Northern Territories. I sold AR 721 to a colleague who was retiring on health grounds. When I visited him in Herefordshire I found the little grey car happily charging over the hills of the Welsh Borders.

OP 83 (May 2002)

Journeying to Cape Guardafui

by Colin Everard

In the late fifties I undertook two journeys by land and sea to Cape Guardafui. At that time I worked for the East Africa High Commission (based in Nairobi) in one of its far-flung departments called the Desert Locust Control Organization. We were not only much preoccupied with controlling the invading swarms of desert locusts and their progeny, we also spent much effort in trying to understand the migratory patterns of the vast invading swarms. In the latter connection, as I settled into my work in Mogadishu, I became intrigued concerning the locust situation in the north-eastern part of Somalia. I therefore planned a journey to the tip of the Horn of Africa, namely Cape Guardafui.

As an aside, in ancient times, the general area was regularly visited by the Egyptians for the purpose of collecting myrrh; the Egyptians called the area The Land of Punt. In Roman times, the area was called Promontorium Aromata. The name *Guardafui* stems from the name of the tribe of the area; the tribesmen are called Guardaf.

After a three day journey, we halted near the top of the mountainous escarpment at a small village called El Gal. The villagers told us (I spoke fluent Somali) that although the Italian authorities were beginning to survey the area with the intention of constructing a road, there was no road linking El Gal with the coast. It would be necessary for us to hire burden camels. It was explained that although camels were not usually used on mountainous tracks, the local people had bred a smaller type of burden camel. These animals would be quite capable of walking through the mountains to a coastal fishing village called Durbo.

We set off in the late afternoon, with two camels carrying our belongings and water. After descending into a valley in the late evening we made a small camp. We carried on at 5.00 am the following morning. Once in Durbo I made contact with a Somali District Officer who kindly made his small cross-country vehicle available to me, stating that I could drive the vehicle with my helpers to Alula, and decide at Alula how I should reach Cape Guardafui.

At some points on the littoral we found ourselves driving close to low cliffs, which narrowed our passage between the sea and the higher ground.

The surface of parts of the cliffs had been cracked and sometimes broken by myrrh trees, whose bulbous roots had somehow taken firm hold. My mind went back to a visit to the Valley of the Kings in Upper Egypt, and a wonderful wall painting (in the palace of Queen Hatshepsut), which depicted myrrh being collected in about 1500 BC from the Land of Punt, which was later to be called Somaliland. The aromatic tree was an important ingredient for scent.

Alula is a small town which is the administrative centre for the tip of the Horn of Africa. I was told that it would be difficult to reach Cape Guardafui, because after a few hours the track would come to an end at the foot of some cliffs which extended into the sea. We drove eastwards towards Cape Guardafui and reached the end of the track at Bereda just before nightfall. There we asked the villagers how we should reach Cape Guardafui. They advised us that the best way would be to travel by canoe during the night to Olloch, from where one could walk to Cape Guardafui. At 10.00 pm I was invited to sit in a canoe and I enquired whether I should paddle or assist in any other way. The answer was immediate, "You are a tall man and skill is necessary to paddle the canoe in the sea so that it will not capsize. The sea is shark-infested. The best thing for us would be if you could lie on the bottom of the canoe and remain as still as possible!"

The next eight hours proved to be the most comfortable part of the journey. The canoe made its slow progress in a smooth and stable way, following the shoreline about two hundred yards out to sea. The moon was clear and the air was pleasantly warm. With the gentle lapping of the sea against the sides of the canoe, the experience was positively refreshing.

At 6.00 am the following morning we reached Olloch, and the canoe was beached some way from the shore as the water was shallow. I left the canoe with the helpers and waded through the surf towards the village which had been established on a sandy slope just above the sea. As we walked out of the sea, the villagers streamed towards us. Clearly, the villagers were surprised to see us and some of them touched my skin. Most of these individuals had never before seen white skin and were clearly intrigued by the difference between the colour of their skin pigmentation and my own.

At 8.00 am we began the walk towards Cape Guardafui. The first part of the walk remains unforgettably imprinted in my mind. It was extremely hot and the soft sand burnt our feet as we tried to force our way upwards. The first part of the journey was strenuous and it seemed to last an eternity; as we took each step forward, the soft sand dragged us back. Eventually, the trying first stage of our walk was left behind and we continued for a few hours over a gently rising plain until, at last, the lighthouse at Cape Guardafui came into view.

The lighthouse was maintained and operated by Alfredo Polidari. Although he spoke no English and my knowledge of Italian was superficial, somehow over the next day and a half we managed to communicate effectively. Alfredo had looked after the lighthouse for two years and was proud of his ability to maintain and operate it; he gave me a detailed guided tour of the lighthouse complex. All was immaculate and clean. The metal parts of the equipment were highly polished, which added lustre to the general appearance.

Evidently, Alfredo was a self-sufficient individual. He had lived on Cape Guardafui with three or four Somalis for two years. Although he was totally preoccupied with the maintenance and operation of the lighthouse, he seemed well-versed in current affairs and referred to the Suez Crisis, the German question and other events of the day with knowledge. If someone has been virtually alone for a protracted period, when the person receives a visitor it is quite normal that the person begins to talk, sometimes uncontrollably. During my visits to various field officers, the tendency for them to talk continuously for long periods was much in evidence. As far as Alfredo was concerned, he showed no inclination to talk at great length; on the contrary, he was interested in the purpose of my visit, asking questions and listening to the answers with interest. Alfredo explained that he had recently accepted an offer of a short holiday in Mogadishu, but had cut it short; he had not enjoyed the noise on the streets and the general hubbub of the city! He also explained that he rarely received visitors. He had been visited a year previously; there had been two men, one of whom was a Catholic priest. Unfortunately, the priest had suffered a heart attack and had died. Alfredo then pointed towards the grave which he himself had dug about a hundred yards from the lighthouse.

After having spent two nights at the lighthouse and having obtained as much information as was possible about movements of locusts, I told my helpers that we should leave, returning the way we had come. Apart from the information I had received, we had walked over the general area and collected samples of many species of the vegetation and these were placed in a press. Subsequently, they would be sent to the herbarium in Nairobi for further examination. It later transpired that at least one of the plants we had collected had become an addition to the recorded African plant species.

We returned to Durbo over the next two days, using the same route. The overnight canoe journey proved to be as pleasant as the earlier one. We reached Durbo, west of Alula, by about midday and the helpers suggested that we should return to our Land Rovers at El Gal that evening. I responded that it would be unpleasant to walk in the heat of the afternoon and felt that perhaps we could leave at about 3.00 pm; from this time, the temperature should progressively cool. We should be able to reach an altitude of about three thousand feet above sea level by nightfall and we could then walk the remaining part of the journey to El Gal the following morning.

At about 2.00 pm, we were making final preparations for the walk and the helpers were loading the camels. A man then began to talk to us and it transpired that he too would be walking to El Gal. We invited him to walk with us. He then explained that the camel track which we had used was a rather long route. He knew a much shorter route and offered to show us the way if we would like to use it. We were fatigued and the prospect of a shorter walk proved attractive. We therefore asked the camel driver to meet us with the camels near the top of the escarpment; by the time he arrived we would be waiting for him by the track. At 3.00 pm the group of four of us (including our new-found guide) set off and, initially, we made good progress. After about an hour, the terrain became steep and rocky. Our guide explained that once we had reached the top of the ridge, it would be a steady walk to the track where we were to meet the camels. We laboured long and hard up the mountain and, after scrambling for two hours, we became extremely tired. Our guide had stopped his easy conversation and looked a little anxious. Shortly after we had carried on, one of my helpers collapsed with exhaustion. When I asked for the goatskin of water to help revive him, I found that the rest of the group had already drunk about two thirds of the available water. After a few minutes, the man slowly began to regain consciousness and we told him that we would try and half-carry him onwards with his arms on our shoulders. After another hour's hard scrambling (by this time no one spoke), we had reached what seemed to be the crown of the mountain. We then stopped to rest.

I noticed that the lips of the guide were quivering and I looked at him with concern. He then announced that he had missed his way and we had climbed a mountain which was too far to the west. In order to gain the ridge where we were supposed to meet the camels, we would have to descend into a valley and climb the side of the next mountain. At this juncture, the helper stared at me with piercingly deadly eyes. With a look of hate on his countenance he blurted out "Shall we kill him?" For one ghastly fleeting second, I felt I could identify with his exasperation. Then I simply responded "No!" But I could understand his frightening emotion.

Not only had the guide misled us, but one of our group had collapsed with exhaustion, and the remaining helper and myself were in a pitiful state of fatigue. I for one felt terribly alone on the mountain. The barren mountains were uninhabited. Although the sun would soon set, it was still hot. If we were soon to find that we were all in a state of collapse from exhaustion, would we be able to summon the strength to forge ahead the next day after an overnight rest on the mountain? Would we be prey to wild animals? How long could one maintain one's strength without water? We could not evade such questions and we did not know the answers. All we did know was that we had made a dreadful misjudgement; we had separated ourselves from our water!

I gathered myself and announced that we had no option, we must try and reach the ridge before the camels, otherwise the camels would pass and we would be without water. We scrambled down the mountain and into the valley. As we began to climb up the other side, I realised that dusk would descend within the next 45 minutes. We were beyond the point of goading one another to greater efforts. The only question was whether we could keep going at all.

The final part of the climb up the mountain entailed scrambling over some huge rocks. Fortunately, the man we had been dragging had now partially recovered and I tried to explain to him that if he could keep moving for another half hour, we would be on the ridge. When we reached the camel track on the ridge it was dark. We sank to the ground amongst the bushes in a semi-exhausted state. By now, the silent night air felt cool, and I hoped that a breeze would bring more relief to our weary limbs. As a faint wafting of air filtered through my shorts, which were saturated with sweat, I began to feel livelier. I wondered about the whereabouts of the camels; were they in the area, or had they already passed?

In terms of co-ordination, the planned separate movements of the camels and our group had turned out to have been a terrible mistake. In any case, within two minutes of our arrival on the track, we heard the unmistakable noise of wooden camel bells. Although we were exhausted, we managed to generate mild feelings of relief.

The next morning, fed and rested, we walked the remainder of the journey to El Gal. At lunchtime, we began the long drive back to Mogadishu. On our return to Mogadishu, a comprehensive report was prepared covering our expedition and a number of possibilities were highlighted which merited further exploration. In fact four years later, in 1961, I was to make another expedition to the area. Alfredo, the lighthouse keeper, was still enjoying his lonely work. In that remote region, in his friendly way, he asked me whether I happened to be 'passing again'? I asked him how many visitors he had received during the previous four years. He became thoughtful for a few moments; then he made his response. "One."

OP 86 (October 2003)

Somaliland Protectorate

British Somaliland was administered by the Government of India from 1887 until 1898. Responsibility was then transferred first to the Foreign Office, and then in 1905 to the Colonial Office. The badge for the Protectorate depicted the head and shoulders of a kudu. In 1950 the design was changed, with the kudu's head reduced and altered, shown as a crest above a shield, all within a white disc. The Crown was shown between the kudu's horns. The shield below had a complicated three-part design of crossed spears with a round shield, a minaret and a dhow at sea with an anchor below. This design was used until the Protectorate's Independence and subsequent incorporation into Somalia in 1960.

Anuta – An Island from Paradise?

by James L O Tedder

Naturally one of the attractions of the Pacific throughout history has been that somewhere there is an island paradise. This has led people into doing all kinds of unusual stunts and going to the edge of the world to find this island paradise. Thor Heyerdahl in his splendid book *Fatu-Hiva Back to Nature* told of how he and his wife went to Fatu-Hiva in the Marquesas before WWII to find paradise on earth. But, as you may read, all was not well in that paradise. There were the tropical ulcers, there were the disputes with their landlords, the diet, and there was the question of religion, or rather the way people practised it, that finally was the undoing of their dream. Of course Thor eventually returned to the islands because I suppose he found them the nearest to what he thought was paradise that he could find on earth.

Many people who came to the Solomons as their first experience of the Pacific were disillusioned by what they found. All the stories they had read of the Pacific, particularly of places like Tahiti and Raratonga, had not prepared them for the reality of the equatorial high islands. These islands, with the help of the early white contacts, had succoured a people who were not so open or welcoming as the Polynesians, and whose democratic systems had prevented the rise of powerful chiefs who, in places like Samoa and Tahiti, ruled whole islands. But here in the Solomon Islands there were no large and important chiefs, and many villages barely spoke to each other. But once you were past that natural reserve of these people and they knew you, then you could not hope to meet and have better friends who were always loyal and steadfast. The other shock to the visitors arriving in the Solomons was that, with exceptions, many of the islands did not have golden beaches, and it rained a lot, and it was hot and humid and the bush was thick and the ground was muddy.

There was an island which was a story book island, but it was so far out in the Pacific that it was closer to Tuvalu (Ellice Islands) than it was to Guadalcanal. It was within the boundary of the Protectorate and, what was more, it was part of Eastern District where we lived for four years. This was the island of Anuta which lay in the blue, blue Pacific of the large lazy swells some 450 nautical miles east of the island of San Cristobal. This tiny island, a green hill and a small flat of sandy spit covered with coconut palms in this huge expanse of blue ocean, was less than three kilometres in circumference. The beaches were wide and golden. The Polynesians were of the same colour and their smiles were as wide. Just over two hundred people lived, loved and of course argued, as do all humans, on this beautiful island.

The only safe way for the Government ships to reach Anuta, in the days before the captains were trained in deep sea navigation techniques, was to island-hop. First, the 250 miles from Kira Kira to the large island of Santa Cruz, discovered in 1592 by Mendana in his second voyage to the Solomon Islands to set up a settlement. It was fairly easy to find Santa Cruz though several times we found ourselves thirty miles off course. If you were too far to the north then the 700 metre cone of the volcano Tinakula would act as a marker to set you on course for Graciosa Bay, Santa Cruz's huge harbour, where Mendana died. The second section of the voyage occurred during the next night when the ship sailed 110 nautical miles south east to the island of Vanikoro. On the south coast reefs of this island France lost its famous explorer, La Perouse. At least that is where the wrecks of his ships *Boussole* and *Astrolabe* lie today, though what happened to the explorer and his men has not been solved. In the days that we visited the island it was the site of a logging operation. Vanikoro was not the ideal South Pacific island. There were no beautiful beaches, the place was full of midges and mosquitoes, the rainfall averaged 300 inches a year and much of the coastline was protected by mangroves. It certainly would not have impressed La Perouse who had previously called at Botany Bay.

Then it was a mid-afternoon departure from Vanikoro ESE into the ever-present SE swell. Now there was a definite change in temperature and if you had done the trip before you now reached for your woollen jersey and breathed in a much cooler air. Generally the SE wind was blowing and rain squalls came scudding across the sea, limiting the horizon to a few hundred metres and driving the deck passengers to huddle closer together. In ten minutes the squall had passed, leaving the white horses gleaming in the sun and the dark blue of the rolling swells reminding you it was the Pacific. If the fates were kind, you would expect to see the grey bulk of Tikopia on the horizon at dawn and by 10 o'clock be safely at anchor off the NW beach of this island. The Tikopians were made famous by the anthropologist Professor Firth. They were Polynesians with a well-developed chieftain system. There were four *Te Arikis*. In the mid-1950s three were followers of their ancient religion and one, with his people, were adherents of the

Church of Melanesia (Anglican). As this chief lived nearest the only safe anchorage it seemed obvious to assume that the Church's proselytising had been done on the beach. The ancient beliefs had been strong and it was not until the 1956 and 1957 cyclones, and many deaths from influenza, that the other three chiefs and their followers became Christians. It was always a busy day or two at Tikopia as formal calls had to be paid on each *Te Ariki* in order of seniority before any of the more mundane work of administration could commence.

The departure for Anuta was usually with a full ship of passengers, as the Tikopians took the rare opportunity to visit relatives, buy coconuts, or just have a look. At nine at night the click-clank-clink of the windlass marked the anchor coming up, and soon the ship started to roll as we cleared the shelter of Tikopia on a NE course. Dawn at sea with the large swell like a series of grey hills over which the ship wallowed, the sky brightening with a grey light, then a pink-tinged line of cloud giving way rapidly to the first rays of the sun appearing above the horizon. The deck passengers leaning over the rail or sitting on their bed rolls on the hatch covers, clearing throats, chewing betel nut, or just lying listening to the hum of desultory conversations. Climbing to the top deck the bosun pointed ahead to a small cloudlike bump – "Anuta now", he said, "should be there by 8 o'clock". And by 8.00 am we were anchored off the SW beach, rolling heavily in the swell. There was no question of going ashore by ship's boat in a dignified manner with the ship's crew in uniform performing their drill with oars. There were but two ways, and by now the islanders were demonstrating in fine style one method, as the first of the swimmers were climbing the ship's side, their faces wreathed in smiles, their long hair streaming and their *tapa* breech clouts looking distinctly fragile.

The second method did not look much better, as the first tiny canoes with an inch of freeboard arrived full of laughing children. It was always difficult to know how many had travelled in any one canoe, as bodies kept falling out and half the passengers seemed to be in the water at any one time. But the larger outrigger canoes had by now negotiated the surf and these looked far rnore suitable for conveying an officer of Her Majesty's Service in a dignified manner to pay his respects to the *Te Ariki*.

But first one had to move out of the cabin, or was it a fish bowl? There were two ports and one door, and there were two faces at each port, and possibly six at the door, absolutely fascinated by all our doings and possessions. The Melanesian boat's crew were very suspicious of these wild Polynesians and kept warning Margaret and Claire, the wife of the Forest Officer, that we had to lock up everything, otherwise there would be losses. The cheerfulness, wild abandon and curiosity, made these people attractive but their size was daunting. Thighs like tree trunks supported huge barrel chests with hands like soup plates. The women were not the little Polynesian beauties but matched the men in size and stature, not rotund like some modern-day Polynesians but of huge frames. The women wore vast wrap-around skirts of *tapa* and equally large smiles. Most wore a necklace with a barbless *bonito* fish-hook attached. Some had bleached their hair with lime but all wore their rather curly hair quite short. Most had tattoos featuring the *bonito* tuna fish down their front, on their arms and backs of their hands. Many of the men were tattooed on their thighs and the backs of their legs.

With the canoes alongside it was just a case of standing on the gunwale and waiting until the ship rolled close to the canoe, and then making a leap into the narrow hull where there were always plenty of willing hands to stop you falling overboard, or to pull you from the sea if you did miss. The approach to the beach was across the reef and it depended on the size of the swell whether it was hair-raising, exciting, or just another canoe trip. On the beach you were surrounded by the rest of the population, who all wanted to shake hands or, with some of the braver ones, touch noses in the traditional Polynesian greeting. Then off along the beach to *Te Ariki* who was sitting cross-legged in his house. The houses, like those in Tikopia, were basically a roof with walls only two feet high, and a floor of beautifully woven mats, the finer *pandanus* ones placed on the coarser ones of coconut leaf, so that the whole effect was indeed very comfortable. The doors at the gable end of the house were so low that one crawled in on hands and knees, and that ensured that your head remained below that of *Te Ariki,* which was socially required.

Introductions were made through the interpreter and gifts were exchanged. The Administration permitted the District Commissioner to purchase gifts for the *Te Arikis* of Tikopia and Anuta from the Station vote. Such gifts were often a drum of kerosene, a knife, lengths of cloth, anti-mosquito spray or a hurricane lantern. Gifts from the chief were one or two beautiful finely woven mats of *pandanus* leaf.

After the formal proceedings other pleasantries were exchanged and inquiries were made of the people's gardens, fishing, health, and whether there were any outstanding disputes. As the atmosphere relaxed there would be jokes and much laughter. On one visit the *Te Ariki* admired my shirt. There is only one thing to do in those circumstances, so I took off my rather grubby and sweaty shirt and handed it over with much ceremony. He also admired Claire's blouse but she voiced strong opposition to the suggestion that she should strip off and hand over her new blouse. "Where would such a practice end?" said Claire.

Anuta was obviously well able to look after itself. Very few of the people were in other parts of the Protectorate, a couple of young men on plantations or with the Honiara Town Council, and two or three were at the Church schools. Consequently there were not the demands for assistance to have some errant husband return home, or requests to take boxes to relatives, or disputes on the distribution of goods or money sent home.

After the formal meetings there was time to walk around the remainder of the small village and exchange pleasantries with people sitting outside their houses mending fishing equipment or exchanging gossip with visitors from Tikopia. The return to the ship was done by canoe, in the same way as the landing, but the tide had changed by this time which could add to the uncertainty of crossing the reef without being capsized. Margaret was too slow to make the jump on to the ship's rail, or so thought the large Anutan who helped her up with a slap upon her bottom which certainly helped her make up her mind.

There was occasional canoe traffic the 90 nautical miles between Tikopia and Anuta, but some administration and Church officials had tended to discourage such voyages. I thought this was wrong. This was part of their culture and their way of life, and to deny them this occasional adventure was similar to discouraging our young people not to climb in case they may fall. As it was, the Anutans travelled regularly some 25 nautical miles to the easternmost island in the Protectorate, which was a small shaft of rock called Fataka or, by the Europeans, Mitre Rock. Here the Anutans caught seabirds and fish.

So this was an island which to the outsider seemed a paradise untouched, or barely, by the wicked outside world. Untainted by the tourist, the commercial world seeking to profit from the people or their resources, and inhabited by a cheerful people content with their home and not seeking a 'greener field'. Imagine my disgust, concern, and jealous thoughts when I found a travel book just the other day advising people how they could visit Anuta. Is no place sacred in this modem world?

OP 74 (Autumn 1997)

Not a Wisdom Tooth

by Jane Shadbolt

The Noble Army of Martyrs has included me in its ranks for many years, ever since my marriage in fact. Membership almost went with the job description of a Colonial Service wife. It was taken for granted that one would be a splendid little woman, bravely coping with hardship and isolation, always ready with hospitality for all-comers and bearing and raising children with the minimum of fuss and inconvenience to one's husband.

By the time I was into my third pregnancy, in 1958, I found that my martyrdom was taken for granted and I began to gild the lily with a few little extra sufferings. I let it be known that I had toothache, though I may not have mentioned that it was very mild. We were stationed at Loliondo, on the Serengeti, at the time two hundred miles across the grassy roadless plain to the nearest hospital or dentist, so I did not expect my bluff to be called. I just hoped for another credit for being cheerful in adversity. I had reckoned without my husband's strength in problem solving, however, and I paid dearly for my bid for admiration.

One morning in the rainy reason my husband appeared in the house mid-morning saying "Get your stuff together, Baghwan Singh is going to Arusha and will take you to the dentist". The Indian shopkeeper took a monthly trip to the nearest town for supplies, and he was at the door with his five-ton lorry, ready for the journey. At that point I should have admitted that my toothache was very slight and not worth a ghastly bumpy ride in the rainy season. I did not argue with my husband in those days, as I do now. I was much too intent on being the perfect wife, so in ten minutes I found myself climbing up into the lorry, parting with two tearful little girls and wondering why on earth I was going.

Baghwan Singh and I could only communicate in Swahili, our only common language, so conversation did not flow too freely. Something else did, however, and that was the contents of his lunch tin which was beside me. After a few miles I felt a puddle seeping through my skirt and found that I was sitting in curry. Turmeric is a strong dye, and mixed with the blue of my skirt it left a khaki stain on my rear which could be open to a very unkind interpretation. We moved the tin down onto the floor and thumped along for several more hours.

By late afternoon we came off the Serengeti and began the ascent to Ngorongoro. There is a notorious sticky patch of black cotton soil on that hill and it was raining again. We were soon bogged down to our axles. I was not much use to Baghwan, although I did my best to dig while he jacked up the lorry. Soon it was getting dark and desperate. Not only would we not reach Arusha that night, we would probably have to sleep in the lorry. Then the first of two miracles happened (the second came at the end of the trip). The light of a vehicle appeared behind us, the first we had seen since we left. Father James, a Roman Catholic priest whom we both knew, came out of his Landrover and offered help. It was so totally unexpected and such an answer to prayer that I would have put Father James forward for sainthood. He took me up to the District Office at Ngorongoro while the rest of his passengers helped Baghwan on his way. I had a meal and a bed for the night from the District Officer's wife, and next day I rode on to Arusha with Father James. I had always rather fancied Father James, but I doubt whether my tubby shape and stained skirt posed much of a threat to his vows.

My poor appearance was brought home to me at the hospital where the nurse at the desk, after hearing of my need of a dentist, phoned through "There's a woman here who wants to see Mr Martin", as if I should really have used the tradesman's entrance. I didn't like her any better when she put down the receiver and said "I'm sorry, Mr Martin is on two weeks local leave!"

You may well wonder why we had not phoned ahead to make an appointment, regardless of my hasty departure. The only communication between our home and the outside world was a daily radio session with Monduli, the headquarters of the whole District. This took place very early each morning. I did have help from that contact from now on, however, because someone from Monduli who had to be at the hospital looked out for me and took me back there in the evening. Meanwhile I booked in for my confinement in four months time, though I could have done that by letter of course. It hardly made me feel that my journey had been worthwhile.

The Townsends at Monduli made me very welcome. I was starving hungry but I had to wait as they were going out to dinner at a nearby tea plantation and I was also invited. My journey back was also arranged. A Veterinary Officer was going to Loliondo the next day and would take me, but he was leaving at 4.00 am so as to go the long way round and avoid Ngorongoro. I decided to enjoy the evening as the next day promised to be pretty grim.

The dinner party was wonderful. The house was an elegant old German colonial building with large high-ceilinged rooms filled with vases of long-stemmed Persian roses. I had been lent a very becoming dress by Helen Townsend and felt very happy. We came back to their house at midnight and my alarm seemed to ring almost as soon as I fell asleep. The rain was lashing down and it was pitch dark as we drove off. The Veterinary Officer was a South African called Peter Anderson, and he liked to smoke a rather heavily scented tobacco. After a few miles I had to ask to stop so that I could lose the previous night's meal. For the rest of the journey I was hollow with hunger.

We promised ourselves that we would stop in Nairobi for some food, but by the time we passed through it was after lunch, and the friends we called on gave us a dainty afternoon tea! The few miles of tarmac around Nairobi soon ended and we went back to muddy earth roads again, on into the Rift Valley and into Masai country again at Narok. There were still many miles to go and it was still raining as darkness fell. We had the Mara river to cross before we entered Loliondo district, and it would be swollen. The ford where the track crossed would be well under water. We were both rather quiet by now, weary and worried.

About midnight we approached the river, and here the second miracle happened. Lights shone across the water. We climbed out of the car and heard my husband's voice calling us. He had guessed that the river would be swollen and had come to meet us. He had been waiting for hours as we had taken much longer than any of us expected because of the mud.

Peter and I had no idea of the depth of the water, or the strength of the current, but we held on to each other and headed for the headlamps opposite. I think we were too tired to be frightened so we just went on and reached the bank, wet to our waists but safe. The whole journey back had taken on a nightmare quality, but it wasn't over yet.

About ten miles from home we came upon an upturned car, with its wheels in the air in the road before us. We walked towards it in silence, expecting to find bodies either in it or under it. There were none, they had escaped through one of the windows, whoever they were, and had walked away.

I remember leaning wearily against a wall when we finally reached home at 2.00 am and my husband saying "Whatever is the matter with you?"

I'm afraid the splendid little woman image had slipped for a moment. But I suffered no ill effects and the baby boy who was born later that year became a Colonel in the Royal Marines so perhaps this was the first part of his training.

OP 83 (May 2002)

Journey in the Hadhramaut

by Mary Reid

At the beginning of 1963, the children having returned to school after the Christmas holidays, I received an invitation to accompany my husband on a visit to the Eastern Aden Protectorate and, as the guests of the Commandant of the Hadhrami Bedouin Legion (the HBL), to go on a 5 day drive through part of the Hadhramaut and down the West Road to Mukalla on the coast. This really was a once-in-a-lifetime opportunity and one which I was thrilled to grasp since, apart from intrepid travellers such as Freya Stark (*The Southern Gates of Arabia* and *A Winter in Arabia),* few women have ever been welcomed in that part of the world – and particularly in its upper reaches which constitute the Hadhramaut.

As I am sure many of you are aware, a 'Wadi' is a rocky water-course or river bed, dry except in the rainy season, and the Wadi Hadhramaut stretches roughly 350 miles and almost due West to East, is some 50 miles wide, and lies to the south of the great Northern Desert which, in turn, runs along the southern edge of the Sand Sea and the Rub-al-Khali Desert or 'Empty Quarter' (much written about by that noted Arabist and desert traveller, Wilfred Thesiger).

The Eastern Aden Protectorate comprises the states of Qa'iti, Kathiri and Mahra and it was to the two first named that I paid my memorable visit in 1963. As a result of territorial and constitutional changes, Wahidi State, which was formerly one of the member states of the East, had become part of the Western Aden Protectorate by the time of my visit – but it may be of interest to know that legend has it that the biblical Wise Man who bore the myrrh on the occasion of the Nativity hailed from Wahidi State.

Our journey started from Khormaksar Civil Airport where our party of three (my husband, myself and a member of my husband's staff) boarded a vintage DC3 (Dakota) of Aden Airways. To anyone who has never flown in these parts, at that time, and possibly even now, an air passage in South Arabia was an experience never to be forgotten – 'charter' and 'bucket-shop' flights are the height of luxury in comparison! This wonderful, old, aerial work-horse of World War 2 had been converted so as to be a combined passenger/cargo carrier – humans up front and goods and livestock at the tail – dispensing with the need for 'in-flight entertainment' since goats and / or chickens invariably escaped from their netted confines at the rear and sought out their owners! But it was our fellow passengers (we three were the only Europeans on board) who got our trip off to an exciting start – entirely male, of course, since the place of the woman in the Eastern Aden Protectorate was very much in the home and in the village. However, the men-folk more than made up by their colourfulness. Young soldiers of the HBL returning from furlough, strutting proudly in their gay 'mufti', olive-skinned Kathiris with their distinctive oriental features (about which I shall be commenting later), fine-featured merchants from Mukalla, immaculate in white, almost Indian-like garb, and, of course, the ubiquitous dark-skinned Bedouin tribesmen, fierce of eye and beard and wild of hair, with *jambias* (curved daggers) at their waists, crossed bandoliers and loaded rifles across their bare knees.

As was to be expected, our take-off was delayed and I leave you to imagine the atmosphere inside the tight-packed cabin in that least comfortable, albeit most reliable, of old planes – a heady mixture of sweat, goats, fruit and vegetables, chickens, petrol fumes – and over all the smell of the cheap perfume with which even the humblest of Arab males loves to douse himself. However, we eventually lumbered into the air and headed out to sea, thence along the coast, skirting the white line of the surf where it broke across the sands of Arabia and so to Bir Ali on the furthermost edge of Wahidi State. Thereafter we turned inland, almost due north, over lifeless craters and volcanic outcrops and the sprawl of the mountains on the route which I would be taking on my forthcoming journey, up to 6,000 feet high, a sepia mass that ruled a straight line across the brilliant blue of the sky. And so, about two hours after take-off, we touched down at Ghuraf Airstrip where we were met by Qaid (Lt/Colonel) 'Pat' Gray, Commandant of the Hadhrami Bedouin Legion since 1959 and who had previously served under the famous Glubb Pasha in Jordan and latterly in Muscat and Oman – a great, ruddy-faced bear of a man with magnificent handle-bar moustaches and with his red and white Arab head-dress at a jaunty angle. With him was his tall, lean second-in-command, Major David Eales, seconded from the British Army, who was to be our guide and mentor over the next five days, and standing by were two long-wheel-based Landrovers with their attendant HBL drivers, immaculate in their khaki drill, knee-length, skirted tunics, crossed bandoliers, red cummerbunds, putteed legs and bare feet, all topped by the same head-dresses as their officers. Whilst our baggage was being off-loaded we took shelter from the blazing sun in the shade of the Dakota's wings, and took stock of our surroundings, noticing amongst other things that each of the Landrovers bore a foot-wide, painted red strip across its bonnet and this, we were told, was to identify them as 'ours' in open country in the event of punitive RAF air-strikes into tribal territory! Eventually all was ready, the plane had proceeded on its southward way to Mukalla, our kit had been loaded onto the vehicles and we were off on the 20 mile drive to Seiyun, the capital of Kathiri State.

The words 'South Arabia' and 'desert' understandably conjure up visions of searing heat, limitless stretches of rolling sand-dunes, camel trains, the occasional oasis and swash-buckling Arab horsemen as portrayed by Rudolf Valentino or Omar Sharif. Admittedly, my first impression of the Eastern Aden Protectorate was of dry, glaring heat but there any preconceived ideas ended and our drive from Ghuraf to Seiyun, with a back-cloth of jagged, inhospitable hills, was along a reasonable 'murram' (baked soil on a stone foundation) surface road winding between pocket handkerchief sized fields of millet, yams and a variety of pulses, all with strategically laid out irrigation channels fed from deep wells, from which the precious water was being drawn by either 'Persian Wheels' (a large, multi-spoked, wooden wheel rotating a sort of conveyor belt of tin or pottery vessels which scooped the water from deep down in the ground, brought it up to tip it into one main distribution area, the whole Heath-Robinsonish contraption being operated through a series of cogs and shafts turned via donkeys or mules walking in constant circles alongside) or by simple block and tackle and pulley systems mounted over the wells' openings on crude wooden tripods with camels trudging up and down ramps and hoisting goatskin bags of water from the depths to be hand poured into the channels. In the field – this being a male chauvinistic society – it was the women-folk who were doing the hoeing, weeding and harvesting, dressed either in shapeless black, or equally shapeless but much more colourful, red shifts and wearing on their heads tall pointed straw hats which made them look like witches without their broomsticks. And it appeared that the donkeys and camels at the wells were the responsibility of ragged urchins of both sexes, encouraging their charges with shrill, throaty cries. Children were also to be seen in the fields, with equally unkempt pi-dogs, scaring the birds from the crops, but stopping to gaze wide-eyed as we passed.

After about 15 miles the periodic clusters of shabby village houses, with their scratching chickens and foraging goats, began to give way to much more affluent looking dwellings – white-painted villas much decorated with plaster curlicues and lattice-work edging to their roofs, surrounded by low walls enclosing gardens with cannas, oleander, zinnias, frangipani and bougainvillea creating a riot of colour in the shade of groves of date palms. Seiyun is a prosperous town, known as the 'Paris of the Wadi', its wealth stemming from a long-standing tradition of emigration to Malaysia, Indonesia and Zanzibar, in particular of the ruling Al Kaf family who were reputed to be multi-million sterling millionaires, and it was on remittances from their Far Eastern cousins that the merchants of Kathiri State had built up their prosperity. It is a gentle, civilized world of its own, set somewhere between Arabia and South-East Asia with its high cheek-boned, semi-Malay faces, its ginger coffee and its elaborate Indonesian-style mosques.

It was evening by the time we reached Seiyun. We were hot and dusty and stiff after our drive so we drove straight to the Sultan's guest house – a three-storeyed villa on the outskirts of the town, furnished a bit like a Victorian boarding-house, but with high-ceilinged and refreshingly cool rooms, and charmingly set in a large date-palm grove. There was the luxury (for South Arabia) of electricity but, in true Arab style, our toilet facility consisted of a 'long drop' down the side wall of the house to a deep pit. I did bless another true Hadhramaut facility in the form of a large, indoor bath-house on the ground floor (called *ajabia*) where, in four feet of deliciously cool water, I was able to wallow, after standing by the side and soaping off the travel grime. With the dust and fatigue removed, we ate a leisurely, and not too Arab meal (with the inevitable tinned fruit and condensed milk, of course) then sat on the flat roof amongst the palm branches and watched the moon over the surrounding hills. All was quiet except for the distant barking of dogs and the hum of the nearby electricity generator – and so to bed.

Seiyun is, by comparison with the claustrophobic air of Tarim, gay and genuinely justifying its reputation as 'The Paris of the Wadi'. A town of palm groves and gardens, gleaming white villas of up to three storeys and, in its centre, the Sultan's palace which looked as if it was made of marzipan, towering over the market square – white, of course, but picked out in candy pinks and blues and greens and with a gaudy standard flying from a central tower. In the glare of the noonday sun, the vast market place sprawling out in front of the palace presented a vivid scene of hustle and bustle, of colour and sound and, if one did not look too closely, of gaiety and even opulence. Market women squatting by their displays of fruit and vegetables spread out on the baked ground red and green peppers, ginger, yams, sweet potatoes, corn-cobs, fresh dates on their stems, oranges and limes. Ramshackle stalls with flimsy canvas awnings over bolts of cloth – coloured cottons, cheap satins and silks and brilliantly woven camel saddle-cloths. Coffee and fruit juice vendors crying their wares and rattling their cups, cooked meat sellers enveloped in spicy wood-smoke, woeful little donkeys, and groups of supercilious looking camels with their equally haughty drivers. That evening we were invited to dine at the palace as guests of the Kathiri Sultan, who was hosting a party in honour of a visiting dignitary from the Foreign Office in London. This was to be no desert meal, with basic fare by guttering oil or pressure lamps and attended by down-at-heel, fierce-looking tribesmen, but a true, 5-star, Arab-Sultanic banquet (clearly organised to impress 'the Man from the Ministry' who had, hopefully, come bearing gifts from HM Government!). As you undoubtedly know, Arab dining is done squatting on the ground around the dishes of food, and etiquette demands that feet must point decorously away from the food, and that only the right hand must be used with which to eat. The guest of honour, however, was clearly more accustomed to the eating habits of the West End and, at well over 6 feet in height, his initial contortions as he endeavoured not to offend, caused not a little discreet amusement amongst the other guests! Eventually he succeeded in disposing of his limbs in something approaching an acceptable position, and the feast commenced, and feast indeed it was: not the usual goat, rice and chuppaties, rather steaming platters of saffron, pillaf and brown rice, haunches of mutton and lamb straight from the spit, curried chicken and guinea fowl, great dishes of assorted vegetables – okra, beans, tomatoes, peppers, onions, yams and others I did not recognise – cheeses made from goat's or camel's milk, little earthenware pots of wild bees honey and, of course, the ubiquitous, piping-hot, flat pancakes of coarse, unleavened flour. All this in the surroundings of a large, airy chamber carpeted in richly-coloured oriental rugs, and with plump cushions for the guests comfort; chandeliers shining from the vaulted ceiling, and everywhere a positive army of white-clad retainers. This gargantuan meal finished, to the accompaniment of appreciative belches and burps, we were offered bowls of rose-water with which to rinse our fingers before adjourning to an ante-room, equally sumptuously furnished, where we were served tiny cups of sticky-sweet and milkless tea and offered bowls of fruit and sweetmeats.

It was an entirely different face of South Arabia that presented itself to us as we drove westwards out of Seiyun the following morning. As we passed through the outskirts of the city, the villas and gardens gave way to isolated clusters of village houses; the palm groves to clumps of wind-blown camel thorn; and the trim, cobbled streets to dusty desert tracks stretching mile after limitless mile into the distance. But on either side it was far from a scene of desolation, and what might have been viewed as a desert waste was, in fact, a land awaiting the onset of the rainy season – the season that would fill the irrigation channels and bring the desert back to green life. But this was the dry time of year and we drove along in the hot desert air. I was in the leading Landrover with Major Eales and the driver, Saleh, my husband's vehicle lurching along a quarter of a mile behind, well out of range of our billowing wake of dust and sand. From time to time we would halt to stretch our limbs, have a welcome drink from the canvas water-bags hanging on the Landrover doors and take stock of our surroundings. In the distance the rugged wall of the 'johl', with sometimes the crumbling walls of some one-time prosperous town on the long abandoned trans-desert route shimmering through the heat haze, and, by the side of the track, unaccountable piles of massive boulders. And then, away in the distance, like some Stonehenge transposed from the green downs of Wiltshire to the sand dunes of Arabia, there appeared our immediate objective, the astonishing sky-scraper town of Shibam.

If Seiyun is known as 'The Paris of the Wadi', then Shibam can rightly be called its 'New York'. The town simply burst upon us like one of those Italian towns that are built facing inwards, so as to present a rampart wall of houses to the outside world; no towers, no grand entrances exist, just a solid facade of windowed buildings constructed solely of mud, bound with straw (as in biblical times) with interior support pillars of straight palm-tree trunks and soaring to ten, twelve and even fourteen storeys. The approach road swung in a wide detour, past white mud villas, each in its own walled garden, and our little convoy entered Shibam up a ramped approach and through a great archway into the public square. Those towering mud buildings all lean against each other and that square with its massive gateway is the only way in or out of the city, a sombre place and yet with an air of dignified wealth and tradition. Shibam is a place of great antiquity but, in truth, there is no reason for its being. It is not an agricultural centre but is purely residential, maintained by the wealth of its men folk who traditionally depart as youths to the four corners of the globe to make their fortunes, but always to return in middle and old age. As a consequence, there are reputed to be three women to every resident male, many of them known as *sharifas* or descendants of the Prophet. But women were conspicuous by their absence at the time of my all too brief visit, and I was told that, unlike other places in the Hadhramaut, purdah is enforced most rigidly within the high walls of Shibam. After a meal in the ante-room to the 'city hall', a 12 storey pile like a white wedding cake, we resumed our trek across the desert. I looked back and watched Shibam fade into the distance, a lonely, white fortress mass in its desert of sand, one of the most Alice-in-Wonderland cities in the world, the memory of which I shall carry vividly for ever. I often think how privileged I was to be permitted to see it for myself and to feel its aura of mystery.

OP 62 (October 1991)

Aden

Aden became a Crown Colony in 1937, having previously been governed as a part of British India. The Governor, Sir Bernard Reilly, suggested that the colony's badge should be a traditional two-masted dhow on a stylised sea, similar to that shown on the colony's first postage stamps. The first design showed brown hills in the background (see the defaced blue ensign on page 323) but when it was drawn up by the Royal Mint the hills were omitted. The flag at the stern appears to be flying against the wind! The badge was used until January 1963 when Aden became part of the Federation of South Arabia, which had an entirely different flag in an Arabian style.

Journey to Mongu

by B H

"**P**osted to Mongu." Such was the tail-end of a telegram we received at Cape Town on our return from home leave some years ago. On arrival at Lusaka, we learnt, not without some surprise, that a road had been cut through to Mongu and we were to make use of it. A large car, complete with driver, was put at our disposal and we left for Barotseland on a bright and sparkling morning at the end of September. The first part of the run was easy and we lunched with some good friends of ours at Mumbwa where we collected the auditor whose duties led him to Mankoya. Trundling some miles behind us was a weary old lorry with all our equipment and we only hoped that it would catch up with us that night as we had barely anything in the car with us.

Shortly before dark, we reached the Kafue – a grand sight after the heat of the day and, to our astonishment, we found a young cadet camped there. He had been, as far as I could remember, only three weeks in the country and had been sent out on tour almost immediately after his arrival. He proved a delightful creature and his camp appeared to us the acme of comfort. Longingly we looked down the road for any signs of our lumbering old follower but the night air was not broken by any sound of a mechanical nature. So it came about that our friend proved host and served a most excellent dinner which we ate under the stars. After dinner we sat over the fire for a while until the time arrived for my young daughter to go to bed. The snag was that there wasn't any bed to which she could go. Our young host, however, insisted that we take over his tent for the night, so we wrapped the child in a rug and put her on the floor of the tent and told her to go to sleep. This she had little difficulty in achieving – it had been a hot and tiring day.

Still no sign of our lorry. We gossiped for another hour or so with one ear cocked into the night. There were lots of noises, certainly – quite a symphonic night – but none the one for which we sought. We were camped in the middle of a big game reserve and the auditor remarked that there was known to be a large herd of elephant in the vicinity and that possibly may have accounted for the non-arrival of our trailer. My husband and I couldn't help feeling that the fault was much more likely to lie within the bowels of the lorry itself. Subsequent events proved us right. The time came when sleep was essential so we set about fixing ourselves up for the night with what spare equipment the cadet could lend us. The auditor, a smallish man, purloined the canvas bath which he filled with grass and snuggled down into it like a small bird in its nest. He declared that he had never been more comfortable. Everyone behaved very nicely and said nothing about straws in his hair.

In due course we all settled down though I confess to a feeling of disquiet when I heard a lion roaring in the distance. All I hoped was that it would keep its distance. Despite these feelings, it was not long before I was well asleep. Some time later, I wakened with a start and lay rigid listening to a scuffling noise all round the tent. With some excuse, perhaps, my mind immediately leapt to the larger carnivora and it was some time before I mustered sufficient courage to switch on a torch. I almost laughed aloud at what its beam revealed. There was my young daughter – the latter half of her still wrapped in the rug – crawling round and round the bare earth looking for a softer resting spot. "I feel so cold and uncomfortable", she complained. The matter was duly adjusted.

In the early hours of the morning, the crippled old lorry snorted into camp and Africans tumbled off her in all directions. Why or how they came to be there was something which was never explained satisfactorily. The driver of the dilapidated old vehicle muttered things about the differential and we promised that it should receive attention in the morning. It had necessarily to be a makeshift job as we were pressed for time the next day. The crossing of the pontoon (with no guide rope) was something which had to be accomplished as early as possible – before the rising wind which made it dangerous. After a hasty breakfast, the packing-up business was soon completed and our car was run on to the pontoon.

A slight mist lay over the river and the occasional hippo puffed up to blow it away. We pursued a somewhat circuitous course and the crossing took the best part of half an hour. From the other bank we watched the paddlers steer the clumsy craft back for the lorry. By that time, little fingers of wind were scraping the surface of the water. The lorry was run, loaded, on to the pontoon and, from where we were standing, looked most precarious. The superstructure, formed mostly of our kit, was out of all proportion to the vehicle itself and it still had its human cargo clinging to it like flies. By the time it was getting towards mid-stream, the wind had risen in earnest and we watched the canting over of the whole outfit with some dismay. Steering obviously became an impossibility. Riding at a sharp angle, the pontoon with its big burden was being pushed steadily up river and we despaired of ever seeing our belongings again. However, our driver assured us that they would make land higher up and paddle down to the bank where we were. Such fortunately proved to be the case though there were times when it seemed an impossibility and in defiance of all the accepted laws of gravity.

It was hot when we started on our way again hoping, against all advice, to make Mongu that night. We took the bare essentials from the lorry knowing that it would have to take the trip very slowly while we decided to push straight through that night. The run to Mankoya was a relatively easy one and we reached there in time for lunch. Our hosts almost implored us to stay over for the night but we pushed doggedly on. The next ninety odd miles were heartbreaking. The 'road' was a mere track hewn from the bush and not properly stumped. The soil was pure sand and necessitated travelling in second gear for the most part. It would have been suicidal to stop where the sand was particularly deep or we should never have got going again. So on we ran through the baking afternoon. Bush fires were the order of the day; frequently we found a smouldering tree lying across our path. The driver would then swing out of the sandy rut and go snaking through the bush, missing trees by inches while I closed my eyes waiting for a rending sound.

Quite early on, we had found that some enterprising African had at some time during our journey made off with our water sacks. A bitter blow! Our thirst was terrific. Fortunately we were carrying a drum of water for the car and a single flask of drinking water for our little girl. We had to ration her with this as we were not too keen on her drinking the other which was both dirty and oily. The car's thirst was prodigious and whenever we struck a piece of hardish ground we stopped and filled her up. It was a gruelling trip for any car. The driver assured us that there would be a water hole at Luampa so our minds busied themselves with this pleasant thought as we swing from side to side in our seats while the car waggled her way through the sand. Alas! When we reached the much-vaunted water hole it was dry. Three eland gazed at us speculatively as much as to say "You've been had too". It was then that we broached the drum for our own thirsts. Our lips had cracked, our tongues doubled in size and felt like a thick pile carpet stuck to the roofs of our mouths. That drink was one of the best I remember.

As dusk fell, so some of the stinging heat of the day was left behind but we still had a good way to go. With headlamps picking out all the eccentricities of the road, we roared on through the night and then – what we had dreaded for so long, happened. We stuck. Well and truly. We all got out of the car and dragged branches from the trees to push under the wheels. Fortunately, we were by that time on the outskirts of Mongu and evidently within hearing range of an African village as various leaping, shouting people came speeding through the night and we soon had a willing band of helpers. Those wheels seemed insatiable. We piled leaves and branches under them and every time we tried the car the foliage was pulverised, while the smell of burning rubber from the whizzing tyres filled the air. So we continued to scrape and dig and fill up until finally there appeared to be a reasonable chance of getting going again. The driver levered himself into his seat and started the engine. Rocket-like the car shot into the night with a roar and, as she fled her long resting place various bodies jumped the running boards. In the soft moonlight I noticed a white shirt on the far side and thought it was my husband. The driver, we learnt later, had spotted a white shirt on my side and had thought the same thing. We didn't dare stop in that treacherous place so flew on to Mongu.

On arrival, we found that my husband was not of our party! Consternation sat heavily on the driver's face. "I can't go back", he said, "not tonight, I'd stick as soon as I stopped."

"Quite", I said, not very helpfully.

"Do you think your husband could walk in?"

"Of course", I replied airily as though walking through the bush with a nice sandy bottom was one of his favourite occupations late at night. The driver was afraid that he would prove somewhat irascible on arrival but I assured him, not without some misgivings, that he would be certain to understand. I only hoped that I had not over-estimated the big-heartedness of my husband's nature.

Fortunately, by the time he did turn up, he had walked off any spleen he might have felt and there was nothing but a happy reunion. Our hosts had not thought it possible for us to be there for at least another two days and they were reaching the tail-end of a dinner party – the men all dinner-jacketed, the women in flowing gowns. We were offered whiskies and the faces of the guests were a study when we asked for a water sack. As it was so late, we were asked to join them at table there and then. I squeezed between two immaculately clad men. One turned to make a remark to me and I saw his nose ruffle up in disgust as I swung round suddenly and sprayed him with a shower of dust from my hair. I could not have cared less.

We had arrived.

OP 42 (November 1981)

Stomach Ache in the Solomons

by James L O Tedder

It was a recent visit to the Republic of Kiribati, setting for Grimble's wonderful stories of *A Pattern of Islands* and *Return to the Islands,* that stirred memories. Not only had Grimble, and later Eric Bevington in his book *The Things they do for England if only England knew,* showed how isolated life was on these islands, but they also revealed how medical emergencies could lead to trying circumstances. Even if radio communication was available, the possibility of a ship being close to effect a rescue was rare. Before radio it was not even possible to obtain encouragement or advice from a doctor.

Gazing across the lagoon at Abernama and trying to imagine myself in such a situation I suddenly remembered an incident while visiting the Santa Cruz Islands in the British Solomon Islands Protectorate. Unlike some places, the Eastern District did have a ship, plus radios, plus an Assistant Medical Practitioner. The schedule for touring the Santa Cruz Islands, 250 sea miles to the east of district headquarters, was a tour in April and another in November. That way you hoped to avoid the cyclonic season and the stronger SE winds in the period June to September.

On this particular trip the tour was delayed until late May – possibly due to the late arrival of *Margery,* a sixty-foot single engine vessel after an overhaul. There was already a load of 25 deck passengers returning home when the ship reached Kira Kira bay, and we added a few more including Mike Russell the Agricultural Officer, Francis Kikolo the Assistant Medical Officer, and myself.

As the anchor was weighed, I leant over the rail talking to Francis and complained about a stomach ache. He assured me in the best medical terms that it would soon pass – possibly tension he suggested. I was inclined to agree with him as the departure had been the usual frantic rush to ensure that the station would look after itself, that the mail had been loaded, the payment vouchers, the cash imprest, the necessary files, and the bank forms were on board. A last look through the mail from the Secretariat in case there was some urgent request. Audit queries were not even opened. Then a check on personal matters such that Margie and the children were going to be comfortable during the next month.

Some thirty hours after leaving Kira Kira the ship entered Gracioza Bay on Ndende where some passengers and cargo were unloaded. Then it was a short night voyage across to the Reef Islands where Mike and I were to go ashore. Francis would take the ship to Vanikoro, 120 sea miles to the SE, to deal with some medical problems among the timber workers, some of whom were from Australia. He decided to take the Reef Islands medical assistant and the nurse for on-the-job training. He calculated that he would be returning within a week, by which time we would have completed our work on the Reefs.

The Reef Islands consist of a coral atoll raised on the eastern section to some three or more metres above the sea, with the major lagoon stretching thirty kilometres to the west. Here it is possible for ships to anchor for protection from the SE trade winds as long as they can thread their way through the reefs to anchor off the large island of Fenualoa. This is 10 kilometres long and only ½ kilometre wide, and it is separated from the other islands by a narrow but very deep channel through which the swell moves. Then on the eastern section there are a host of islands ranging from a tiny half hectare to larger ones of over one hundred hectares, but all connected by shallow water which at low tide has to be waded through to move from island to island. The population is dense and the whole of the islands are a veritable garden of coconuts, breadfruit in season, yams and other vegetables and fruit.

After a battle with Treasury a grant of fifty dollars had been given to the district to erect a rest house on a tiny island off Ngadeli; far enough, said the Headman, for visiting officers not to be 'in the hair' of the villages. The owner of the island had the contract to erect the three metre by three metre house, and a small shelter over a fireplace formed the kitchen. It was not the height of luxury but it seemed that way after the smelly cramped ship – and it remained level all the time. It had been a battle to obtain this small grant from Treasury but it was pointed out that the ship could go off on other duties, and that being on shore we had more contact with the people and were able to be more efficient.

This then was the setting, and though the island and the position of the house were idyllic, I was not comfortable being doubled over with my stomach ache. Mike was quite cheery and said it would soon pass but I wasn't so sanguine. Next day the pain had localised to my right side and I announced 'appendicitis', and I was going to lie very still and eat nothing and drink water for the next twenty four hours. I suggested to Mike he take a trip across to the medical clinic an hour or so across the sand flats to another island, and see what may be in the cupboard to deal with this problem of mine. He returned in the afternoon to inform me that there was no anaesthetic, one rusty scalpel, some aspirin and a fungicide for a common skin complaint. Mike said, I think as an aside, that he was quite a whiz at dissection in his biology classes. I decided I was not that sick, and we would wait for another day and then assess the situation. Naturally I applied a lot of willpower during the following days to see whether I may be a faith healer. Certainly I felt a little easier next day, but I did not move off my sleeping mat, uncomfortable though it had become, and continued to drink the very unpalatable well water which was very salty but made even worse-tasting tea. Mike went off to count coconuts and talk copra drying to some nearby villagers.

About 1100 hours the next morning the cry went up 'sail ho' and several villagers arrived to point out a ship in full sail coming up from the SE. As it sailed nearer I struggled out to look and recognised the *Yankee* which every two years sailed around the world with a crew of rich young Americans. "It will have a doctor, Mike", I said, "so you'd better grab a canoe and see if the doctor will do a house call." As the ship was obviously making to anchor in the western lagoon, it was going to take some time for Mike to hopefully return with the doctor.

Some time after three o'clock I heard the approach of people and Mike introduced me to the doctor. She was very young but full of confidence, and I thought that was an advantage as she would remember her course and be up to date on all modern medicines. She climbed the steps into our tiny house, felt my stomach and said "Yes, it does seem like appendicitis". Then she looked around and said she would not wish to operate here in such 'appalling conditions' which rather upset us because as far as we were concerned it was a fine new leaf house still without the 'livestock' likely to inhabit an older house. The doctor suggested I was possibly over the worst of the attack so an injection of tetracycline 'the new wonder drug' would be the solution.

"Roll over and pull down your shorts, this may hurt a little" she said as she rammed a large needle with a large dose of the 'wonder drug' into my bottom. There is such a thing as a counter-irritant and I completely lost the pain in my stomach. Next day I felt much better but the doctor arrived for another injection and suggested that when the ship returned I make all haste to the Honiara hospital.

The very next day the *Margery* arrived with Francis who was very keen to operate on the spot. Apparently he hadn't done such an operation for some time, and thought the practice would be useful. The offer was refused quite politely by me and we rearranged the programme. Copra loading was commenced at once and news was sent out that the ship was to return to Honiara. That evening we crossed to Gracioza Bay and took on more cargo and a couple of passengers. By now the SE trade wind was in 'full voice', steady twenty knots with rain squalls reaching thirty to forty knots. As we cleared the shelter of the island the full force of the weather hit us. The swell was most impressive and as it was on our quarter we rolled very well indeed.

As I was the patient, I was in the only bunk. Hans, a timber worker with a bad toothache, had the three foot settee and Mike placed a thin mattress on the cabin floor. Under my bunk were several drawers which kept on being thrown out by the ship's motion onto Mike. There was little space to put them elsewhere as the cabin only measured two metres by two and a half metres. Every time we wanted to use the wash basin, we had to stand on Mike's head. The cabin was on the after-deck which in calm seas was some two metres above the sea. The motion of the ship became more violent and the ports in our cabin had to be screwed tight and the door firmly closed as the seas were breaking against them. Unfortunately none were really water tight and soon Mike's mattress with him on board was not only sliding back and forth across the cabin but he was now afloat in several inches of salt water.

We moved the dozen deck passengers who had become very frightened into the tiny galley which was quite a tight fit. Normally one person was a tight fit, but they certainly did not wish to stay on deck any longer. At three that afternoon the Bosun (Captain) Basi, normally and even in this situation a very phlegmatic middle-aged man from Guadalcanal, came to tell me that the crew were so frightened they would not take the wheel any longer. The large five foot diameter wheel was kicking so violently that it was taking two men to hold it. He and one crew member said they would 'try' to steer the ship. If we had changed course to run with the sea, who knows where we would have ended up, as no one knew deep sea navigation. Many a canoe had disappeared in similar fashion. The swell was indeed so large that we slid down the slopes, and climbed laboriously up the next one only to be hit with four feet of the top being blown back at us. Water had squeezed into every nook and cranny. In a way it was exhilarating but also a bit of a worry. However, all good things come to an end, and just before dusk we sighted San Cristobal where it should be and soon after we had its shelter. Shame-faced crew appeared to take over the wheel from the bosun and at midnight we dropped anchor in Kira Kira bay.

Mike had rubbed his elbow raw from trying to stop his sliding on the floor. Hans said his toothache had cured itself and the Honiara doctor told me it was too late to operate – "have it done on your next leave".

OP 83 (May 2002)

A Kenya Journey

by B W Thompson

It's about 300 miles from Mombasa to Nairobi. In 1952 only some 20 miles of the road was tarmac. The rest was native earth though covered in most places with murram (crushed laterite). This was maintained by periodic levelling with a grader or by the less technologically advanced feat of towing a tree behind a tractor and so sweeping the muck back into the holes. There were four settlements. First was Voi at 100 miles; it had a road and rail junction, a station, a hotel and a goodly number of permanent houses and shops as well as African huts – quite a metropolis. Then came Mtito Andei, half-way; it had a small hotel and petrol, nothing else. 200 miles from Mombasa was Makindu, its existence derived from a water tank where railway locomotives could fill up. A number of track maintenance staff had quarters here and a few Africans were living in the area. Finally came Sultan Hamud, 50 miles further on, where there was a petrol station and a few huts. Apart from these small settlements and others nearer Nairobi the road was deserted and ran lonely through the savannah, climbing from sea level at Mombasa to 5,500 feet at Nairobi.

Views were fantastic and ever-changing – rolling hills, deep valleys and vast sweeping plains. There were distant mountains with Kilimanjaro's snow-covered peak dominating the northern half of the route. The road skirted the majestic Tana River near Tsavo, famous location where the building of the Uganda Railway was held up in 1898 because the local lions developed a taste for eating labourers. Along almost all the route there was game to be seen and run into if you didn't watch out. It wasn't unknown to be stuck in the middle of a herd of elephants as they ate the roadside trees and playfully tossed the branches on to the highway, leaving you to drag them away before you could get started.

The road was always bumpy and often rutted. However, the main problem was the corrugations. Corrugations were the curse of East Africa's earth roads. A few inches deep and six to nine inches from crest to crest, like miniature waves in earth, they developed across all country roads. Cars bounced over them, often almost uncontrollably, and always most uncomfortably. It was claimed that the only solution for reasonable progress was to get to 40 mph. At this speed the wheels were supposed to ride over the crests and not have time to drop into the hollows. The theory was fine, in practice it didn't really work too well, besides which, taking a bend on loose murram at 40 mph was liable to result in an alarming slide into the ditch, a condition in which long-suffering passengers could be most uncomplimentary.

Cars trailed a massive cloud of dust, visible for miles. At least you could always tell if anybody else was about. Most often there wasn't and you were all alone. However, should someone happen to pass, especially if you were stopped, you'd find yourself in his dust cloud, covered in a layer of road dust, spluttering and choking and with visibility reduced to nil. A good shower of rain would lay the dust and make life more comfortable, but at the same time might well convert the surface into a thin layer of slithery mud, almost as effective for uncontrollable skating as ice on tarmac!

Given these various potentials for disaster the cognoscenti would rarely set forth without a variety of items, such as a shovel, panga, spare petrol and water and a goodly supply of food, all intended towards simple self-preservation. In addition it was desirable to allow plenty of time. Indeed a couple of days with an overnight stop at the half-way hotel was often a wise planning precaution, especially during the rainy season. It was into this maelstrom of uncertainty that I pitched myself one day in February 1952. The weather was and had been dry and warm, the forecast the same. There was no reason to expect unusual difficulties. If I left at 7 am, I'd have 10 hours to do the 300 miles. Average 30 mph – should be no problem – in fact I'd more likely average 40 mph and be home before 3 pm. I phoned my wife the day before and assured her I'd be home at the latest by 5 pm.

I set off from Mombasa at 7 am, exactly to schedule. The journey went fine. I was in Voi by 9 am. 50 mph average. Fabulous. At this rate I'd be home for lunch. But I had a small job to do in Voi. No more than just a quick drop-in, I'd been assured. I dropped in. They were thrilled to see me. They'd got a serious instrument problem, they said, could I please take a look at it. I looked. They were right, they had a very serious problem. It needed over three hours of determined impatient struggle to get the thing working again, my mind throughout far more attuned to schedule than problem. But all things come to an end, and in due course, success achieved, I bade farewell and hurried to the hotel for a quick lunch. I was on the road again by 1 pm, 200 miles from home. I'd have to push hard to meet my 5.00 pm deadline.

I pushed hard. Police patrols on remote Kenya roads hadn't then been invented and there was little or no other traffic. The road over the Voi-Makindu section was wilder than before Voi – narrower, much more twisty and hilly and mostly with a bumpy, corrugated, loose murram surface. Being young and all alone I travelled in competitive mode. Accustomed to loose murram, a superb surface for drifting the car round sharp bends at speed, I made rapid progress, helped in no small measure by a succession of both intentional and unexpected skiddy thrills. I completed the 100 miles in just over two hours. This was so good it was almost unbelievable. I persuaded myself I'd meet my self-imposed schedule.

There was another visit to be made in Makindu where two lonely Africans of my Department worked from a small office. Luckily they had no problems and by 3.30 pm I was happily on the road again, revelling in speed, sunshine, and the optimistic determination to do the final 100 miles in an hour and a half.

I was busy revelling, and doing a sprightly 80 mph on a flat bit, when I spotted a length of wood on the road in front of me, obviously dropped from a passing truck. It had been broken in two, though the two halves were still joined. One half was lying flat on the ground, the other half was sticking up at about 45 degrees away from me. I saw it. I thought about it, all in the same flash, decided it wasn't harmful, and went over it. Bad decision. The bit sticking up hit the front of the car and went down flat, the bit lying flat pivoted upwards and there was the hell of a crash as it pierced my petrol tank. The car jerked to a sudden ragged stop. I happened to be looking at the petrol gauge at the moment of impact. It collapsed to zero in one fell swoop. My heart went with it. The ecstasy of life abruptly evaporated as I realised I'd been precipitated into the sort of predicament I daren't even dream about. My future had suddenly become decidedly uncertain, if not exactly desperate, and my schedule was all set to be upset. Getting away from here would be a problem. There was no telephone and little more hope of a tow than of Cinderella's coach arriving at midnight. I felt furiously unhappy.

In a quandary the wisest thing to do is think. I thought. Black thoughts. It seemed sensible to crawl under the car and have a look. I crawled, a dusty crawl, the back of my head scraping the ground, my nose wiping dust off the bottom of the petrol tank. Why can't cars be three feet off the ground? A piece of wood about 2 by 3 inches was stuck hard into the bottom of the tank. The other end was jammed so firmly into the road surface that I could only shift it by hammering hard with my shovel handle. I took off the tank, there seemed no point in leaving it there. The hole was frightening. The wood had struck the front corner of the tank and driven a hole through the bottom and the lower part of the front face. The edges of the hole were jagged metal bent into the tank. My grandfather would have said it was a 'fine how d'you do'. It was too.

In times like these human companionship is always helpful. I walked back to Makindu and was hot and dusty by the time I arrived. I consulted my staff but they could tell me nothing I didn't know. The next passenger train wouldn't pass by until the early hours of the following morning, but I might hitch an earlier freight train to Nairobi. Alternatively I could sit on the side of the road and hope to hitch a lift. I sipped some tea whilst one of my lads went to ask when the next freight train would appear. He came back in jubilant mood accompanied by a railway plumber who'd been dropped off an earlier train to do some work on the water tank. He was going to be picked up tomorrow. He had a soldering iron and some solder. Might he be of any use?

Would solder stick to petrol tanks? He didn't know, nor did I. There was only one way to find out. I borrowed a bicycle, returned to the car and, with the tank unsteadily balanced on the handlebars, took it back to Makindu. To repair the hole all we needed to do was solder another piece of metal over it. But I didn't have another piece of metal; nor did the plumber. We'd have to use what we had and all we had was the jagged metal bent into the tank. What could we do? We began to debate the question. Now Africans are good at debating. Give them an issue and they'll debate it non-stop, everybody having at least one say. That's why things often don't get done. The fun's in the debate, not the doing. So when the plumber and I began to consider how to get the jagged edges back together again, my two lads joined in, three or four railway workers came over, then a few of the folk living nearby. One man brought his wife and another brought a cow and a big talk ensued. Soon the wife fetched some home-brewed beer – *pombe* – and before long the debate began to get shrill.

Long before this stage, I'd decided that action was needed, not talk. So the plumber and I hack-sawed a big hole out of the top of the tank in order to get at the damage from inside. Then, using a length of wood and a hammer, we banged the metal back into shape until the jagged and torn edges more or less lined up. Some of the cracks were pretty wide and didn't look at all promising. Nevertheless we optimistically heated the soldering iron in an African cooking pot, fuelled by charcoal, and tried to run solder into the cracks, cheered on by the assembled community, now debating our chances of success. A lot of solder fell through the cracks and for some time the project didn't look at all hopeful but with persistence, spluttering and swearing the job eventually seemed to be finished. There was extreme tension when we put water into the tank. We all held our breaths. There was no leak. Encouraged, and by now semi-expert, we re-soldered back the bit we'd cut out of the top of the tank, no easy job this as it kept falling in, and then sat back and contemplated the achievement. The community, by now somewhat slurred in speech, cheered the success.

Fine, I now had a petrol tank. Unfortunately a petrol tank without petrol isn't a particularly useful possession. Maybe I could borrow some from a passing motorist, if there was one. We all went back to the car. I re-fitted the tank and tried to borrow some petrol. Time went by. No car passed. No borrowing was achieved. Even had a car stopped, there was no means of transferring petrol from his tank to mine unless he had a rubber tube, a somewhat unlikely possession, or a spare can. There didn't seem much cause for optimism.

But then, out of the blue, came sudden salvation; the cavalry galloping up. An African walked along the road carrying a bow, arrows and a guinea fowl. He stopped for a chat. He'd been hunting and had passed the camp of a white hunter some way back. He'd bet his guinea fowl there'd be plenty of petrol at the camp, and maybe I could buy some. I'd have to go along the road for a mile or two until I came to a deep dry stream bed, make my way up it for about a mile, and look for tents on the top of the slopes on the right. The going was pretty rough. I borrowed a bicycle from one of the group. It had no brakes and a chain that missed a beat once in every revolution. Still, the niceties of the Highway Code didn't seem appropriate in this situation, and I optimistically pedalled away, accompanied by a gaggle of merry supporters, some rolling about on bicycles and some on unsteady feet.

I was able to cycle along the road, brakes or no brakes, but I had to push the bike up the watercourse, struggling round enormous boulders, over sheets of shingle and up little dry waterfalls. I abandoned the cycle after a while and climbed. I made it in the end, too, though my supporters gave up. Maybe I'd had less *pombe* and more incentive. I found the white hunter and his clientele, all dressed up like white hunters and getting ready to go out on a shoot. I told my story. They said I looked a bit dishevelled and gave me a couple of strong whiskies, a four gallon drum of petrol and a hand back to the bicycle. Then I was on my own. Have you ever tried riding a cycle with no brakes down a rocky watercourse with four gallons of petrol balanced on the handlebars after about a tumblerful of whisky? Progress was exhausting and very erratic and I kept falling off.

Back at the car I tried to pour the petrol into the tank. It wasn't easy, the can gurgled and the hole wouldn't stay still. However, eventually much was in and at last I was ready for departure. I cycled back to Makindu where the community, still gathered in discussion and reminiscence, welcomed me with acclamation and something sobering to eat and drink. At last, bidding fond farewells to a now raucous assembly, fully convinced of its inventive engineering expertise, I trudged back to the car and set off, very gingerly, for Sultan Hamud, 50 miles away, where I could get more petrol. By now it was dark, but moonlit. I purposely ignored my decapitated schedule. No more speeding. I was too terrified my petrol tank might spring a leak and I'd have to start repairs all over again. I had a headache and tried not to sleep.

[After further incidents with an elephant and an impassable road-blocking truck, he eventually reached Nairobi early the next morning.]

OP 89 (April 2005)

On Being a Pacific Sea-Dog

by R E N Smith

I served in the New Hebrides Condominium from 1961-67, most of the time as a British District Agent for Central District Number One. Since the New Hebrides (now Vanuatu) is an archipelago of many islands, and since air travel was only just coming to them, most travel was necessarily by sea. To me, a native of an inland county in Britain, and a newcomer from an eleven year sojourn in a landlocked Nyasaland, the sea was a new experience, and one to be savoured to the full. There were numerous ships plying the New Hebrides waters, including the Messageries Maritimes *Polynésie* of happy memory, several trading ships, the British and French National Service vessels and finally the Condominium Joint Administration's own two touring ships, *Roçinante* and her newer rival, *Navaka*. The odd name of the former is due to her having been an intended companion to the *Don Quichotte,* a handsome almost yacht, which had proved a little fragile for the often turbulent waters of the group, and had been sold.

These two little ships, neither much over forty feet long, were extremely active and hard worked, not only taking the French and British District Agents about their duties, but also carrying departmental officers and various official visitors on theirs and in addition finding room for a modest amount of government cargo. Though the two worked at the same duties, they were considerably different, the one from the other, not only in design, but in style. The *Roçinante* was not in her first youth, and arrangements aboard were a little on the spartan side. The only accommodation for Condominium officers and their staff was a single cabin at the stern, about ten feet wide and long, containing five bunks, no cupboards, and a bottlegas domestic refrigerator whose fumes discharged at the level of an upper bunk, making it necessary for you to be careful which way your head lay. The dining area was just outside and consisted of a single bench the width of the ship with a table in front of it. The captain slept in the wheel-house / bridge, and the 'deck' passengers dossed down anywhere free from cargo or other clutter.

Navaka was fresh from her Australian builders, but had had an unusual problem on her trials. While she answered her helm well in one direction, on the other she did not. Her captain (Jack Barley) investigated and discovered that one of the steering arms fetched up against a traverse beam. In the carefree way of the time, a chunk was cut out of the beam, and the trials proceeded satisfactorily. She was slightly better provided for in accommodation than her rival, for she had a small dining saloon (with sleeping accommodation of sorts) but the one 'First Class' cabin was no more than about seven feet by five, so that with two bunks in it, you had great difficulty in dressing or undressing!

Each tour by sea started at five minutes to midnight; this was because the captain was paid £1 Australian per head per diem as a victualling allowance. If he sailed before midnight, that counted as a full day. On return, however, he always tried to arrive back at dawn, for whatever time he actually reached Vila he only received 10/ for that day. The system must have worked well enough, for Captain Guénet was able to build a small block of housing flats out of his pay. The departure of the BDA and / or FDA on tour was far from impressive – none of the clerks, cooks or servants, messengers and bevy of carriers and applause from the attendant multitude of my African days. You and your clerk rolled down to Vila wharf at about 11.30 pm, climbed aboard an apparently deserted ship, found a bunk and turned in. A few minutes later the ship came to life, all was bustle and away you went, ready for another island in the morning.

Going ashore at the various islands in the district was sometimes a little tricky, for as there were no jetties or wharves except in Vila, you had to use the tiny dinghy that each ship carried. This were driven by a small outboard motor (2½ hp I think) known, perhaps rather derisively, to my colleagues as 'Le British Seagull'. While these engines were reliable, they were not very powerful and you could spend an awful lot of time trying to find the landing place. Fortunately many of the New Hebrides islands were high ones, very steep too, and therefore one could get in fairly close with the ship, but there were exceptions. At Mataso there was a considerable reef, and in inclement weather the young men would wade out onto the reef up to their chests to grab the dinghy as it putputtered its way inshore. Being steep too was not always an advantage either, for Tongariki beach was not only steep, but made up of fistsized pebbles, which rolled up and down with the tide and waves. If you could not get into your boat easily, you would have to swim for it. Buninga, next door, was even worse, for the landing spot consisted of large boulders, each slippery and a trap for unwary legs. In spite of this my Waterloo came at Tongoa, where the beach was gently shelving. I went ashore in poor weather, the dinghy was upset, and I found myself being rolled upon by it, but I was younger then and no harm done!

The dinghy also served as the only method of unloading cargo, a long and tedious process, though sometimes assisted by canoes from the shore. Since it was so small, the skipper often had to use some ingenuity with his cargo. My colleague and I once went to Emai with a load of timber and aluminium roofing to build a clinic. This was to be on the weather side of the island, where four of the six villages lay, and there was no convenient beach and a difficult reef passage. This did not worry Guénet at all; he just made a raft of the timber, mounted the roofing on top and sent the dinghy off to tow it all inshore. There was an unhappy moment when the roofing shifted and started to tip up the raft and seemed headed for the reef below. It was saved by the swift and efficient action of Willie, a crew member, a villainous looking and indefatigably cheerful 'man bush' from Tanna. Without a second's hesitation he leaped overboard from the dinghy, swam to the raft and put his weight onto the side lifting it into the air, thus balancing the whole contraption and getting it ashore, only a little damp. Willie, not a man used to overmuch praise, basked in our gratitude and the clinic was soon built.

The British and French national services had their own touring vessels for the New Hebrides, but their usage was based on different attitudes. For us in the sixties there was the *Euphrosyne II,* a handsome sixty foot or so motor vessel, meant for the British Resident Commissioner and captained by Harry Kirkwood, retired from the Royal Navy after a long and distinguished career – he had been in charge of the base at Singapore and had commanded the *John Biscoe* in Antarctic waters. A hospitable and sociable man ashore, at sea he was a fierce stickler for discipline – the crew were always smartly uniformed and quick to obey orders, as indeed were the passengers. I rather think that in his heart, Harry felt that passengers aboard his ship should neither be seen nor heard, and while the Resident Commissioner found himself received with deference and courtesy, these were both rather formal, as if he were an admiral, unwillingly accepted on board a fighting ship. His presence was perhaps necessary, but could he not have picked another flagship? When entering Vila harbour, the crew lined the side in their best uniforms, and the officers saluting their distant masters – an event that on one occasion resulted in the ship bumping a buoy.

There was also a startling occasion when the helmsman walked away from the wheel at sunset one day; when Harry had recovered from his almost apoplectic fury he asked the miscreant the reason for this incredible behaviour, and received the improbable reply "But Sir, I am a Seventh Day Adventist, and it is now my Sabbath, so that I may not work." All the same, long after Harry had left the country, and even after independence, *Euphrosyne II* continued to ply the waters when most of her contemporaries were wrecks, a tribute to the high pitch of efficiency that Harry had inculcated in his crew. Not only that, but the hero of the wheel episode just mentioned, rose to command the ship! The *II* added to the ship's name commemorated her predecessor, the British Service ship of prewar days. This was sold on the orders of London, on the grounds that it was too expensive – a decision that effectively marooned all the British officials in the country. Without a ship they just could not do their job – apparently a matter of total lack of concern to the Colonial Office of those days.

Naturally it was impossible for French national pride to accept any position of inferiority, so they indulged themselves with two ships. One was the *Aquitaine*, a sleek custom built and fast ocean greyhound puppy. Before its arrival the French District Agent was wont to expatiate on its magnificence and virtues, most of them apparently due to his advice. After its arrival he invited me on an inaugural tour of the district with him. I will not call it a disaster for we did return safely, but *Aquitaine* was an unsatisfactory sea boat and extremely wet. The forecabin, where we slept, was stiflingly hot and if the skylights were opened was soaked with sea water at even a moderate speed. On top of that the seats and bunks were leatherette – hot, sticky and uncomfortable. I heard no more of the ship's virtues, and she was soon palmed off on the FDA at Santo. I trust that he was duly grateful.

About this time Vila was visited by a New Zealander with an old trading schooner, the beautiful and graceful *Trade Winds*. It took the acquisitive eye of the French Resident Commissioner, who summoned the skipper to his office and asked what he would take for the ship. This worthy, who had paid £7,000 (Australian) for the vessel quite recently, promptly asked £12,000. On observing that Delaunay did not even blink, he thought rapidly and added "Sterling, of course", which in those happy days was worth twenty-five Australian shillings, thus adding an extra 25% to the price. And so the deal was struck. The story and prices may be apocryphal, but were never denied by either side, to me at any rate. Delaunay may have paid rather a lot for the ship, but all the same she proved extremely useful. Whereas neither the *Euphrosyne II* nor the Condominium ships could carry much cargo, the *Trade Winds,* now renamed *Alize,* could manage about 70 tons. This was just what the French office needed, for after years of *dolce far niente* it was entering upon a programme of educational expansion into the outer islands, and *Alize* was perfect for this sort of work.

She was also a good ship to travel on, for there was a large 'owner's' cabin, a capacious saloon (with bunks) and a couple of single cabins, a little Victorian in their appurtenances, but entirely adequate, and she was as steady as a battleship. She is gone now, a total wreck on a northern island of Vanuatu, but her memory stays with me. I well remember how on one perfect evening, Michel Lajus and I, together with another French Office man, sat on the deck with our drinks and watched the sun go down in glory over a tranquil ocean.

The other fellow remarked with a contented sigh "Et on nous paie pour faire çela".

A week or two later Michel and I visited Emai aboard the Condominium work horse, the *Roçinante.* Our business demanded that we go ashore, even though dusk was upon us and the rain was pouring down; it did not help either that we were anchored a considerable distance from our intended landing spot. As we made our miserable way, squatting on wet seats in sodden discomfort, with Le British Seagull driving us along at a good two knots, Michel turned to me and solemnly intoned "Et on nous paie pour faire çela!"

OP 75 (Spring 1998), OP 76 (Autumn 1998)

By Motorcycle in Uganda

by S Nicholl

There was a time in my life when I thought I had premature Alzheimer's disease. The suspected affliction occurred during the time that my wife was pregnant with our first child. We lived at the time in a little town called Gulu in Northern Uganda and, during the pregnancy, I was the most absent-minded member of the Gulu community. To put it mildly, I was worried about my condition. In fact it had me worried stiff. A perversity of life of course was that the more I secretly worried, the worse the condition seemed to get. I was not to know then that many first-time expectant fathers tend to suffer from a variety of mental aberrations during their wives' pregnancies. Luckily the various symptoms seemed to disappear with the birth of the relevant child. Probably the most notable of my numerous lapses, during this period, resulted in an unwanted and unplanned motorcycle trip.

For the confinement my wife was to be admitted to the European Hospital in Kampala, Uganda's commercial capital. A couple of weeks before the expected event, on our doctor's advice, I took my wife to stay with some very good friends of ours who lived on a coffee estate near Kampala. They had kindly offered to do the needful, and take my wife to hospital at the required time. I then returned to Gulu to plot and plan a way to be in Kampala at the time of the great event. I had applied for some leave but 'sorry old chap, no reliefs available'.

My plan, which I thought foolproof, consisted of amassing long lists of required items of stores, repairs to vehicles, mechanical spare parts for maintenance of water supplies equipment, etc etc. Some of the instructions were deliberately ambiguous thus requiring my personal attendance at headquarters for the purpose of elucidation. However, I had forgotten the immortal words of Rabbie Burns 'The best laid schemes o' mice an' men gang aft agley.' Well, my plans certainly went agley. You see, quite often during this period, I absent-mindedly forgot that I was absent-minded.

A couple of days before parturition day, I left Gulu bound for Kampala, fully confident that little could go wrong with anything concerning me in the immediate future. The road from Gulu to Kampala in those days was dirt road all the way to the outskirts of Kampala. Something of an obstacle

221

on the journey was a poles-and-paddles pontoon ferry across the Nile about fifty miles south of Gulu. It was desirable, when intending to cross the Nile by this ferry, to arrive at the ferry early in the morning in order to be first to cross. This latter pre-emptive move reduced waiting time at the ferry in the blazing sun. It also reduced the time that one was exposed there to the hordes of malaria-carrying mosquitoes. It was therefore with a great feeling of optimism, that I left Gulu by lorry before dawn on that particular day and headed for the Nile ferry at Atura.

When we arrived at Atura we found to our delight that we were to be the first vehicle to cross that morning. However, my feeling of euphoria was soon to be brought to a grinding halt. As our lorry was negotiating the rickety ramp on to the pontoon of the ferry, I realised that I had left all my stores documentation back in Gulu. Panic.

"Quickly, driver, you and the turnboy help me to get the old motorcycle off the lorry. You then continue on to Masindi by lorry and wait for me there at the Rest Camp. I must return to Gulu by motorcycle for some papers that I have forgotten. I will rejoin you later today at Masindi."

A quick refuelling of the motorcycle from the drum on the back of the lorry, and then I waited on the north bank of the Nile while my lorry, on the ferry, set off across the wide river. Refuelling the motorcycle was not a problem as it was common practice in those days for lorries to carry a 44-gallon drum of spare fuel. This was because of the long distances often travelled in remote areas.

The motorcycle started after a few attempts and then I was on my way. Mindful of the importance of not having an accident, I was riding rather carefully. All went well for several miles and then I detected a faint intermittent jerking in the behaviour of the motorcycle. Reasoning to myself that there was nothing much I could do in the circumstances. I just kept going. Suddenly the rear wheel of the bike seemed to seize up and, as a result, I was thrown, arms and legs flailing like a discarded rag doll, into the long grass by the side of the road. My not-so-trusty steed lay nearby in a way that seemed to indicate that it had had enough of maltreatment and abuse.

As I lay there in the grass it suddenly dawned on me what the problem with the bike really was. Before leaving Gulu, we had emptied the fuel tank and drained the oil from the crankcase. At the ferry, however, we had only filled the fuel tank. For a few moments I scourged myself with a long stream of colourful and varied obscenities. When I had finished, it was then the turn of the poor innocent motorcycle to be the butt of my venom. A string of lurid invectives were launched at the now inert machine. I suggested to the poor wretched machine that certain of its integral mechanical parts would serve a better purpose if they were located somewhere in the lower reaches of a sick cow's bloated intestines. I further added that I hoped the said cow would be constipated.

Eventually good sense and reason returned. I got to my feet, rather painfully I might say, and lifted the bike to an upright position. The rear wheel refused to turn and I found my diagnosis to be correct; the engine had seized because of lack of oil in the crankcase. I then stood the bike on its stand as it didn't look quite so pathetic that way and settled myself by the side of the road to wait for assistance. It was probable that a north-bound lorry would eventually come from the direction of the ferry and, with a bit of luck, would have some spare engine oil; it was unlikely to have room on board for the motorbike.

After waiting for about half-an-hour or so, my patience started to wear a bit thin. My imagination too was becoming rather active, as I listened to a variety of sounds from the surrounding bush. It was after all, wild country. I decided to put the gear lever in neutral and try pushing the bike and perhaps make some forward progress. It worked. After about one mile at slow pedestrian speed I realised that, although it was better than sitting by the side of the road, it was not going to get me to Gulu in a reasonable time. It was then that I decided to see if the bike's engine would start. It did and I leapt on board and took off up the road, giving vent to my feelings with a loud rebel yell.

By freewheeling downhill and stopping when I felt the motorbike starting to jerk, I made quite a bit of progress. Eventually I came to a village and found an African gentleman there who had salvaged some old engine oil from somewhere, and kept it in a lemonade bottle for use on his bicycle. Gladly I paid him the price of a bottle of Dimple Haig for his bottle of oil and I felt I had got a bargain. I quickly filled the crankcase of the motorbike and completed the journey to Gulu without incident.

When I got to Gulu I was obliged to call at the PWD office to get the spare key to our house. Why? Well, you see I had put the key of our house in the glove box of the lorry and forgot it when I left the lorry at Atura. Suffice to say, I recovered my papers from the house, returned the key to the PWD, refused to answer the numerous queries re my appearance and, after checking the motorbike, headed for Masindi and the dubious comfort of the Rest House there.

The lorry was faithfully waiting in Masindi and after reloading the motorbike on board we called it a day. I had a bite to eat and went to bed. To say that I slept would be an inaccuracy; it was more like a coma. Next morning we headed for Kampala and arrived there without further ado.

Lorry, motorbike and requisitions etc were delivered to our headquarters. My boss perused the documents and then looked me in the eye. "I hope you are not in a hurry for this lot. It will take us about a week to complete everything." I looked him straight back in the eye and, hypocritical swine that I was, I said "That's okay. But don't keep me too long. I'm scheduled to go to West Nile District soon after I get back to Gulu."

During the week that I sojourned in Kampala, I visited my wife every day at the hospital. At the end of the week, baby Nicholl had still not arrived, and had overstayed his gestation residency by four days. He managed to extend this by a further six days before eventually making his arrival in the world. My wife still felt reasonably well and the doctor assured me that there was nothing to worry about. However time had run out for me. I had no option but return to Gulu.

Shortly after returning to Gulu, I went off to West Nile District as scheduled. I travelled there by the Northern route through Madi Sub-District which was subordinate to West Nile District. After a few days I eventually arrived in Arua, the principal town of West Nile District, and paid a courtesy call on the District Commissioner. We knew each other from my previous visits. After we had chatted for a while he remembered that he had a telegram concerning me.

"Sam", he said, "some good news for you. First of all, my congratulations. Your wife has given birth to a baby boy. Mother and child are both well. You may pick them up any time next week." I thanked him for the good news and stood up to leave. As I got to the door he said "Sam, there is something puzzling me. Why is it that you, being an enterprising chap, didn't wangle something so that you could be with your wife when the baby was born?"

OP 87 (April 2005)

The Silver Handshake

by J D Kelsall

In 1949 the Lake Victoria Fishery Service's first wooden motor fishing vessel, a 45 foot craft built in South Africa and shipped up to Mombasa and thence by rail to Kisumu for fitting out, had not long been commissioned and sailed down to Mwanza, Tanganyika, when the Chief Fisheries Officer, Lieut Cdr George Cole, RNR, decided that it would be interesting to pay a visit to the little-known Godziba Island. This lies in the middle of Lake Victoria, about half-way between Musoma and Bukoba, and is less than a mile long and half a mile wide. Being surrounded by deep water, it seemed likely that fishing might figure largely in the activities of the inhabitants, about whom nothing was known. Indeed it was not known for sure whether the island was still inhabited, although there was a report to this effect from a number of years previously.

So far as was known, the island had not seen a European since the beginning of the century, when Captain Whitehouse was carrying out the hydrographic survey of the Lake for the preparation of Admiralty charts. George Cole thus had no difficulty in persuading Jim Rowe, the Provincial Commissioner, Lake Province, and Jock Griffiths, District Commissioner, Bukoba, to accompany us on the safari to this remote and inaccessible outpost of their respective domains.

The voyage from Mwanza to Godziba Island took two days, with an overnight stop on the way, and we arrived during the afternoon of the second day. When we had anchored in the little bay on the west side of the island, a small, grossly over-loaded canoe put out from the beach and pursued a rather erratic course towards us. When it arrived alongside, Jock Griffiths leant over the side and greeted the occupants, telling them where we had come form, and explaining that we had brought their 'Bwana Provincial Commissioner' all the way from Mwanza for the first time ever, in order to visit them. This information produced howls of mirth and a torrent of comments in Luhaya, and several of the occupants of the canoe almost fell overboard in their convulsions of merriment. The PC grinned at Jock and remarked that he did not appear to be making much impression on his subjects. He then addressed the visitors and told them that the Bwana who had just been speaking to them was their District Commissioner who had come all the way from Bukoba to visit them, something which had never happened before. This statement produced even greater merriment and further comments in Luhaya. It was, in fact, very evident by now that the occupants of the canoe were, to a man, blind drunk. However, when the mirth had finally subsided, an elderly man in the stern managed, in spite of some alcoholic impediment in his speech, to convey to us that he was the island's Headman and that he would be very pleased to welcome us at his village at the north end of the island if we cared to come ashore the following morning.

We walked up to the village in the morning to find some 20 to 30 people – probably the entire population of the island – assembled outside the Headman's hut. We were warmly welcomed by a now sober, if somewhat hung-over, gentleman who introduced us to his wife and seated us outside the entrance to his hut.

An interesting *baraza* now took place, with information on various aspects of island life being provided and numerous questions being asked on life in the 'outside world'. We learned that the inhabitants were much occupied in fishing at certain seasons, and that they supported themselves on this and on the produce of their *shambas*. Contact with Bukoba, some 80 miles away, was very infrequent, normally being through the medium of sailing *karuas** which occasionally called in to buy dried fish. Very rarely, crossings were made by canoe in fair weather, but this was considered extremely hazardous, even in a sailing canoe – understandably, in view of the great expanse of open water, and the risk of sudden, violent squalls.

In the course of conversation, the PC mentioned that he would shortly be going on home leave, and might never have another chance to visit the island. At this point the Headman's wife disappeared into the hut, to re-emerge shortly and whisper something to her husband. He explained to the PC that she had been sorry to hear that he might never return, and she would like to make him a farewell present. This she did in a most courteous manner, presenting him with a silver shilling piece which, she explained to him, was 'to help him to have a good time while he was on holiday at home'.

I have never seen a more genuine and touching gesture. The widow's mite indeed . . .

OP 43 (April 1982)

---

*Karua – a small undecked open boat with lateen sail

Railways and Motive Power

by Don Owens

Had it not been for my RAF training as a Flight Engineer, East African Railways might not have selected me for special training in diesel electric traction, first at English Electric in Preston, then Napiers in Liverpool, Brown Boveri in Switzerland, British Railways Staff College in Derby, and Nairobi Polytechnic. This augmented ten years experience in various steam locomotive depots in East Africa, and with my name listed on 27 March 1959 in the register of the Institute of Locomotive Engineers in London as No 4398 D J Owens, AMILocoE, my transition from the steam to the diesel locomotive age was clinched in the mid 1960's with my promotion from Shedmaster to Diesel Motive Power Superintendent.

Kenya Colony was created in the 1920's out of undeveloped country through which the Uganda Railway tracks led to Uganda, and the railway was renamed the Kenya Uganda Railways and Harbours (KUR & H). Then in 1948 when the railway, road and marine services in Tanganyika were taken into the fold, the whole new system was named the EAR & H. This resulted in the need to reclassify and renumber the locomotives in each of the three territories, which presented some difficulties for many non-English speaking African drivers. For example, KUR & H locomotive No 162, stabled by its crew for overnight maintenance, was stripped of its former identity and fitted with the new railroad letters and number plates, making EAR & H No 2401. Imagine the crew's consternation when they signed on for duty next morning to find they were rostered to work 2401, and exclaimed "Where is our loco number 162?" As locomotive letter and renumbering progressed over the next few months, many African crews resorted to wrapping coloured rags around the boiler handrails to enable them to recognise their locomotive on renumbering.

Locomotive maintenance and boiler washouts, entailing a 16 to 20 hour period in shed, matched crew rest periods. This enabled us to allocate crews to locomotives on a permanent basis. Crews took great pride in their locomotives. The driver's cab would be scrubbed clean, copper pipes, brass control valves, and gauges would be highly burnished. The mechanical condition and external cleanliness of locomotives reflected the pride of the Shedmaster and his staff. A friendly inter-shed competitive

227

spirit existed between the sheds at Nairobi, Nakuru, Mombasa, Eldoret, Kampala, Kisumu, Tororo and Voi (Kenya and Uganda sheds listed in order of fleet size).

The long distance 'Top Link' trains carried two crews. One drove while the other rested in a specially fitted 'Caboose', which had bunk beds, showers and kitchen facilities. Crews were usually European or Asian drivers with African firemen, but gradually a few of the best African drivers got on the 'Top Link' work. After some six hours driving, the crews changed over, but to ensure all was well both crews would remain on the locomotive for some 15 to 20 miles to the next station stop. On the 40 hour Uganda Mail round trip between Eldoret and Kampala, there were two drivers who fell out with every driver they partnered, but I settled matters by rostering them to work together permanently as a team. I think they were scared of each other for they caused no further trouble.

Throughout the world there are many different gauge railway systems. America, Britain, Canada, most of Europe, Mexico and many other countries operate on standard gauge 1435 mm track. In the north and south of Africa they have a narrower 1065 mm gauge system which cannot be linked up with the even narrower 1000 mm gauge systems of Kenya, Uganda and Tanganyika – a major snag for Cecil Rhodes' dream of a Cape to Cairo Railway.

The terrain and rail gauges dictated the type of steam, diesel electric or electric locomotives best suited to the railway operators' requirements. On railways where there were no significant gradients, high speeds were achieved by conventional steam locomotives fitted with large diameter driving wheels. The UK railway races of the 1890s were won by locomotives with single 7 foot driving wheels, but for heavy loads maximum tractive effort required locomotives with four, six or eight driving wheels.

In the UK, high-speed trains had difficulty climbing up to the British rail summits of Shap (1,015 feet), Slochd (1,315 feet), and Druimuachter (1,484 feet), where their trailing loads of eight to ten coaches would pull their speeds down to 25 to 30 mph on the gradients. These UK summits are mere mole hills when compared with the Kenya line's 8,322 feet Mau Summit and 9,136 feet Timboroa Summit (highest altitude reached by any railway in Britain's former Colonial Empire), the former 495 miles and the latter 524 miles from sea level at Mombasa. Nairobi itself at 5,453 feet is 330 miles from Mombasa. To master the gradients on East Africa's metre gauge railway system, articulated Beyer Garratt locomotives with a tractive effort of 40,252 lbs and a weight of 138 tons were introduced in 1926. In subsequent years as traffic built up and the need for greater power arose, more powerful Garratt locomotives were introduced between 1939 and 1957, by which latter date the railway was operating 252-ton locomotives with a tractive effort of 73,500 lbs. Designated the 59 class, they were the largest in the world to operate on track gauges up to 1065 mm, and all 34 in the class were named after mountains in East Africa. They had a water capacity of 8,600 gallons and a furnace oil capacity of 2,700 gallons.

There were lots of Big Game incidents on the East African Railways. Two of many which occurred in my time as Shedmaster at Nakuru are worth recountimg. The first was circa 1955 and involved a lumbering old 52 class Garratt on the climb from Rongai to Visoi (rhino country). With a maximum trailing load the locomotive was struggling up the gradient at a steady 12 to 15 mph, impaired in its efforts by a leaking piston gland on the right hand lead engine which was emitting a periodic snorting squirt of steam with every revolution of the wheels. This noise attracted the attention of a rhino which charged out of the bush and followed the locomotive for almost a quarter of a mile, desperately lunging at the offending piston gland, until eventually tired and bleeding from the base of its horn, it gave up the fight.

The second incident circa 1956 took place on the down Uganda Mail en route Nakuru to Nairobi along the floor of the Great Rift Valley (giraffe country). I was on the footplate of the locomotive driven by the late Pete Harrison who invited me to take over for the next 20 mile section of line. We were doing about 45mph when two groups of giraffe emerged from the acacia trees where they had been browsing on either side of the line. Inevitably one group decided to amble across the rails to join the others, completely disregarding the speed of the approaching train. If Pete had been driving he would have made a gradual brake application, mowing through them as he brought the train to a gradual stop. (Game Department laws required locomotive crews to report all giraffe deaths on the line and produce evidence by cutting the tails off all dead giraffes). But Pete was not driving, and yours truly slammed the steam regulator shut and threw on a full emergency application of the brakes. I stopped the train without killing any of the animals, but I cannot commit Pete's language to print as he mentioned something about it being lunch time, and my sudden stop would have had the soup course sliding off the tables in the dining car and on to the laps of an irate bunch of passengers.

In the early 1960s the massive 252-ton 59 class locomotives ceased to work Mombasa / Nairobi / Nakuru trains, which were taken over by the newly arrived 1800 hp Diesel Electric locomotives built by English Electric in the Dick Kerr and Vulcan works in Lancashire. These new D/E locomotives, designated the 90 class, were vulnerable to head-on contact with big game – giraffe, elephant and eland – and impact at speed with any of those would dent the front nose compartment, breaking internal air pipes, electric conduits and severing control circuit wires. This resulted in a total failure of the locomotive, and the all important passenger train having to be rescued by commandeering a locomotive from the nearest freight train. This problem was overcome when the locos were fitted with the Owens designed giraffe guards, formed from ½" steel plate. Kenya trains killed big game at the average rate of a giraffe every six weeks, an elephant every six months, and the rarer eland once a year. Smaller game kills were not reported. These were the statistics before poachers began decimating herds, but still current in 1973 when after 25 years service, I opted for premature retirement on offer to all designated officers of HMOCS, and took up an appointment with Bombardier/MLW in Montreal (leading to other assignments in the railways of Jamaica, Greece, Sri Lanka, Bangladesh and Canada).

OP 83 (May 2002)

Part 4
DOMESTIC

The Lap of Luxury

by R E N Smith

It is now the established and unquestioned belief amongst the British public and intellectuals of all varieties and nations, that not only were wicked colonialists conscienceless oppressors of the poor, but also that they lived in the lap of luxury such that they, as really mere lower-middle class *arrivistes,* could not otherwise have contemplated in their most technicolour dreams. This belief is not entirely new, for in 1949 we First Devonshire Course neophytes, peacefully pursuing our studies at LSE and SOAS in London, were often greeted with the derisive hail of 'White Masters' from the more radical of the students there. I still remember the horrified incredulity with which a group of these gentry greeted the arrival of John Pepys-Cockerell, immaculately clad as if for the city.

Arriving in Nyasaland in January 1950 I spent my early months in a one-roomed Tobacco Buyers' office (with no facilities) on Famine Relief before going to my first district station. This was Port Herald, whose sonorous and historical name has now been replaced by the more Malawian one of Nsanje. This will not have changed the climatic conditions – it was extremely hot, humid and cursed with a remarkable variety of insect pests, all distinguished by size, persistence and ferocity. It was no more than 150 feet above sea-level and 150 miles or so from the sea, with a vast swamp on the other side of the Shiré river, on whose right bank it stood. I can only hope that the housing conditions have changed for the better, for in my time these were simplicity itself. Even though as Assistant District Commissioner – a grandiose title for a brand new probationer chicken just out of the egg – I was allotted a large and imposing two-storied house; it had just four rooms plus an outside toilet. I shared it with the Assistant Superintendent of Police, the Rhodesia Native Labour recruiter, and at night, the Customs Officer. This unusual arrangement came about because the last-named was awaiting his decree absolute, and to avoid putting it in jeopardy, since he had his lady love living in his own house, came over after dinner and slept in our joint living room. I cannot remember if the country sported a King's Proctor, but if we did, this simple system foiled him, for it was a legal dogma that adultery could only take place at night.

Thus I had just the one room to myself and here I kept my state – a bed with skin thongs and a lumpy kapok mattress, a Roorkee (collapsible – and it was) chair, a canvas-covered camp table, and a side-board/bookcase/drinks cabinet-cum-whatnot made by piling empty petrol boxes on their sides. The boxes had previously contained two four-gallon flimsy cans for petrol but were now a major element in our living; there were stacked boxes in my room for clothes, books and other valuables. I had lids put on several and these contained all my gear from pots and pans to food, clothes, grog, for *ulendo* (safari). Another had side doors and folding legs and held paperbacks and my one great luxury, the famous 'saucepan' radio. Central African veterans will remember these hardy and useful wirelesses, conceived as a cheap means of receiving news and music for villagers, and sold in vast numbers; they were indeed built inside 'saucepan' shaped containers and made one's lonely tent on *ulendo* seem in touch with the world – even if it was only Radio Lusaka.

Modern political correctness will undoubtedly contrast my lordly state most unfavourably with the miserable and abject poverty of my oppressed subjects in their mud huts, but in fact these buildings were little, if at all, inferior to my single bare room and sparse furniture. A 'mud' hut is a more sophisticated and solid construction than the title indicates, for it is not mud, but wattle and daub, and is similar to those buildings that housed my Anglo/Saxon-Celtic-Welsh peasant ancestors for centuries, and where they bred, lived, brought up their families (and often the livestock) and died in conditions that they probably considered to provide a reasonable and cosy familiarity.

There were other snags with home-making. Not long after my arrival in Port Herald we were blessed with a brand new experiment, in the form of an Agricultural Supervisor. This was a large and innocent young man named Mike, even newer to Africa than me. Before leaving England he had been assured that he would be provided with a house, but on arrival what he actually received was a sum of money and instructions to build himself one. In order to have somewhere to put his Government refrigerator (kerosene), bed, table and chair as well as himself, he started off with the kitchen, which was a small separate building from the house. For the time being his cook had to make do with a thatched shelter and a fire amid some stones. Mike also had to arrange the making and burning of the bricks, and to this end he had a large clay pit excavated. Whilst doing this he heard a commotion among his workmen and went to investigate. They were all highly agitated and pointed to a large snake they had unearthed. In his virginal innocence, Mike promptly picked it up and turned to his men for its identification. Finding himself suddenly alone, he walked over to his kitchen to ask his cook. That worthy took one horrified look and not being able to get past Mike, crashed out through the wall. Putting the creature in a sack, Mike sent it to the camp of a Game Department man, a keen herpetologist, who sent a note of thanks, adding that he hoped Mike had not tried to handle it. Apparently a burrowing viper (for such it was) possessed the ability, unique among snakes, of being able to strike backwards over its own head – and even skilled and devoted snake lovers were reluctant to handle it.

My next palace was the District Commissioner's house in Chikwawa. The proper incumbent had gone sick, and for a glorious few weeks I was elevated into the position – at no extra pay, of course. The house, however, had lost its former good size and status, for it had been perched on the cliff edge above the Shiré river, and as the river had progressively undermined the cliff, it had had to be demolished. My house was built from the salvaged materials and consisted of two long high thatched buildings, with a verandah for sleeping on, for Chikwawa was as hot and sticky as Port Herald.

I moved from Chikwawa to the sub-district of Mwanza, where once again any incipient delusions of being of a superior clay to the local population were soon dissipated. This time I had a 'bush-house', and any officer who served in Nyasaland at this time will remember these misbegotten constructions. Allegedly designed by a qualified architect, who allegedly never had to live in one, these creations boasted two modestly sized rooms – living room and bedroom, joined at one side by a miniature dining room, and on the other by the bathroom and loo. For some highly technical reason the room farthest from the (outside) kitchen was the dining room, so that to avoid continually falling over the Bwana and his guests (if any), food had to be brought through the bathroom and bedroom to reach it, while the loo access from the living room was through the dining room and bedroom. Being then a bachelor, I was comfortable enough, but in Zomba and other metropolises families were expected to occupy these huts – and huts they were, being often thatched.

On my first leave I married and brought my bride to our first house, down in the Shiré Valley below Zomba at the lonely Land Settlement station of Chigale – hot, malarial and on the wrong side of a deep (in the rains) stream. The two 'officer' type houses had been built in the usual confident if unskilled manner by a previous Land Settlement Officer (we were jack of all trades – with the inevitable corollary), and were the essence of simplicity – living room, dining room and bedroom all in a straight line and with bathroom attached to the bedroom. This latter had been built over a not properly filled-in well, and its bricks sagged dangerously outwards. This was no problem and was easily solved by a brick buttress suitable for a modest sized cathedral. The kitchen was some distance away, on the far side of the road leading to the next door house, again no problem as no-one lived there. The house chimney was also simple – it just went straight up so that at midday there was a bright patch of sunlight at the bottom. This too did not matter, as I never had occasion to indulge in a fire. There was a store-room attached to the house, which had been the abode of a spitting cobra until Tony Smith, my predecessor, had been temporarily blinded by it.

Not long afterwards we found ourselves, via a thatched house on a prison farm and a nicer one-and-a-half bedroom one in Zomba, once again on our own, at the sub-district station of Kasupe, where the house (formerly in part the post office) had a beautiful site on a col between two mountains. It was, therefore, on the main route of wild animals in their travels, and there were plenty of them, even though we were no more than thirty miles from Zomba, the then capital. We were often regaled by the grunts and roars of itinerant lions – romantic Africa at its best – if one's security had been better than the mosquito-wire-gauze doors that our bedroom sported in hot weather. Water was a problem, only solved by my messengers catching enough tax defaulters to supply a work force to hump an old 44-gallon container (cut in half) up the hill from the well in the *dambo* (marshy area). This house had another 'first', for its septic tank had been recently installed, but as the house was built on solid rock, the tank had to be above ground, and one's first sight of the house was of this fine and impressive concrete construction, standing several feet in the air and all but alongside the front path and steps to the house. Luxury was lacking, but all the same we spent three very happy years at Kasupe.

And so our luxurious progression went on. In twenty five years we had about twenty houses in three different territories, and while the houses were adequate enough, none was ever really suitable for grinding the faces of the poor or lording it over anyone. British colonial standards in the Pacific when we went there in 1967 were modest, even by the poverty-stricken standards of Nyasaland. They had been much grander in India, but while the Heaven-born members of the Indian Civil Service (in its upper ranks at least) had had to maintain a certain dignity, we lesser lights of a newer and more plebeian service were permitted no such prestige fashions.

In the New Hebrides we occupied a ramshackle and elderly wooden 'colonial' Pacific affair, square and hot, where the central rooms were almost too stuffy for human endurance and we slept, ate, dined and wined on the filled-in all-round verandah. Since the childrens' bedroom's only window was immediately above our own bed, my wife and I led a rather public private life. The house survives to this day – as the Women's Interests Office. There were a few more modern houses, but they were uniformly undistinguished in size and appurtenances – a separate dining room was unheard of, apart from the houses (grandly named Monument and White House) of the two senior British Office administrators.

I finished up in the Gilbert and Ellice Islands, where for many years after the war the country had been run by a former naval officer with a strong personality and an economical soul. By this time I had reached advanced years and some dignity as the Senior District Commissioner, but I still only qualified for a standard 'B' grade house – two bedrooms and a large living/dining room, the rooms separated by soft-board partitions (soft-board meant that you could poke your finger through it). In all the older 'B' grades, the house was thatched, but my elevated rank was recognised by the provision of a soft-board ceiling. This was not an unmixed blessing, for since the PWD only renewed the pandanus thatch when daylight and rain broke through, the ceiling was marked by circular brown stains accompanied by an ominous sagging of the soft-board and the room looked rather seedy. These houses had been built when officers were not encouraged to have families and two bedrooms presented a problem if your family, like mine, included adolescent children of both sexes. This is where the elevated status bit came in handy at last, for the District Commissioner was actually provided with a separate guest-house – a bedroom with loo and shower attached. You just had to try to avoid having official guests during the school holidays.

In a country distinguished by incessant heat under a blazing sun the provision of a covered verandah was rare, unless you paid for it yourself. I managed to 'bounce' Authority into approving a verandah at the DC's house, provided that the work was carried out at minimum cost, achieved by an arrangement with the Betio Town Council, whose chairman was the District Commissioner. In my final year when the District Commissioner was abolished (and the district run from the Secretariat) I was promoted out of harm's way to be Secretary (for Natural Resources) under a Minister whose previous official contact with me was when I had fined him for causing a disturbance in a police station! To mark my rise in importance I was allotted a new two-storied house in an obsolete cemetery; it still had only three bedrooms and a living-dining room and no covered verandah. Quite unofficially I prevailed on the Betio Town Council, which was no longer under my control, to put up a good thatched lean-to verandah, while my family and I humped coral and sand and water, mixed concrete and laid a proper verandah under the thatch.

There were only three grander official houses in the entire colony – two 'A' grades, for the Chief Secretary and the Attorney-General (they actually boasted an en-suite bathroom for the occupants) and the Residency itself. This was not much more than a larger version of the 'B' grades. It was distinguished by being blessed with a huge reception/dining room, but the building was thatched and did not even sport a covered verandah, which is perhaps why the Resident Commissioner was not too keen on my efforts to get one for a mere District Commissioner. When the colony was separated from the Western Pacific High Commission in January 1972 the Residency was upgraded to a Government House, but it had no improvements added. It was just the old building re-christened.

Looking back over a highly varied career, the most resplendent accommodation I ever had in my overseas service was in Government House, Cuttack in the province of Orissa, when I was Aide-de-Camp to the Governor there in 1946-47. This establishment was only modestly grand, having been upgraded from a mere Commissioner's bungalow about five years earlier on the promotion of Orissa from a Commissioner's bailiwick to a full blown Governor's province, but in the 19th century even Collectors and Commissioners had of necessity to present a lordly façade. After all, quite minor Indian potentates had palaces. I lived with my master and his lady in this graceful pillared and porte-cochèred Government House, with a suite of my own – an enormous bedroom with attached bathroom and a large office/sitting room, where, promptly at 6pm every evening, a soft-footed, white-clad and gold-badge blazoned *khitmutgar* brought me a silver tray on which reposed a small decanter of Scotch, soda water, ice and a glass. Now that was the lap of luxury.

OP 83 (May 2002)

A Nigerian Garden

by Muriel Barnett

When first I went to live in Southern Nigeria in 1937 my most outstanding impression of the landscape was the monotony of the dull green of the trees. Strange too was the lack of seasonal changes. Except for the heavy rains in March, there was heat night and day. Seeds sprouted whatever time of the year one entrusted them to the soil, provided one kept them well watered. The sight of the ubiquitous palm tree brought little joy. All year round its lower branches hung bedraggled, while its topmost ones reared clownishly erect. Providentially other trees were kinder to the European eye, displaying vivid red-gold blossoms like the umbrella-shaped flamboyant tree.

Gardening in Nigeria is not so much the art of encouraging things to grow as of preventing the unwanted from taking over. Wooden fences, even telegraph poles, have been reported to take root on occasion. Making a hedge is a simple affair in Southern Nigeria. One just shoves short rough cuttings of African prickleless holly criss-cross into the ground. I used to feel sorry for the slender cassia trees which reproduced themselves so fast they were viciously hacked down to provide a daily supply of firewood for the kitchen stove. Three colours of bougainvillaea cascaded over the balustrade of our verandah. The usual purple, the dramatic crimson and the rarer coral pink. At times before its pruning we seemed to be living in the Palace of the Sleeping Beauty. Some Europeans had all ground-vegetation scraped off round the house to create a sandy weedless desert, while others cultivated a carpet of runner-grass to protect their eyes from the harsh glare of red laterite.

Except in the forest where rotting leaves yield rich humus, continual cropping tends to exhaust the soil, so that while plants may grow fast they are far from Chelsea Flower Show standard. The same can be said of the local fruits. Cucumbers mature rapidly to produce comparatively tasteless fruit which during the night is often rendered useless by nocturnal insects munching over them haphazardly. Lettuces run to seed, never heart, their leaves drooping floppy as a Dali watch. Tomatoes grow swiftly but have none of the tangy flavour of the Scottish variety. Grapefruit trees bear large green-skinned spheres which taste sweeter than any we could buy from the greengrocer at home. Mangoes are plentiful but have a turpentinish flavour and were not eaten by Europeans, but the avocados and the soursops – although they did not look like our peaches and strawberries – tasted not unlike them. Bananas and melon-shaped paw-paw grew in profusion, as well as coconuts, but not apples nor pears; and how one longed to sink one's teeth into a crisp apple or a well-ripened plum.

Having to move house at short notice often prevented colonial gardeners from embarking on elaborate schemes. Besides, frequent house reallocation discouraged ownership of heavy tools such as lawn-mowers. Trimming the rough lawn was referred to by the garden-boy as 'barbing de grass', which entailed taking savage swipes at it with his machete. If one craved flower beds then trenches had to be dug two feet deep ready for an infill of fertile black earth fetched from the forest by one of the garden-boys using a head-pan for lack of a wheel-barrow. Every evening it was his task to water the flower-beds using water in buckets from the stand-pipe at the kitchen doorway, which he scattered by means of a raggedly perforated cigarette tin. Such was the strength of his habit that even in the torrential rains of March he would keep up this routine in the late afternoon.

Plants and seeds brought hopefully from Britain seldom arrived in Nigeria in good condition, since once the ship reached the heat of the tropical latitudes they tended to deteriorate beyond redemption. One friend of ours created a garden with nothing but blue blooms. And a great success he made of it, although he was telling no secrets! Many people managed a creditable show of colour using plants such as scarlet zinnias and balsams as well as deep red canna lilies.

Our compound in Yaba, six miles north of Lagos, grew from its sandy desert six varieties of hibiscus shrubs of different colours. One of them put on a show which seemed pure magic. I would gather a bowlful of its white blossoms in the afternoon, keep it in the fridge and place it in the centre of the dining-table just before guests sat down to dinner. As we munched our way through the courses, we would be granted a magic exhibition. Its colour change would range from white through pink to deep red by the time we were drinking coffee.

I have pleasurable memories of the cool-looking ice-plant and pink oleander as well as blue morning glory – no association with the drug scheme in those days – which climbed the wall on one side of the kitchen door. It jostled with another creeper with feathery leaves and bright scarlet flowers whose name I never managed to discover. At the lower end of the garden a massive magnolia covered itself with cream-tinted flowers in the evening. The door at the front of the house was flanked on one side by dutchman's pipe and on the other by my great joy the moon-flower. It has often been said that West African flowers lack scent, but the moon-flower puts paid to all that. Its delicate perfume is out of this world. At dusk, especially at the time of full moon, I would stand in front of it watching its buds slowly unfold like a rapid-camera film presentation. Once its white saucer-sized flowers opened to their fullest extent, they exuded an exotic perfume, which pervaded the house for the rest of the night. In the morning its dead petals drooped fawnish yellow. Nonetheless the show was put on again the following evening. Many times I think how fortunate I am to have experienced the magic of the African moon-flower.

We were posted for a short time to Northern Nigeria in 1942 while my husband was seconded to the Royal West African Frontier Force. There our garden presented us with an enormous delight. It was alive, friendly and had the most lovable of garden inhabitants, a reddish-coloured rhesus monkey. He slept at night in some secret place and played in our garden during the day. We christened him Archibald.

One of my self-imposed duties was to change the flowers and the water in the vases every day to prevent the spread of mosquitoes. As soon as Archibald saw me approaching with the secateurs in my hand he would run to meet me and hold up his hand for me to take as I would a child's. Then he would lead me down the path and point out to me what he considered the brightest blooms. And I would go along with his choice. Sometimes a particularly pleasing spray would be at the end of a tree-branch beyond my reach. So Archibald would let go of my hand, shin up the tree and gingerly ease his way along the slender branch so that his weight brought the prize within my reach. I would hold on to it and give him time to streak back to safety before I applied the secateurs. Then he would leap to the ground, take my hand and escort me back to the house. Archibald seldom entered our living quarters although I once caught him sitting at my writing-desk examining a lead pencil with wondering eyes and inquisitive fingers. He split it down the side seam, then threw it to the ground. Nothing magic about it, his expression said.

We had to leave the house hurriedly when our turn for a passage home by boat came our way. We couldn't take Archibald with us, but that was no problem. Archibald watched us go sitting half-way up our acacia tree.

He made it plain he was not leaving 'his' garden. We heard two or three years later that Archibald had been found one morning at the foot of the magnolia tree stretched out peaceably in his final sleep.

OP 85 (April 2003)

It's a Dog's Life

by Duncan D McCormack

By early 1958 all was ready for the great Kenya adventure; medicals, the rather disconcerting interview with Lord Cobham at Government House in Wellington, letter of appointment from London, car sold, packing and personal arrangements completed, but what about the dog? Ruff had come to us eighteen months earlier, wandering in off the road as a nervous, hungry stray with a frayed rope around her neck. Slowly built up to health and trust, we'd become inseparable. She couldn't fly with us from Auckland; in those days the flight took a full week via Sydney, Melbourne, Perth, Cocos I, Mauritius, Johannesburg and Salisbury to Nairobi, with six one-night stopovers. So we put her on one of the Royal Dutch Interocean Line freighters that travelled about the globe, assured that she would be well cared for in her kennel on deck. As a typical New Zealand farm dog, an Alsatian-beardie cross, we were confident she had the hardiness to survive the voyage. Our flight was not without incident, with mechanical problems out of Cocos, violent thunderstorms at Mauritius and, finally, arrival at the newly opened Embakasi Airport a day late and no one to meet us. Fortunately, an Asian clerk from Survey of Kenya had gone out for a look at the new facility and reacted to our paging. The first weeks in Nairobi passed in a blur; introduction to Survey of Kenya, tentative trips up the Rift Valley to other newly-arrived Kiwis at Nakuru, the new excitements of Africa.

Then the message to say Ruff's vessel had finally reached Mombasa, via eight or nine Australian and African ports along the way. Our shiny new little VW Beetle was to be tested on the ever-changing conditions of the 300 mile Mombasa Road. First traverses are always the most memorable; out of Nairobi before first light, a pause beyond the tarmac's end at Athi River on the plains for a roadside thermos of coffee, the rolling landscape full of game and wild flowers from the first touch of the long rains which heightened that magic, and the heady smell of damp earth and animals. Then the brilliant glitter of mica schist on the murram road and the diabolical, rocky surface before Sultan Hamud, strewn with troops of baboons and massive elephant dung. Finally, out onto the plains, the teeth-rattling corrugations ineffectually swept by a tractor towing a large thornbush, on past the Teita Hills and Voi, southeast to the beginnings of narrow tarmac at Mariakani, the start of villages with goats, chickens and laden women on the road, coconut palms, the hot, steamy mashed-potato smell of approaching sea – the Coast, Mombasa.

After a night in the old Tudor House Hotel on the Island, we drove down Kilindini Road through the arched tusks next morning and found our vessel. The huge, jolly Dutch skipper welcomed us aboard where Ruff was beside herself in welcome, no doubt having given up hope on the tossing ocean and during the long tedium of ports. We were treated to a marvellous luncheon of sauerkraut, sausage, potato and Amstel. Over coffee and cigars the skipper said "She would have died on deck. She's spent the voyage here in my quarters behind the bridge. Don't forget, she now has warm coffee with a little sugar mid-morning and she shares my meals."

Our euphoria turned to emptiness when we finally bade farewell and the captain, tears streaming down his weathered face, made a last plea for us to leave him Ruff as a ship's dog.

Then her real adventures began – a dog's first sight of antelope, warthog, baboons, elephant and all else Africa had to offer. Even before leaving Mombasa, she was pelted with small green mangoes thrown with unerring aim by the resident monkeys at Tudor House (they'd thrown none at us earlier). Unlike colleagues, we were never pole-fished and our car was never interfered with. If we stopped at some distant, remote spot and the normal knot of children materialised from the bush we were never crowded. Ruff simply silently retracted her upper lip to reveal a smile of formidable canines, tail still wagging. Over the years she traversed the Rift Valley from the heat of Magadi, the craters of Suswa, Longonot and Menengai, splashed in Lake Victoria, camped at Lake Baringo and put up half a million flamingos at Nakuru with a few barks.

She had only just reached her prime when the winds of change were at full blast throughout Africa. To my later regret I opted out. With ageing parents in New Zealand, the only way to get Ruff home was via quarantine in UK, then by sea to New Zealand. So she flew off to London ahead of our leave to a kennel in Mill Hill. Arriving by sea early in the bitter January of 1962, our car slung off and eventually started, we headed for a B & B we knew off Edgware Road, then drove out to pick up the dog. We were in need of a flat for the several months before we were due to sail for Wellington, and a large dog didn't help matters. We located an ideal one very near Wimbledon Common, but the owner insisted on seeing the dog. I guess my wife and I also had to pass muster. That evening we drove to a quiet mews off Bayswater Road, to be ushered in to an Aladdin's Cave of luxurious carpets and vases that looked suspiciously Ming. The landlord stood erect and dapper in reefer jacket and regimental tie beside an extremely stern old mother. Ruff sat obediently beside me, while they appraised this large hairy animal of very dubious lineage. We assured him she only barked when she had to. Then, as if on cue, Ruff rose, crept across the carpet, tail and ears down, and gently licked their hands. We were in!

For a few months, sporting 'Visitor to Britain' bumper stickers which helped with minor parking infringements, we frequented the City and West End where Ruff, guarding the car, became a familiar to the beat policemen who were very impressed with her teeth on approaching the car. She slithered on icy ponds on the Common, chasing ducks, barked at the winter kite-flyers and visited the Keeper of the Common's cottage. Derek had been a boyhood neighbour of mine in Auckland. It was an anticlimax on arrival in Wellington after a 34-day voyage from Tilbury via Curacao, Panama and Tahiti when no one asked to see Ruff's quarantine papers until we finally proffered them. She lived with my parents for our final short tour of Kenya. Then again in 1966-67, when I returned to Kenya for the New Zealand Government. Back in Wellington when Ruff was 13, one day she failed to rise to my call, only the eyes flickered. I held her paw while the vet injected her, and as she slipped away, it was as if the whole African adventure was finally laid to rest; the heat, the safaris, tick fever, tongue bitten by *siafu* (soldier ants), chasing crabs at dusk on Malindi Beach. *Kwaheri,* Ruff – you did well.

OP 85 (April 2003)

Mail Day

by James L O Tedder

In the Solomon Islands as with many other parts of the world where the Colonial Service was stationed, there were many variations of waiting for the mail. It was an important event particularly for the wives who didn't always have a busy work schedule, and who hadn't left home so long ago. Then there were the old timers who were at home where they were, and didn't care for mail to remind them of a different life, or who had such long intervals between mails that it was no longer looked forward to, if it had been more regular. Of course mail days also in the outstations meant that the audit queries, the judicial comments on the last few months of court work, and the usual impossible requests from the Secretariat arrived as well as the personal mail.

In Honiara in the 1950s the plane arrived every fortnight via Papua New Guinea in the late afternoon. The new arrivals in the islands would be seen gathering outside the post office before the truck had arrived from the airstrip. People with longer residence would turn up just as the mail was being thrust into the boxes. Then many adjourned to the club to read their mail and some even to pen replies. Others rushed home to enjoy their mail in peace, and do their replies before morning, when the mail closed at some very early hour before the plane flew back along the islands to Papua New Guinea and connect with the rest of the world.

To those living in the outstations this mail ritual was not so serious or, if serious, it was not on a regular basis. Mail flowed to the outstations as and when a ship went that way, and if the ship's bosun managed to remember to notify the post office that he was sailing. Some forgot or went off in another direction and ended up by chance at a post office in the outstation without mail.

Even given these problems there were other obstacles for people to receive their mail, whether they were villagers receiving news from their relatives in Honiara, or expatriates dreaming of 'home'. Many of the locally originated letters were addressed in rather a perfunctory manner, with a name, a village and the island. But sometimes the village name was one that had been applied by the Church, and what many knew as Forte was actually St Johns. It took a lot of skill on the part of the outstation postal clerk, who often came from a different language group, to decide where the letter was to be delivered. If the District Officer was taking the mail with him on a tour, he had to go over the mail with the clerk for instructions as to where the letters were to be delivered.

Then the actual physical nature of the islands added their difficulties. Sometimes the rivers were up, and the district tour diverted, so those letters were either left at another village to be delivered by the headman or medical assistant or some other person later in the week. How many letters did not reach the recipients is not known, but there were few complaints about the mail service. In any case news would travel by word of mouth as well, and this was always reliable even if the text was sometimes garbled.

For an expatriate living on the outstation there was less trouble in the addressing, but just as much as in the delivering. Malu'u was an outstation in the north of Malaita and some 50 km from the 'capital' at Aoke. Just to ensure that the District Officer Malu'u had something to do when not touring, the District Commissioner sent a weekly police patrol north to a half way point where the constables exchanged the mail bag with a patrol from Malu'u. So audit queries and requests for information reached the District Officer within a day of the mail closing at Aoke. At times, if a ship had brought mail from overseas via Honiara, then the District Officer might also receive air letters. Parcels and any large letters were not carried by the patrol which had to travel fast, both sections doing the 50km trip in the day. The patrols were also useful in that people could send in their complaints and worries once a week, and the presence of the police helped to ensure law and order. Such patrols did not always meet up. Many times the rivers were up, and even the strong constables thought twice about crossing a really high river.

District ships were not always available, either taking officers on tour in another direction or sitting at Tulagi, the marine base, awaiting their regular check-up, or even having been borrowed by other districts. There were two ships stationed on Malaita. One was the *Margery*, a 20m vessel, apparently built for the US Armed Forces on a tug design. It looked as a small ship should look, carried a lot of ballast and even rolled like a ship. It operated out of Aoke, with the District Commissioner deciding on the programme, which was made up also to suit other officers, such as the Medical Officer and Agricultural Officer, who wished to tour to various parts of the island. The post office was always informed of its ETD and when mail could be expected at Malu'u and places all round the island.

The second ship was a 12m ketch stationed much of the time with the District Officer Malu'u who used it for touring. It made some trips to Aoke for medical cases, or to collect supplies, transport prisoners and, of course, it always carried mail.

Kira Kira on San Cristobal (Makira) was further away from Honiara than Aoke and received fewer ships – except in the calmer periods when there would be a rash of officers from Honiara on a 'swan' – so mail was less frequent. Sometimes the occasional trading or recruiting ship would bring mail, but that could be infrequent. If the district ship *Mary,* similar to the *Margery,* had been on a freight and passenger run to Honiara when the ship from Australia was due, there was always the excitement that surface mail with papers and parcels and grocery supplies would arrive.

The cry of 'sail ho' always went up on the district station when a ship was sighted. As the *Mary* was expected mid-morning at Kira Kira after its 18 hour journey from Honiara, people were standing by so it was no surprise when a labourer looked up from his grass cutting and gave the shout. Now there was an hour for the station foreman to arrange for the prisoners and station work-force to assemble and launch the work-boat, for the works foreman to bring down the tractor to collect the cargo, and for some excitement to build up. People were always expecting relatives or cargo, or it was just fun to learn at first hand from the boat's crew what had been happening in the 'big smoke' after two months without 'real' news. So excitement began to build up, with a steady procession of people down the station path to the beach, with our children, having been excused school, in the lead. There was laughter and shouting among the assembled people, some of whom were helping launch the work-boat, skipping out of the way of the breaking waves as they pulled up their lava-lavas clear of the water, while the children from the local school were already swimming around the boat and getting in the way. The station work-boat was a prize after a long fight with Treasury who could not understand why the ship could not moor at the wharf, or why we couldn't just use the smaller ship's dinghy. The crewing of the station boat was always eagerly sought after, but the station foreman usually managed to be the steersman and his friends manned the oars.

By this time the boat was on its way out to where the *Mary* was anchoring. The dinghy was lowered and quickly filled up with passengers' colourful painted Chinese tin trunks, sleeping mats and bed rolls. But the priority was for the mail, and the first boat had the mail bags which were collected by Mathew, the postal clerk, and carried up with Reuben's assistance to the leaf-built post office. There, as the bags were tipped out on the floor to begin sorting, the radio schedule would start and call Mathew away to take and send telegrams. These schedules always seemed to coincide with the ship's arrival and be extra long.

The station routine had been broken and it was fun. Most of the medical staff were on the beach, the agricultural assistants were eyeing the new copra drier parts, prisoners and station labour were in the thick of unloading, all the police were there except the desk officer and those on patrol, many people from the surrounding villages not in their gardens were there, even the District Commissioner had abandoned his desk to ensure all at the beach was in good order.

Meanwhile the first sorted mail was being heaped up on the office desks, the official letters to be opened and registered and placed on the DC's desk and the private mail was now coming through. By official lunch time the boys and I were able to walk up to the house with a few air-letters which were not opened until after lunch, and the hour's siesta had begun. At two it was back to the office to stare at the official mail heaped up on my desk. Why could such a pile be generated in only four weeks by the Honiara bureaucracy, and just before I was due off for a two week tour? Most of it would have to await my return. But just to make sure there were no nasty surprises, or some pleasant ones, it would all have to be read and filed. Some at least could be answered by Silas Sitai, a local man who later became the District Commissioner, while the rest were left to mature. Some could be solved by time alone, some could be dealt with on tour and the rest would await the tour end.

Unlike most days I would leave the office at 4pm with a large bag of mail, and over tea we spent time sorting out the personal mail – the letters from parents, sisters and brothers, and friends. Then there were the official looking ones suspected of containing bills. Finally, there were the parcels of magazines, papers, books and other exciting articles. The number of these increased as Christmas drew near. The personal letters were read at once, while the others waited until after dinner of the next day. Not having electricity meant there was a rush at dusk to ensure all the kerosene lamps were operational, and in any case we had to divert attention to the grocery order but that is another story.

OP 90 (October 2005)

Supermarket – Island Style

by James L O Tedder

In the mid 1950s there were only two sources of European style groceries in the Solomon Islands: the Trading Company in Honiara which was often out of stock or the item was on 'the next ship', and the old firm of McIlraths of Sydney. This firm had been supplying wholesale groceries to the South Pacific since well before the war. The firm supplied a catalogue and price list and several evenings were spent making up the order based on what was necessary or what couldn't be resisted from the lyrical description. The pantry had to be checked, the consumption rate of various items calculated, taking into account the delays that could occur between sending and receiving the order. Then allowance had to be made for visitors, and functions such as the Queen's Birthday. Finally the budget had to be considered.

One of the problems was that the new order often had to be dispatched before the current one was received, and you never knew what could not be supplied or what was certainly not going to be ordered again. Even though the Sydney ship came every six weeks, a cyclone or a strike could delay it by two or three weeks, so that uncertain period had to be taken into account. Then when our order was complete and ready to post, was there a ship likely to be going to Honiara within a week or two? Of course, the letter could arrive in Honiara the day the fortnightly plane had already departed. So that would be a minimum of two months before we could see the order on the back verandah. We considered ourselves lucky: times in the Gilbert and Ellice Islands were much longer.

So it was a long time between the making up of the order on the back verandah – under the glare and hiss of the pressure lamp – until we opened up the cases in the same position. There were other problems due to the long wait. Some items had fallen out of favour by the time they arrived; children had switched from baked beans to spaghetti, tins of meat ordered by the beauty of the label and the glowing description in the catalogue had by now been uncovered for their false advertising, and here was another case ordered before we had decided how to dispose of the first case. So the arrival of the *Mary* off Kira Kira was exciting not just for the mail, but whether our new grocery order had been shipped. Had the station orders been supplied? Was there rice for the hospital patients? And drugs, what about the new drugs promised two months ago? And was the drum of petrol for the radio battery charger, missed from the last ship, finally on board? And what about the vital building materials holding up work on the new hospital?

Our other concern was whether there had been sufficient time between the arrival of the Australian ship and the sailing of the *Mary* for the customs agents to have cleared and loaded our grocery order, and whether unloading was going to be accomplished without any dinghy capsizes. Kira Kira had only a bay protected from the worst of the SE weather but open to the north and north-west. During the SE period, landing was no great problem with only a small surf onto the sandy beach. During the months of November and December, though, there would be occasions when a huge low swell would be running, and then the surf could be horrendous, breaking far out and giving little warning of its coming.

It was strange that so much food had to be imported, but it was the lack of variety in the local produce. Living on the coast one could be expected to have plenty of fish, but not only were they difficult to catch but the local people were gardeners not fishers. The few Polynesians on the station sometimes would have fish for sale but even they found fishing difficult. There were always sweet potatoes for sale and some local 'greens', but there was no established market, possibly because of the low population density. Fruit was hard to find. We did grow paw-paws, tomatoes and sometimes managed to buy a bunch of bananas. One group of people to the east had as their basic diet green bananas, usually boiled – not very appetising. There were two ancient grapefruit trees which yielded wonderful fruit for several months of the year. This seemed to coincide with an influx of visitors from Honiara, or there would be a plea from Honiara as to whether we could spare a few for an important visitor. But these fruit were no respecters of authority. Sir Christopher Cox, then the adviser to the Colonial Office on Education, caught an eyeful of juice one morning. Many Europeans even imported potatoes and onions, but they were often a mass of rot when they arrived, so we decided very early to make use of the yams, taro and sweet potatoes. We did, however, keep a tin of dehydrated potato in the pantry for our visitors whose taste buds couldn't take to the local root vegetables. Several times we tried to bring down from Honiara fresh meat and butter, and as there was no refrigerator on the ship I suggested if the parcel were put high on the foremast, it would keep cool for the eighteen hours – but of course it didn't. Whenever there was a local feast in which a bullock or pig was killed, then we usually ended up with some meat – usually very tough but a nice change from tinned meat.

There were at times errors in our overseas grocery order which could not be easily corrected, such as ordering a case instead of a bottle of coffee essence. We sold on bottles, used them for presents and even bequeathed the remaining bottles to our successor. Large rounds of cheese wrapped in cheesecloth were wonderful for the first month, but then tended to develop strange moulds. But there must have been a stage in the maturing process which we did not see in our cheeses. Father Devlin at Dala in Malaita invited me in for lunch one day as I walked by. After lunch he asked if I liked cheese and sent off his house servant to 'fetch the cheese from the shed'. A few minutes later I detected a very strong odour closely followed by the cheese held at arms length by the small boy. Holding noses we cut pieces and the flavour was wonderful and there was no mould; perhaps the mould could not stand the stench. Apparently the cheese had been lost in Honiara several months before being 'found'. A side of bacon packed in salt was imported and hung over the fuel stove in the kitchen. It remained in good condition for a number of weeks before turning rancid. Even then I found that taking slices packed in salt on tour, then grilled over the village fire, removed the rancid flavour.

So with the groceries opened and the next order sent off, the next few weeks would be devoted to answering the personal mail, paying the bills, reading the magazines and enjoying the whole process and even looking forward to the next mail day. Meanwhile, I had a tour on the morrow and attention would be turned to other matters. It was only after I had left that the station could lapse back into its routine, not to be disturbed until I returned or the next ship arrived from Honiara.

OP 91 (April 2006)

Bumps in the Night

by J S A Lewis

I went out to the Federated Malay States in 1928 as a Customs Cadet and was stationed at Ipoh, a fairly large town in a tin-mining district. After passing my language and law examinations I was transferred to Tampin, which was an out-station on the borders of the Federation and the State of Malacca, as the Asst Superintendent in charge of the Customs station there.

There was only one road into Malacca at Tampin and, as the State boundary ran through the town, there was a Customs gate in the middle of the town to make life more interesting. Malacca was virtually duty free so there were no Customs controls on the Malacca side of the boundary; smuggling was one sided, ie into the Federation. Consequently most of the town, consisting of Chinese and Indian shopkeepers, lay on the Malacca side of the boundary. The town on the Federation side of the border was the usual small out-station with only five European Government officials – the District Officer, the doctor, the PWD engineer, the Police Officer and myself. We had the usual Club, with billiard table and a hard tennis court, which was also used by neighbouring rubber planters. There was a fair sized playing field in the town where the local Asians played soccer and hockey. The Government offices overlooked this field, and I had a pleasant office next door to the District Officer where I was kept cool by a punkah over my head pulled by the office boy.

I was allocated a bungalow to live in which was about one mile out of town and rather secluded. It was a three bedroom wooden bungalow raised three feet above the ground, solid but somewhat primitive. I had an open verandah around the house with roll up blinds known as 'chicks' to keep out the rain. There was no electric light, so I had to make do with Chinese oil lamps and candles. A good torchlight was therefore essential. A block of ice was delivered daily for the ice box to keep the drinks cool and the food from going bad. The kitchen in the servants quarters only had an open wood fire and a few pots and pans. For an oven the cook used an old empty four-gallon kerosene tin placed near the fire. How he was able to produce the meals he did, I cannot imagine. Each bedroom had its own bathroom, which was a small concrete room at ground level and contained a large earthenware jar of cold water and a 'thunder-box' loo. Snakes had a habit of visiting the bathroom via the water drain, presumably to cool off, and small scorpions had a nasty habit of dozing under the thunder-box seat. One had to be constantly aware of creepy crawlies and be always on guard.

One night during my sojourn there I was woken up by the sound of padding footsteps on the verandah outside my bedroom. I suspected a thief, and so got out of bed with my torchlight and revolver, which I kept under the pillow, and opened the swing doors of my bedroom quietly. When I turned on my torchlight to see who was there, the sound of footsteps immediately stopped and there was no-one on the verandah. I was somewhat surprised and assumed that the noise must have been caused by a civet cat or possibly rats thumping about in the roof. The revolver may sound melodramatic but at that time there was a world wide recession which hit the Malay States badly. Many rubber estates and open cast Chinese mines had to close down, shedding their labourers, as the price of rubber and tin had plummeted. Consequently robberies and burglaries had increased considerably. As my bungalow was wide open to intruders and I was on my own I felt a bit safer with a revolver under my pillow.

Some weeks later the same thing happened again. I woke up to hear the distinct sound of footsteps on the verandah. I got out of bed with my torch and gun and listened by the swing doors, as I did not want to be fooled a second time. I thought to myself I am wide awake, the noises are not from the roof, this time there is definitely someone on the verandah. I was not the slightest bit frightened, as I had had nearly two years experience of grappling with bootleggers and smugglers at night in the jungle, so that catching a thief would be child's play. I opened the swing doors quietly and turned on my torchlight fully expecting to find a thief on the verandah. You can imagine my astonishment on finding no-one there and the sound of footsteps had stopped as soon as I had shone the torch.

Some time later the District Officer obtained a young ADO to help him, and I was instructed to share my bungalow with him. I welcomed his company and between us we were able to buy a kerosene oil pressure lamp for the house. This gave off a bright light which made life easier at night. One night I was again woken up, this time by the noise of banging and thumping coming from the ADO's bedroom which was across the dining room from my bedroom. Thinking that he might be in some kind of trouble I went across to his bedroom. When I reached his swing doors commotion still reigned in his bedroom but as soon as I opened the door and flashed my torchlight into the room, the noises stopped. The ADO, to my astonishment, was fast asleep in his bed. He woke up when I entered his room and I explained what had happened but he had heard nothing. Years later I met a colleague who had lived in the same bungalow before me and he admitted he had also heard footsteps in the night. I was also told that the bungalow had been built over an old Malay graveyard, which may have had something to do with it.

OP 64 (October 1992)

Who's Afraid?

by Janet Wimbush

When you leave the Plateau Province in Nigeria by the road to the West, you come to the Escarpment. You then drop three thousand feet and three thousand years. The Plateau is the tin-bearing district of Nigeria, and it is the only part of the country where Europeans have ever made settled homes. And very lovely and very sophisticated many of their homes are. The indigenous people of that part of Nigeria are the Birom tribe, known generally as the Pagans. Their standard of living must be something like that of Neolithic man.

Thirty years ago, when my husband was stationed at Jos on the Plateau as a Government Surveyor, there was a district at the foot of the escarpment called the Marma country, which had for some years been closed to mining. There were two reasons for this. Some of the Pagans had been so hostile to Europeans that there had been violence and bloodshed. And sleeping sickness and yellow fever were rife. It was before the day of inoculation against yellow fever.

The day came when the authorities decided that the hostility and the disease had both abated and that the district could be reopened to mining prospectors. Before that could happen survey beacons had to be erected. That was where we came in. My husband was despatched to do the job, which was to take about a month, and I went with him. I was rather excited at the thought of going to bush for the first time.

"We are going to the Marma country tomorrow," I said to the Nursing Sister, when I met her at the Club.

"I hope you are taking a doctor with you!" she replied facetiously.

On the appointed day, we set off in our Ford truck, with the cook, steward, and odd-job boy, and the inevitable sordid-looking paraphernalia of beds and baths, lamps and filters, tin trunks and camp chairs. Our own luggage looked grim enough and the servants' loads crowned it. Among their bedding rolls and tin kettles there were always some muddy yams rolling about and a couple of squawking hens with their legs tied together. Behind our truck came the lorry carrying the survey gang. This consisted of a Headman, two chainmen and a dozen labourers. They were all Hausas, and their chief characteristics were cheerfulness, beautiful manners and bone idleness. I was very fond of them.

The name of the Headman was Mallam Dogo, which means literally the Tall Teacher. Anyone who could read and write was given the title of Mallam. He and I became great friends. He used to carry me on his back over the streams when we were on trek, and seemed to look on this as his privilege. But the really important member of the party was the Dan Sander. The literal meaning of this title is the Man with the Stick. He was a policeman in the service of the Native Administration, and was lent to us to act as interpreter with the pagan tribes.

We drove on the first day to the bottom of the escarpment and went on till the road came to an end. From there the journey was to be done on foot, with carriers recruited locally, and our nights were to be spent in rest houses. The word rest house is a misnomer. They were neither houses nor restful. They were circular mud huts with a thatch of palm leaves. Doors and windows were rectangular openings in the mud walls. They contained no furniture. But all the same a rest house can look like home to you when your camp beds and chairs are erected and your books and crockery set out on camp tables.

Each rest house was on the outskirts of a Pagan village. The way of life in these villages was primitive in the extreme. The men went naked. The women wore two bunches of leaves attached to a bit of leather around their waists, which waggled as they walked. They carried their babies on their backs in slings of monkey skin. By way of ornament they threaded short pieces of stick though their nostrils. The Pagans ate what they could grow or kill and had little use for money. In order to earn the few shillings a year that were needed to pay their tax, the women would walk for days to the nearest township with bundles of firewood on their heads. The men carried long knives fashioned from any strips of iron they could lay hands on. Barrel hoops were a favourite material.

We had been moving on for several days and were three days' walk from any road when the cook reported that our tinned food was running out. He had taken for granted that the usual local food would be obtainable and he had miscalculated. The Marma country seemed to provide no food that could be faced by Europeans. Feeling that Cook was being defeatist, I told him in English to find some chickens and eggs. Cook told the Dan Sander in Hausa to find some chickens and eggs. The Dan Sander told the village head to find some chickens and eggs. (I never knew how the Dan Sander managed to communicate, for the language of the Pagans changed every few miles.) The answer that came back was quite clear. "There are no chickens. There are no eggs."

"Never mind," said my husband, "I have heard guinea fowl squawking up on that hill. I will take the gun up there tomorrow morning".

Next morning at first light he had gone, taking some of the gang with him. Others had gone off to cut firewood. The cook was presumably out looking for chickens. The odd-job boy and I had the camp to ourselves. He was an engaging child of about twelve, called Audu. He put out my deck chair, put a table beside me, and made me some tea. I relaxed with a six-week old copy of the Daily Telegraph. It was deliciously cool and there was a faint and pleasant scent of wood smoke wafting from the village. I was at peace.

After a quarter of an hour, something caused me to put down my paper and look up. Fifteen yards away stood silently in a straight line ten naked Pagan men. Each one had his eyes fixed on me. Each one had a leather thong round his waist into which was stuck a long knife. None of them moved or made a sound. Very deliberately I picked up my paper again and disappeared behind it. Perhaps I had dozed off and dreamed it? I would count twenty and look again. I counted twenty and looked again. They were still there. I looked round for Audu. There was no sign of him. I looked at the rest house with its open gaps for doors and windows. There was no sanctuary there. The bush round the rest house had been cleared and we were in the middle of a large open space. It looked to me about the size of the Sahara desert. I could not run away. There was nowhere to run. Not a flicker of expression appeared on the ten faces and the ten pairs of eyes never left me.

After twenty minutes or so I found that I had torn the front page of my newspaper into small shreds. I folded the remainder of it neatly and told myself that my husband would be back any minute now. But then I heard the distant sound of his gun from the hill-top. The hill-top was at least half-an-hour's walk away. The sun was up now, but I was very cold. I found I was biting my nails (a habit of which I had been cured at the age of six). I folded my hands, shut my eyes, and sat rigid. It was half-an-hour later that my husband got back, flushed with success, laden with guinea fowl, gossiping cheerfully with his Hausa men. He looked in astonishment at the row of Pagans. They had relaxed now, and ceased to stare at me. They were talking to each other. They did not look like the same people at all.

"What do these chaps want?", asked my husband. I forbore to say that I did not know whether their object had been rape or murder. "Perhaps", I said, "we could start the process of asking them?" "What do they want?", I said to Mallam Dogo in English.

"What do they want?", said Mallam Dogo to the Dan Sander in Hausa.

"What do you want?", said the Dan Sander to the Pagans in their own tongue. The answer worked its way back to me. They wanted money for their tax. They had heard that we were moving on the next day. They wanted jobs as carriers.

"Why did they stand so long and stare at me?", I asked. And the answer came laboriously back. "They have not seen a white woman before. They were afraid."

Afraid? Of me?

OP 45 (April 1983)

One Christmas in the Gold Coast

by Faith Dennis

My husband had done some small service for the local chief. To express his appreciation, this gentleman wished to give a gift to Madam.

"I go dash her a fine, fine turkey" he promised.

It was to be for Christmas, then some weeks hence, and he would send it in good time to where we lived some twenty miles away. Nevertheless we prepared, with the aid of our somewhat surly boy steward, some quarters for the bird at the back of the compound. We consulted friends in the Department of Agriculture about suitable food, and our reluctant and rather sceptical cook was dispatched to the local market, hinting at a rise in view of the difficult time ahead.

It was necessary next to read up about the daily care of turkeys. There being no public reference libraries in the 'bush', the nearest equivalent seemed to be the bookshelves of a monks' seminary some fifty miles distant. I cannot now quite remember whether these saintly gentlemen were called The White Fathers or the Brown Brothers, but whichever they were they rose magnificently to the occasion and lent me a spotted and mildewed tract *Poultry for All*, published 1903. This dealt with chickens, ducks, guinea fowl, bantams and geese, but turkey were dismissed with *prone to pneumonia: must not drink from lead gutters*. We hastened into our compound. Were our gutters made of lead? They were. The cook's mate was drafted in to make wire cages over the ends where water might collect. We thought it best to forget about the other problem of pneumonia.

Still no signs of the turkey arriving, but invitations for Christmas dinner were sent out and everyone accepted. It was now only ten days before Christmas and it seemed politic to refresh the chief's memory about his promised gift. So, one Saturday afternoon we happened to find ourselves driving slowly through the chief's village. We were duly seen and asked into his house. I was filled with excitement at the prospect of a plump succulent bird for our dinner party, but first, etiquette demanded that we partake of roast groundnuts and palm wine. This was not my idea of suitable refreshment on a hot sultry afternoon but I reminded myself that of course this was a very minor chief who could not be expected to know the tastes of English ladies. Minor he may have been but he was surrounded by his court (all male, I noticed) and waited on by submissive youths whom I assumed were poor relatives. There was just a hint of bygone slavery days in the air, or had I a touch of fever?

There was a commotion on the back verandah.

"For Madam. Christmas dash." announced the Chief regally.

We all stood up, and my 'turkey' made a lunge at me. It had four legs, long curling horns and went 'Baa'. With true British phlegm I said at once that a ram was just what I wanted. My husband rose handsomely to the occasion and according to custom and Colonial Regulations made an exchange gift in His Majesty's coin to the value of the animal. Fortunately we had brought the cook's mate along with us in the car, thinking that he could cradle the expected bird all the way home. It was not a simple matter to get an elderly demented ram into the back of the car. He stuck his shaggy head out of the window, restrained only by a length of grubby string. All the way home he loudly voiced his complaints, 'Baa, baa', and the unhappy cook's mate let forth his tribal expletives non-stop.

Anyone who has lived in the tropics will know that Saturday afternoon is almost a sacrosanct time, a quiet rest period after the labours of the week. Windows were shuttered, and blinds drawn in the residential area, but "Baa, baa" shattered the peace. Unloaded at last in our compound, the ram proved impossible to tether, expensive to feed and horribly unpopular with the entire population, both black and white. We did have our Christmas dinner and all the guests turned up at the party. I chattered loudly of my 'dash' from the chief lest I should hear a whisper that the meat was old boots.

OP 50 (November 1985)

Hurricane Janet, Barbados 1955

by Winifred K O'Mahony

It was during the small hours of the night when I heard the telephone constantly ringing. Befuddled with sleep I could recognise the voice of the Commissioner of Police asking for Dr O'Mahony. Apparently there was an hurricane alert – but I was not to be 'alarmed'. Shaking my husband awake I handed him the 'phone. Yes, Piarco Air Base in Trinidad had alerted us that Hurricane Janet had altered course and was heading for Barbados. Several hours could elapse before it reached us but there was much to do.

In less than 10 minutes Dr O'Mahony was dressed, had taken out the car and was headed for Police Headquarters and the big General Hospital nearby. My first job was to close the big hurricane shutters on all 20 windows, jamming each one of them with the great wooden bars to ensure their security. Then to telephone various friends to whom we had promised shelter in the event of a severe storm. So far the public had not been alerted and the time was around 3 am. I left the radio on as I knew that in due time the Government would be broadcasting general instructions as to what to do. Then down to the big flat beneath our apartment which belonged to the Director of Public Works, now on vacation in Trinidad. Again I had some 20 big windows to secure, doors to bolt and in agony I had to decide that all the beautiful plants on their verandah would have to be left to the mercy of the oncoming storm.

Dr O'Mahony rushed in for a few minutes, swallowed a cup of tea, a bite of toast, and was away again in an endeavour to visit the many outlying country hospitals – about 7 of them, a few of which were below or at sea-level. Now I could hear Police vans with hailers telling the public to clear the roads, batten down their homes and remain there. The streets were no longer safe. Meanwhile the wind increased and our friends were arriving with emergency cases, and even a young baby with his nurse.

In an endeavour to be shielded against the coming storm, a huge Shell Tanker had been left against the great old boundary wall of the Garrison. Later I realised its worth when it served military and other lorries as they subsequently went out on various missions. Beside the tanker were parked a big number of Public Works lorries, hopefully left there for later salvage work. Inside the ancient fort walls lay the big old ammunition store, and this was now receiving military personnel and soon we could hear the purr of a huge radio which was installed inside the walls which were about 10 ft thick.

Returning to my flat I heard the Government broadcasts which were now on a more urgent note. The hurricane was now expected rather earlier than anticipated and would probably pass to the south of the Island. All business firms, banks, offices, etc were to close immediately and everyone was urged to get off the streets. Our good Canadian friends, Mr & Mrs Garrett, had now arrived, together with their little golden cocker spaniel. Alas they had not had breakfast so I had to set about cooking as big a meal as possible for them, not knowing when the next meal would be.

Up until then the weather had been fairly normal but now I was aware of sharp gusts of wind from the North West – an unusual quarter for us – and gradually these were increasing with squally rain. Then Mrs Merrivale Austin arrived with her daughter, son-in-law, their babe of 2½ years, together with Nanny. Multitudes of baggage were carried in by their butler and chauffeur, who then hurriedly left for their own homes. Then I allocated a great big spare bedroom to the nanny and babe and gave out the necessary items for food preparation, etc. Mr Austin was supposed to be in Grenada with his brother, the Chief of Police, and in an endeavour to alleviate his anxiety we put through a telephone call. Luck was with us and we got through, only to learn that Merrivale had left for Trinidad. To our amazement, Grenada had then had no intimation of the approach of 'Janet'. It was then approximately 10 am.

Dr O'Mahony was still not home and the wind was increasing all the time. Eventually however, he arrived, put his car in the garage and battened it down as securely as possible. The wind had now shifted to the north and we could still stand on our sheltered verandah, watching the trees being blown hither and thither. Reduffusion had been off the air some time, and electricity now was cut off. Hurricane lanterns had to be lighted as the hurricane shutters at the windows completely precluded all light. Then came the deep murmur of the emergency generator from the Military HQ nearby. I prayed that the aerials, both there and at Police HQ and at Government House would stand up to the fury of the gale which was now ranging around us. Through a tiny gap in the kitchen jalousies we watched the torment of a quadrangle of tulip trees some 80 ft high, as limb by limb they were torn apart, one of them flung across a building behind us. Then a great evergreen tree, a centenarian at that, had its branches torn off like shreds of paper. Corrugated sheets from nearby Nissen huts were being thrown around in profusion whilst the noise was utterly terrifying. The wind was shifting again and we realised that the peak of the storm was at hand. The men folk kept a constant check of windows, doors, etc, which were taking a tremendous battering, but we heard the wind now approaching from the south and our front door, which was of immense thickness, with four big bolts and two locks, was beginning to give way. Hurling our full weight on it, my husband and Bill Duncan were able to jam a huge 3 ft square piece of timber under the main lock and then wedge the other end with further pieces of timber which they nailed to the floor. Now the great gusts of wind were shaking the whole of this huge old building which had been Military HQ for well over a hundred years. The wooden staircase leading up to the flat was another anxiety – it was laced with a huge bougainvillaea – but if it were torn down how on earth could we get out of the building in an extreme emergency? We had Julian Garrett, a man of 76 years, and Mary Ann Duncan, a pregnant woman, amongst our 'refugees'!

The turning point soon arrived and by 1.45 pm we realized that the winds were diminishing. Carefully opening the kitchen door, which had been protected by trellis on its verandah, my husband carefully stepped out and I followed him. The great lawns around us were smothered with leaves and torn-off tree limbs, as well as many entire trees completely uprooted. An acrid-like smell assailed us from everywhere; it turned out to be sap from the tortured trees. The Adjutant and his staff, together with some of the personnel, were now coming out from their shelter in the old Ammunition Hall nearby. Almost immediately orders were being given for squads of men to start out in convoys of lorries with lifting tackle in order to clear some of the main roads and to re-establish communications. A squad was allocated to Dr O'Mahony and he immediately got out his car – intact, thank God! – and they slowly started out to try and get down to Medical Headquarters at the General Hospital.

Marion Garrett and I struggled through the debris towards the road, which was blocked by fallen trees, and a medley of telephone and electric light wires lay everywhere. Several huge gas lamps from the huge holders had been snapped off and lay in the littered road. Any trees which remained upright had been stripped of leaves and had turned a dark brown. Venturing towards what had been a magnificent copse of tamarind, manchineal and coconut trees which bordered the sea behind our flat, my friend and I found it utterly impassable. The beautiful great trees had been ripped up and hurled against one another, whilst the roots lay exposed some 8 to

10 feet in the air. The erstwhile calm blue Caribbean was now a boiling, roaring horror. Sickened by it all, we crept back home. No electricity, no refrigeration, but thank God I had an adequate supply of food.

It was late at night when my husband returned, deadly tired and very silent. He fell asleep in an armchair immediately, too weary to even walk to his bedroom. I roused him later, gave him a light meal and he retired to bed. At 4 am we were up again, hurried cups of tea were made on an oil stove and once more the poor DMS started off on his island-wide survey. The emergency dynamo from St Ann's Fort was still chugging away, and now lorries and other vehicles were coming and going all the time. Little by little the whole battalion were reporting for duty. By daylight tents were being erected on the surrounding lawns. Sentries were stationed and soldiers with rifles were being sent out to guard strategic food supplies. Soon Army trucks with personnel were leaving to try and open up the blocked roads and clear communications. The Public Works Department called up all available carpenters, masons, etc, and instituted flying squads to commence the immense task of repairing damaged buildings. Then the Electricity Department and Telephone Company co-opted every electrician and every technician available, and with vans, cars, or any possible transport, they started off on the task of disentangling and repairing the hundreds of miles of ruptured and damaged wires. Day and night these gangs of men worked in relays at the immense task.

Later in the day, when there were only short sharp squalls of wind and rain, I ventured further afield from our immediate vicinity. Sick at heart I saw the lovely great trees uprooted and it was a miracle that so many had fallen between the houses or into the road or gardens. Most homes appeared to be damaged in some way and many had lost their roofs. Even strongly built concrete houses had their roofs entirely lifted off. The sea was subsiding but the flooding in many places bore evidence to the phenomenally high seas. Approaching the many hotels bordering the sea, I found the verandahs piled high with sand to a depth of 3 feet or so, whilst fish were floating in the flooded ground floor lounges. The Royal Hotel, with its luxurious air-conditioned bedrooms, once the proud possessor of a restaurant built out on a pier in the sea, which had now vanished and merely the damaged piers were left standing, was now roofless and derelict. The Manager's beautiful bungalow, recently built, was now shifted from its foundations and the roof lay shattered in the middle of the street. Further up the road I saw the home of a distinguished merchant completely cut in two, as if from bomb damage. My courage failed me here, and a passing Staff Officer in a military jeep gave me a much needed lift home. No servants and no help were anywhere available. Sand carried in the wind had permeated every corner of the house. I swept and dusted until my hands were blistered. My lovely mahogany furniture was dull and horrid from the salt-impregnated air. I then learned of a further horror which had occurred near our home. The big Picture House, solidly built of concrete, had been used as a shelter for a large crowd of people. The storm in its fury had ripped off the roof and so caused the walls to collapse. There were many killed and seriously injured.

OP 54 (October 1987)

Barbados

The first Barbados flag badge was introduced in 1870 and the design was used until Independence in 1966. The badge depicts Britannia on a sea-chariot drawn by two horses, with a dolphin tail. Britannia holds a trident, signifying rule over the seas (or  waves). That became the central feature of the national flag after Independence depicted here.

Part 5
LANGUAGE & LOCAL CUSTOMS

How Do You Do?

by PC 49

Advice in plenty was always freely available from those in Ceylon who had been through the hoop before you – for example, in the matter of passing local language exams on which depended your confirmation in appointment and promotion after two years' probation.

"The trick", they said airily, "when asking a prisoner about the misdeed which has landed him in jail is to put your questions to him so that he answers in not more than one or two words. If you ask him why he did whatever he did, you will open the floodgates and you will drown miserably."

The dear old pundit who waited patiently every morning on the mess verandah for his pupils to appear after early parade and breakfast tried to instil the same technique. Unfolding his copy of the *Dina Mina* (*Daily News*) he would point to a suitable court report and guide one's hesitant tongue through the curlicue lettering to an approximate understanding. Whenever a juicy case cropped up, his eyes sparkled and when, eventually, the stage was reached when you practised with real live prisoners in the jail, he could not suppress a shiver of excitement when a flesh and blood murderer was brought in for viva voce practice. They were remand prisoners who had volunteered to break the monotony of sitting around doing nothing whilst awaiting trial, by submitting themselves to interrogation by faltering language students, and certainly they enjoyed twisting our tails a little whilst simultaneously rehearsing their defence in court.

So, every three months, until crowned by success, a small group of probationary officers presented themselves at the main gate of Welikade Prison and were directed to a waiting room. Next door sat the Examiner, accompanied by a Deputy Inspector General (DIG), and the official Interpreter Mudaliyar. (If the Examiner happened to be a senior European civil servant, woe betide you. He would expect to hear the fluent grammatical speech which he himself was capable of delivering to an audience of, say, members of a rural co-operative. In contrast, a senior Sinhalese or Tamil civil servant always seemed to be pleased and surprised that you could utter any words at all in the vernacular.)

When the day came to take the second more advanced exam, I appeared at the appointed time and managed to translate without too much hesitation a crime report written by a village headman in Sinhalese characters. Then a prisoner was brought in for the oral examination. He was an elderly man, polite and dignified in manner, and he took time to settle on his hunkers as gestured by the Interpreter Mudaliyar.

"You may ask him some questions, please" said the Examiner (a senior Sinhalese civil servant, to whom much later I became a devoted and admiring staff officer).

Taking a deep breath, I started off on the well-worn staple questions "Where do you come from? – What offence are you alleged to have committed?" etc, etc. I gathered that he was a peasant cultivator from Tangalle district in the rural south east of the Island, and that he had been accused of manslaughter. Thus far I was in control, although the prisoner had few front teeth and lisped through the gaps in the equivalent of a very broad Devon accent. I gather also that he had been digging in his paddy-field and that he had hit someone with his mammoty or hoe. So far, so good.

Then I made a crucial mistake: I asked "How did you get into this fight?"

He was off in a flash. There was mention of a dead man, mention of two other men, a fight, and yet another dead man. I floundered hopelessly.

At this point the Examiner turned to me with a compassionate smile and said "I think you had better come back and try again in another three months." As I withdrew, I heard him tell the Interpreter to find out what had really happened, and the DIG, who had kept a straight face throughout, told me the rest later. Even the Mudaliyar had difficulty in getting at the facts. The poor old fellow's story was this: He had been digging peaceably in his paddy-field when two men came along the bund separating his field from the next. They were carrying a dead body for burial (Corpse No 1). Our friend remonstrated and told them to take another route, so that the shadow of the dead man would not fall on his rice crop and blight it. The pall-bearers replied that they would be blowed (to put it politely) if he expected them to make a detour of several hundred yards just to oblige him and his superstitions. A furious argument broke out and developed into a fight in which the old man wielded his mammoty to such effect that one of the pall-bearers fell to the ground and died (Corpse No 2). Meantime the second pall-bearer fled leaving Corpse No 1 lying in the paddy-field. The local headman came and called in the Police, who (most unfairly) arrested him and charged him with murder. I hope the Judge was not too harsh on him.

Three months later, I managed to satisfy the Examiner and earned a second pip on my shoulder. And then it was back to square one for another year, learning basic Tamil. Similar visits to the Prison followed, but with a very different type of inmate, mostly a scattering of rickshaw or dock labourers. My Tamil pundit was a purist who insisted on correct grammar, declensions and all, whether or not such high-flown speech was intelligible to humble illiterates. He was right. When in due course I appeared before another (Tamil) Examiner I passed without too much trouble. Whereas a young Tamil-born officer, who appeared for examination at the same time, addressed the prisoners in abominable vernacular (such as used daily by planters or by their wives in the kitchen). He was turned away ignominiously and told not to return before he had learnt his mother tongue properly.

Op 63 (April 1992)

Ceylon

The badge depicts a Buddhist religious building called a Dagoba, with an elephant in front. The elephant was derived from the arms used by the Dutch before British rule, while the Dagoba had been part of the arms of the Ceylon Government Railway. In 1870 the Governor, Sir Hercules Robinson, recommended the design, prepared by the Public Works Department, and the Colonial Office agreed despite the general policy that flag badges should be based on the design for the colony's Public Seal. The badge was used on the Blue Ensign until Independence in 1948.

Massa Gets to Speak Propa

by R R Yearley

On the ship to take up my appointment in the Colonial Service in the Gold Coast in 1948 I expressed some concern as to how I should communicate with the Africans. As well as Ga, the local language spoken in Accra and district, there was Twi, Fante, Ewe and others and I hadn't a word of any of them.

"Don't worry", my colleagues said, "all the people you'll be working with speak perfectly acceptable English and the cook and house-boy and the rest of your staff will speak pidgin which you'll soon pick up. We'll start teaching you now."

Much of the conversation at table from then on was devoted to pidgin, the Anglo-Chinese colloquial speech adapted for Africa. The vocabulary was mainly English with some foreign words like 'savvy' – 'know' (French) and 'palava' – 'talk' (Portuguese), and some local words like 'chop' – 'food', 'eat'. Pronunciation was recognisably English except for some distortions: 'th' in 'this' and 'that' became 'dis' and 'dat'; 'th' in 'thing' – 'ting'; 'there' – dey', 'it' – 'ee' (subject) and 'um' (object). Example: 'I put dis book for table. You want I put um for book-case? Ee dey under dis ting'.

I learned that positive questions began with 'why' and negative were in the form 'why you no?' Example: 'Why you no do dis small ting?' All my colleagues, old Coasters, could speak pidgin effortlessly and without hesitation, so I quickly acquired a working knowledge including idioms like 'unless tomorrow' (no time to do it now), 'lef small' (later) and so many others. But I learned most of all from the stories they told of their experiences.

There was the wife, new to the Coast, who joined her husband a few weeks after the start of his tour. On the first Saturday he went to the office for the usual stint, and at midday adjourned to the Club for a beer or two. When he got home at one o'clock he found no sign of his wife or of any preparations for lunch.

"John, where Missus? Why no chop?"

"Missus dey for bedroom. She asks me where Massa and I say Massa dey for Club, ee come one o'clock time for chop, today ground-nut stew. Missus say she the one to order what for chop. Then she make plenty weep, she go for bedroom and she slam door. I keep chop hot but I no fit make side-dish. I wait for Massa."

"You've done well. All dis be Mammy palaver."

"Dis I savvy too much, me I get two wives."

"Now, you go make fine fine pot of tea. You set table with best cups and you put on clean jacket. I go get Missus. When she come you tell her sorry and she tell you sorry. She order ground-nut for tomorrow. Then you be frens. I take her to Club for chop tonight. Missus new, she go learn. After dis tea you finish duty for today. You 'gree for dis?"

"Yes Massa. Massa savvy woman fine pas all."

Then there was the story of the bride whose husband had been obliged to return to duty straight after the honeymoon, leaving his wife to follow with the freight. When, after several weeks she arrived, she was delighted to unpack and handle all the wedding presents she had hardly seen. She and her husband were invited to dinner soon after by a young, single colleague, to meet other wives and heads of department. She was pleased to see that the glasses were the same sort that she had brought and later the meal was served on the same kind of dinner plates that she and her husband had chosen. But then she realised that the glasses and the rest were in fact her own! She said nothing but when she asked her steward why he had not asked permission to lend he replied: "Dis be custom. Dis young massa, he not get wife, he not get all dese fine tings, but he must en'tain his boss-men, and he want to invite frens so he borrow. All massa and missus do dis. Some ting loss or broke massa replace. Later, when you give fine party for PosMaser Gen you do same ting."

Another recently arrived wife found to her horror, in the middle of a tea-party she was holding for her new friends, that her steward was taking round a plate of cakes among which was a number of foil-wrapped 'Rendells' (a popular contraceptive tablet) which she had put in the fridge. She managed to retrieve the plate and remove the embarrassment without anyone noticing.

The next day the steward said to Massa, "Why Missus take dese sweets away? I chop one, ee be fine fine?"

Massa explained, "They no sweets. They be for stop piccin".

The steward commented, "I get ten piccin. I no tink one small sweet fit stop me." In this way I learned not only the language but the fact that the Africans had a great sense of humour and an unfailing indulgence for Massa's strange ways.

It was a generally accepted custom that if anyone called at a bungalow and the resident Massa was away, the visitor would be served a drink or anything else he asked for. Of course there were abuses, but there was one particular scrounger who regularly looked in for free whisky. The steward was told that if Massa X called he should be told that there was no whisky. So on his next visit when he said, "Pass whisky", the boy said, "Ee finish."

"What do you mean? I see um there for sideboard."

"Yes, Massa, ee dey but ee like ee no dey."

OP 85 (April 2003)

How Not to Learn Swahili

by John H Harris

The idea was you picked it up on the ship going out. This was the 1930s and there was bound to be an old hand on board who would teach you in return for the odd pink gin. This did not work too well for me – those pretty girls and all that sight-seeing. I landed at Dar es Salaam with a few words for food and drink and for things to eat and drink with.

My first assignment was to go down to the Lupa Goldfield to survey the rough and tumble and introduce improved methods and new ideas for recovery of gold. I was accompanied by the then Chief Inspector of Mines and we travelled in the standard 30cwt Bedford truck with the famously uncomfortable PWD body and a local driver.

As we toiled up the Iringa escarpment I looked down onto the plain below and saw with great interest a school of dust-devils, three of them, starting up and moving in a tall and stately fashion along with us.

"What is that?" I asked.

"Dust-devils", said the CIM.

"How do you say that in Swahili?" I queried. But although the CIM was considerably experienced he said he did not know. We could not ask the driver because he was concentrating on the tricky bends and, anyway, it was not long before we had to stop to deal with a blocked carburettor and a swarm of wild bees – but that is another story.

After three days we arrived in Chunya. I pitched my camp in the Inspector of Mines' 'shamba' and was invited to dinner, where I was welcomed as a new boy and asked how I was getting along with Swahili.

"Fine", I said, "and, by the way, what is the Swahili for dust-devil?"

My host did not know either; so he called his head-boy and asked him, in Swahili, what to call the wind that went round and round and up and up and carried all the sand with it. There followed an extraordinary performance. The young man stood on one leg, then on the other. He turned pale grey and finally stuttered a story to the effect that he dare not say the real name of that evil wind which could damage and destroy. The Chief of his village could deflect them with his little finger and would only call them *nyoka* (snake).

"Ha", I thought, "the first in my future collection of African superstitions." My activities on the goldfield progressed and I worked my way, mine by

275

mine, across to the western end where, in one of the larger of the small mines, I was quartered in a comfortably furnished rondavel of mud-brick with a tall, heavily thatched roof and invited to dine with the staff. Talk turned on my experiences as a newcomer and I related how impressed I had been by the beautiful location of the mine, overlooking Lake Rukwa and the distant isolated mountain which resembled nothing so much as a woman lying on a bier, from her upturned feet at one end to her fine head of hair at the other, tumbling precipitously to the valley. That head, I was told, was indeed a precipice down which had been thrown the unfortunates who displeased a chieftain of old. Furthermore, the mountain was thereafter cursed. If climbed, next year's crops would fail. In fact, a few years since, the mountain had been climbed to be mapped by a geologist, and the next year the crops failed.

"Ha", I thought again, "this is the second", and was prompted to ask "Do you know the one about the dust-devils?" Nobody in the crew knew the Swahili for dust-devil. So the manager called in his head-boy and asked the question and the Chunya performance was repeated. The man stood first on one leg, then on the other, turned a pale grey and proffered the story of the forbidden name, the little finger of the chief and the substitute *nyoka*.

Two days later I had to drive back to Chunya for supplies. When I returned, after dark, the manager met me with a hurricane lamp and showed me to my rondavel. That day a dust-devil had cruised through the camp, taken a small corner off the kitchen, settled above my rondavel, lifted off the entire roof and dropped it back on my bed. I asked no more questions.

Note : It seems that over 60 years later there is still no recognised Swahili word for that common phenomenon.

OP 78 (October 1999)

Witchcraft

by R E N Smith

Witchcraft is a most evocative word, conjuring up for European minds visions of naked ladies capering around a horned man; old women being burned for alleged use of the evil eye; Merlin muttering incantations; or, further back, druids doing mysterious things with mistletoe. In my very limited experience of it, witchcraft in Africa had little to do with any of these seductive images, but was far more concerned with the legitimate or illegitimate ways and byways of medicine. I am not at all sure that religion, Christian or pagan, had much to do with it either, though I remember and enjoyed C A W Monckton's story of a New Guinea missionary complaining to government about a native white witch, who brought rain on demand when the missionary's prayer had failed. Monckton's note to Government that he was too busy to worry about quarrels of rival rainmakers, was considered 'contemptuous levity in official correspondence'.

In my subdistrict of Mwanza in western Nyasaland in 1952 I do not think we had any rainmakers, but we did have an eminent practitioner of traditional medicine (and witch-finder), one Black Jiva, who caused me a certain amount of worry. He was tucked away in a far corner of the district on the edge of its junction with Chikwawa and close to the Mozambique border, and in this remote corner he seldom came to my attention.

What forced him into the limelight was the arrival at my office of the badly decomposed remains of a middle-aged Achikunda wornan. She had been brought to Mwanza from the far side of Thambani mountain, a fine pinnacle that stood on the Portuguese border. The story had started in Chang'oima village in the territory of Native Authority Chapananga in the corner of Chikwawa district nearest to Mwanza. Here lived a middle-aged villager, Jasi, his wife Mwangalaine, their two daughters, Feria and Enelesi, the children of these two young women plus other members of the family. A child of each of the daughters had fallen sick, so the family decided to seek professional help. They crossed the district boundary, which of course meant nothing to them, and walked to Kanyani village, where there lived a famed 'doctor' – Black Jiva. To reach Kanyani they had to pass by a Government Dispensary with its trained Government Medical Aide and free treatment, but it never crossed their minds to seek attention from him.

They had a consultation with Black; he examined the children, and treated them next morning by making small cuts on their ribs and giving them medicine. That night Feria's child died. Apparently no blame attached to Black, for he thereupon decided that the children had been bewitched, and gave the family half a cup of *kabanga* each. During this ordeal (for such it surely was) Jasi fainted and died shortly afterwards, and was hurriedly carried over the border into Mozambique and buried, so that he disappeared from my jurisdiction. The family started back for home, but had only gone a short way when Mwangalaine collapsed and died. This proved beyond doubt that she too was a witch, so the family just abandoned her there and carried on home. The poor woman's naked body was found later and its pathetic remains brought to me. As coroner (another of a district officer's many hats) I duly held an inquest.

Feria deposed: "My mother (the deceased) suggested that we go to Black for treatment of the children. When we arrived he asked us for cloths and some coppers, which he would examine overnight. Next morning Black made a small cut on the children's ribs and gave them some medicine. During the night my child died. In the morning (1/1/1952) we told Black we were leaving, but he said 'Do not leave'. He called all the family into his hut one by one. He gave me some medicine and also made three cuts on my chest, back and foot, and put some medicine in the cuts. I went outside and started to vomit. My parents and all the rest of us were vomiting. My father Jasi fell down and I said to Black 'You have made our father very ill'. He said 'If you want your father to stay alive, give me two pounds'. We had no money so Black got some men to carry Jasi back to our sleeping hut. Black told us to go home. We went off, leaving my father unconscious. After we had been walking a little time, our mother lost all strength and looked very ill. Legio (uncle of Feria) said to go on. We went home and buried my child. Legio arrived and said our mother had died and that he was going back to where her body was lying".

I noted for the record that Feria was somewhat evasive and vague.

The next witness was Enelesi, sister of Feria, whose evidence was much the same. She was followed by Lasina, sister of Jasi, who corroborated the evidence of the two daughters. She added the extra detail that Black had "put some medicine on my brother's head" after the unhappy Jasi had collapsed. She asked Black to bury Jasi, but was not present as "it is not the custom of my people for a woman to be present at a burial".

Black then chose to give evidence, and being a pagan was affirmed and not sworn as were all the witnesses.

"I was licensed by Native Authority Ntache in 1948 to treat various simple diseases. I remember when the deceased, her husband and family, came with two children who were sick. They asked me to treat the children. I made small cuts on the children and treated them, but did not give them medicine to drink. That night the child of Feria died. Before that the family had come to me and asked me to give them *kabanga,* because the children were sick and they wanted to find out who was causing this trouble. *Kabanga* is a medicine which I give to people to find out who is exercising the power of witchcraft. If a person is a witch, he or she will faint and die unless I give them another medicine which will revive them. I gave them all half a cup of *kabanga* and saw that Jasi had fainted, which proved that he was the witch. Feria, his daughter, told me not to give him the medicine to revive him, as I was about to do, because he had been troubling them for a long time. I had Jasi, who was unconscious, carried to the small hut, but he died shortly afterward."

Apart from a somewhat feeble attempt to shuffle off at least some of the responsibility onto the family, Black had been reasonably honest about it all, for he obviously believed in his powers both to cure the results of witchcraft and to uncover witches. All the same, I had no hesitation in entering a finding of murder against Black – which was not a conviction – a coroner's court having no such powers so that a finding is not a conviction. The proceedings were typed out and sent to the AttorneyGeneral for his decision regarding charges and a trial.

Parturient montes, nascetur ridiculus mus. The legal opinion from on high was that since there was no trace of poison in Mwangalaine's body (which was hardly surprising as practically no soft tissue was left, and in any case a vegetable poison would rapidly pass out of the body), a charge of murder could not succeed in spite of what was almost a confession from Black. The Attorney-General therefore opined that Black should be charged with pretending witchcraft. Since we mid-20th century moderns could not officially acknowledge the existence of witchcraft, we could only charge an offender with pretending it, which, since Black appeared to have been eminently successful at it, was not really a practical solution. I had also found in my verdict that there appeared to be a prima facie case against Black of demanding money with menaces – but nothing came of that either. So Black went free, having entirely successfully cheated justice – and he was probably utterly ignorant of the reasons!

OP 90 (October 2005)

He Needs a White Cloth

by A S Webb

The office of the Railway Engineer at Zungeru (Northern Nigeria) was behind the railway station, whilst the yard and office of the Inspector of Works was on the opposite side beyond the goods yard. The two offices were connected by a private telephone. One morning, soon after nine, the phone rang. It was the Inspector of Works, Johnny MacCracken, who greeted me with "Morning, Mr Webb. One of my carpenters fell down dead this morning in the joiner's shop".

"You're working your men too hard," I joked, but John was serious.

"No, honest, Mr Webb, he's dead. What shall I do?"

It was a new situation for me and I advised him to do nothing for the time being; I would go to see the Emir.

The Emir's palace was the only structure of any size and importance in what was otherwise a collection of dilapidated mud huts, the sad remains of Zungeru town. It fronted on to the road with a long mud wall, blank except for one opening near the centre giving access to a bare room, the far side of which led into a central square courtyard. The sides of the courtyard had rooms for servants, goats and chickens whilst across the back was a two storey building in which lived the Emir and his family. I greeted the figure squatting on a mat inside the room and explained in Hausa I wished to see the Emir in connection with the death of a man in the railway workshops. He indicated I should wait, and offered me the mat to squat on, but never having mastered the art of sitting cross-legged, lotus fashion, I elected to stand. The wait proved to be a long one and it was well over half an hour before a few people began to arrive, some with mats and rugs, until eventually a dozen or so had assembled, wearing a variety of what I took to be their best *rigas*.

The Emir came in, turbaned and dressed in a very fine embroidered white *riga*. I had met him several times, in fact he used to call on me at least once a month and I would enjoy discussions with him on quite profound subjects, conducted in impeccable English without a trace of accent; he had finished his education at an English University. He greeted me in Hausa and continuing in that language enquired about the man who had died; it was clear these official proceedings would be conducted entirely in

Hausa. I told him the little we knew, including his name, and he turned to one of his councillors who gave a lengthy reply which I could not follow. The Emir had thoughtfully provided an interpreter who informed me that the official 'Registrar' to whom the Emir had spoken, recognized the man. He had arrived from Minna three weeks ago, was about thirty five years old and had no known relatives. The 'Registrar' apparently relied entirely on his memory to keep track of all the people in the district.

The Emir then appointed the interpreter, two councillors and the Sanitary Inspector, who had to be collected from his home, to accompany me to the railway. We set off to pick up the Sanitary Inspector, who lived at the far end of the village and who, judging by the time he took to emerge, was asleep when we arrived. He came, hot and flustered, wearing an enormous brown *riga*. I had a small 1946 Ford Prefect at the time and the two large Hausa men in *rigas* already filled the back seat, but somehow he squeezed in and we set off. Before we had gone a hundred yards, a yell came from the back seat which had me standing on everything, bringing the occupants of the back seat over us in the front. Before I could ask what was wrong, the Inspector was out and tearing back up the road like a huge brown moth with his *riga* flying in the wind. The interpreter explained he had forgotten his apparatus and a few moments later the Inspector emerged waving it above his head, a Flit gun!

It was well past eleven when we arrived at the yard. Johnny MacCracken met us and conducted us to the joiner's shop where about a dozen occupants were sitting on the benches nonchalantly eating whilst between two benches lay a middle aged man looking very dead. We all stood back a little to allow the Sanitary Inspector to step forward and make the most of his moment. He walked slowly round the body, bending now and again to peer at it more closely, then finally satisfied, he announced in firm tones and in English, "He's dead." He followed this pronouncement by walking slowly round the body, vigorously pumping with his Flit gun. His part in the proceedings was clearly over; he joined the councillors and they all prepared to leave.

I quickly spoke to the group, "Is that all? Don't you have to give me a certificate?" They looked blank. "A *taketa*?" I pursued, but they still looked blank and a look of impatience flickered across their faces: he is dead, what more does he want? Eventually I got a curt "No more" and they moved off. Johnny and I walked after them and caught them up.

"Who buries him?" I queried.

This brought them to a halt and definite signs of annoyance showed on their faces. The interpreter slowly and deliberately gave the reply, "He was employed by you so he is your responsibility". They moved on. Once again we gave chase and they sensed we were not satisfied. With growing impatience they waited for us to catch up.

"Where shall we bury him?" I asked. The effect of my query was dramatic; the looks of resignation and impatience changed to ones of incredulity – how could this master race be so ignorant? The leader of the councillors, standing several inches taller than Johnny and me, his bulk emphasized by his black *riga*, turned to the two of us and adopting the attitude of a teacher faced with a couple of very stupid pupils, slowly raised his arms before him, palms turned upwards and dramatically swept the horizon to left and right, implying "the whole of Africa before you and you ask such a stupid question?"

They moved on but the interpreter had a last thought. He turned and after a suitably pregnant pause, delivered what was obviously intended to be the closing speech, "He is a Muslim and needs a white cloth". Johnny and I exchanged looks, yes, and we know who will have to buy that. That is the end of the story except the only cloth in the UAC canteen (store) was a six yard length of double width best quality white drill so we reckoned a third each would give us a pair of shorts each and a shroud. Then it was only a question of bribing four of his workmates with four hours' overtime and a 'dash' of a few shillings to bury him. Where, we never knew!

OP 59 (April 1990)

Part 6
SPORT & WILDLIFE

Golf in the Nigerian Bush, 1948-65

by Iddo Hudo

In the depths of the darkest Nigerian bush, a British District Commissioner had only three duties: (i) to build a Government Store the exact dimensions of a squash court; (ii) to construct an airstrip with a golf 'brown' in one corner; (iii) to maintain law and order.

Nigeria is surrounded on three sides by French territory, and the French M le Commandant also had three duties: (i) to seduce the affections of the wives of fellow officers; (ii) to maintain law and order; (iii) to take long term measures against soil erosion and drought, to minimise the possibility of famine. We laughed at our Froggy opposite numbers for their extraordinary priorities and treated them with genial contempt.

'Browns' were a mixture of sand and oil. The right mix was very difficult to achieve, too little oil and the putting surface was like a bunker, too much oil and the ball would not run. Anyone with expertise in this field was a more than welcome guest. The 'browns' had to be sited discreetly in a far corner of the airstrip, in case some self-important idiot actually tried to land and take off. With different tees and left or right artificial dog legs, one could simulate five or six different holes.

Caddies, average age 14, appeared from nowhere in response to demand, the going rate being half a penny per session, paid in one-tenths of a penny, a coin that looked like a farthing with a hole in the middle. Inflation has swept this coin away and it is now a collector's piece. Intelligence was invariably in inverse proportion to size. I used to take two caddies – one hulking youth to carry the clubs, and another, a sharp eyed youngster about two piss-pots high, who would warn me, in tones of calm certainty, as I attempted an ambitious shot, "Massa more better takey nine iron to fairway; azara tree big too much". Their eyesight was fabulous; I seldom lost a ball.

Apart from the caddies, not much interest was shown by the other natives. Seeing us leaping around the squash court and hacking about in the heat of the noon day sun they used to shrug philosophically, "the ways of the White Man are strange and beyond all reasonable belief". Our activities were generally agreed to be religious ritual to propitiate a particularly fierce and sadistic deity. Three thousand miles away from the patience and tender loving care of a Professional the faults in our swing became accentuated, then indelible and irremediable.

One could become interested in the problems of fairways. Government airstrips had to have a 'laterite' surface, an African soil which compacts well and drains quickly; a ditch on each side and a slight camber is enough to take light aircraft or heavy lorries. To the north, at the south end of the Sahara desert, a thin inch of topsoil held back inexhaustible quantities of sand. In central Nigeria great shards of granite broke through the surface. In the south, where mangrove swamps fringed the Atlantic Ocean, they had their own problems, but I was never posted down there. There is a quick growing grass called *kiri kiri* and for a small bribe the Highways Foreman and Agricultural Assistant would put their gangs on to watering and sowing. In spite of their best efforts, the sand, laterite or granite were a long way from a suitable fairway. Hence every course had a mass of local rulings and case-law, allowing preferred lies, use of tees, and for special situations, eg termites, new ant heaps and the occasional scorpion or snake.

The climate is deadly. Instead of spring, summer, autumn, winter there were three seasons: *Harmattan* – four months of wind blowing from the middle of the Sahara, covering everything with fine dust, sand dunes encroaching week by week. Then the wind stops dead and it is *Bazara* – temperatures reach 130° in the shade, and on the fairway there is no shade. Salt tablets and water at the ready. Then two or three heavy storms and it is *Damuna* – four months of rain every day, sometimes all day. Scarcely a dry inch on the fairway.

Lagos, the Federal HQ, had a course of reasonable club standard, and the three Regional HQs had adequate courses, half a dozen in all in a country the size of Britain and France combined. How we schemed to get on a conference or temporary posting to HQ, but opportunities were rare, bush postings were the norm.

Then in the dry season of 1965/6 came the first of five Revolutionary Military Coups. Golf fell into abeyance as the Coup escalated into widespread political assassinations, breakdown of law and order, massacre of Ibos, and full scale Civil War. It was not safe to be in the open, caddies disappeared; those of the wrong tribe were never seen again.

My mother-in-law, a nine handicap at Wentworth and at Sunningdale Ladies, was staying in Kaduna with us the day revolution broke out. We decided to behave as normal (this was a mistake; with experience we learnt to adopt a low profile and keep inside the compound). She drove out to the links and was arrested by a military patrol. The woods and irons were obviously deadly weapons, the bag was no doubt a home-made mortar, the white balls were high explosive, the yellow balls were obviously smoke or chemical. I had to drive a Sergeant round until we found a caddy from the same tribe before she could be released.

OP 56 (October 1988)

Cricket in Sarawak

by L J Holliday

Clubs played a large part in social life and each club could support several sports such as tennis, cricket, rugby, hockey and so on, many on a seasonal basis. So it was in Kuching, the capital of Sarawak, that cricket was very popular and apart from tossing a coin between two club members to choose teams in the time-worn manner, a signal from a soon-to-visit naval vessel, either RN or RAN, would see a scurry of activity in organising a match. Venues could be a problem as one of our earlier pitches was at the back of Saint Thomas's Church. We normally played on a Sunday morning as Saturday morning was a work time until 12 o'clock. However, and we could understand this fully, the Minister found it most disconcerting to have the punch-line of the sermon destroyed by cries of "How's that?" reverberating through the nave and into his pulpit!

As the Civil Aviation Operations Officer I was at the airport and noticed that the Public Works roller and grader were extending an area, so I asked the Divisional Engineer if he could allow a little extra grading and rolling to be done explaining that a nice big square could be our next pitch. He too played cricket, and it was as good as done. We could then make our appeals as loud and often as we wished. We placed our coir matting in the centre and fixed it with large flat-headed stakes and 'bingo' the games started. The aircraft schedules were known, and the tower would flash a red signal when it was time for them to have precedence. This gave us a break and time for a welcome beer. Invariably when there was a visiting team, the Governor, Sir Anthony Abell, would come and have a chat and watch the game with interest.

Apart from visiting ships and the occasional Sunderland flying-boat from RAF Seletar with personnel keen to have a look at the Borneo Territories and also always ready for a game, the nearest team able to play was the Panaga Club XI from the Shell oilfields at Seria in Brunei, about five hundred miles away. At the beginning of 1953 they flew a team to Kuching and a most enjoyable game was played on Saturday afternoon and Sunday. To say they were a bit strong for us would be an understatement as we were creamed!

Sometime later at an evening function at the Astana, the Governor's

Residence, a group of us were talking cricket when HE joined us and he shortly asked Dennis Bindon, our captain, if any arrangement had been made regarding a return match with the Panaga Xl. Dennis replied that transport was a stumbling block. HE said that arrangements should be made for the game at Seria and he would make available the *Mermaid,* his sea-going motor-vessel. The match was arranged for the weekend 12/13 September 1953, which entailed leaving Kuching on a Thursday afternoon and arriving back the next Tuesday. HE advised Dennis to choose his team and inform governmental heads and company directors or managers accordingly. Any mention of dissension was to be referred to HE – there were none.

Downriver from Kuching we headed north-east along the coast up the South China sea. It was a bit rough on Thursday night, and the vessel developed a considerable roll much to the discomfort of several of the team, but on Friday the roll abated and the trip was quite pleasant. All had recovered by Saturday morning when we arrived at Kuala Belait where Shell had one of their Pembroke aircraft waiting to ferry us to Anduki Airfield at Seria. We were given a tour of the oilfield installations, and the most memorable item was a group of seemingly gigantic bunsen burners lit and burning off gas twenty-four hours a day. They could be heard before they were seen, and nearer they caused the ground to shake.

Then followed a rendezvous at the Panaga Club where we were collected by our hosts. The Club was palatial by any standards and sumptuously presented in decor and furnishings. On Saturday cricket was played from half past two until six with Panaga at the crease. After a shower and change there were drinks and a buffet supper at the Club. Now every home team had its nobblers – a group of supporters whose job it was to keep as many of the visiting team as long as possible out of bed. After the meal the 'Miri Melody Makers' played and we danced well into the night. Some of the hosts, mine included, were only too happy to soldier on and the sun was up before we departed for a shower and breakfast.

The match resumed on Sunday at nine o'clock and Kuching had been well and truly on the ropes, again. When I arrived, Dennis had one look at my eyes, groaned and said that he'd drop me from number 5 to number 10! Panaga were obviously going to 'declare' but left the move just a little too late. One of our players who was a government doctor and an excellent bat, was still at the crease when I padded up and walked to the wicket. He came to meet me and said that there was no way we could get the necessary runs to win, but as the so-and-so's thought they had us, we would play for the draw. For over forty minutes I chose the correct ball to play from the two (or so it seemed to me!) the bowlers dished up to me. Whilst I scrapped and scraped for seven runs, the good doctor scored a magnificent ninety-eight not out and the day was saved. Funnily enough, after stumps when I mentioned the two balls I seemed to be facing, he was only seeing one. His host was obviously more abstemious than mine.

After a delicious lunch we left Anduki in the afternoon to fly to Kuala Belait, thence by boat to return to Kuching where we arrived on Tuesday morning to be greeted by the Governor who congratulated us on a very good draw.

OP 89 (April 2005)

SARAWAK

 Sarawak was taken over as a Crown Colony by the British Government in 1946. The colonial emblem is based on the flag of the former Rajah, Sir Charles Brooke. It shows a shield, divided by an upright cross half black, half red, with an elementary crown in the centre.

The Lion

by E W Bult

"**L**eopards", said Mike Costello, as he came into my office holding a message form. "This signal, which has come in from a railway station down on the Lower Shiré River, says leopards are taking animals of people living in the area and they want police to come and kill them".

The year was 1954. Costello and I were nearing the end of our first three-year tour of duty as junior officers of the Nyasaland Police, and still had much to learn about the territory and its people. Like most young expatriates, however, the prospect of big game hunting offered excitement not to be missed, and we began making preparations for a trip down the escarpment to the tiny station of Lirangwe, from whence the signal had been sent. As Station Officer I controlled the armoury keys and together we selected the firearms which we would take for the hunt, which we arranged for the following weekend. Costello chose a double-barrelled shotgun with a supply of LG cartridges, while I decided on the only longer range weapon available, a .303 SMLE rifle with several clips of ammunition. We taped hand flashlights onto our guns as we knew our best prospects of seeing leopard would be at night.

With plenty of sandwiches, cold drinks, and coffee for the anticipated long wait at night, we left Blantyre by car and reached Lirangwe station about mid-afternoon. The station clerk directed us to the village where the incidents had occurred.

His words of encouragement, "The place is a little bit near", hardly prepared us for a very hot march of about four or five miles along winding tracks between shoulder-high grass and sparse bush. The sun was already below the level of the taller trees near the village when we arrived. We were greeted by people whose goats had been taken by an animal which was clearly powerful; it had torn down the pole and mud-plastered walls of the *khola* where the stock were kept at night. Huge pug marks were evident in the softer ground beside a nearby stream. The villagers were sure that it was a *nyalugwe* (leopard) which had begun nightly visits to plunder their stock.

My colleague and I decided to have a fowl pegged in the centre of a clearing, and to await the arrival of the beast in a couple of trees which were conveniently situated beside the cleared area. As night fell Costello and I bade "good night" to the villagers, climbed up to our respective positions, tested our spotlights by aligning our guns on the unfortunate fowl, then prepared for a long, silent wait for sudden action.

It was not long before rain began falling; at first a few spots, then gradually increasing to a steady downpour. Now and then we jabbed a shaft of light at the centre of our attention, when a real or imagined sound broke through the constant spattering and dripping of the rain. Nothing was spoken between us for what seemed hours until, in almost perfect unison, we called to each other to seek agreement upon a return to the car for coffee and a change of clothing. Needless to say, agreement was speedily reached and, stiffly, we climbed down from our perches and began the long walk to our vehicle. Refreshed, and once more in dry clothing, we started on our return to the village in order to advise the owner of the fowl that we had decided against further hunting that night. Neither Costello nor I wished to spend a moment longer in the fork of a tree, waiting under a cold shower for an event which in all likelihood would not occur. The rain stopped as we neared the half-way point between the car and the village. Shortly after, in the light of my spot lamp, I saw what I believed was a hyena, crossing the path about 25 yards ahead. The beast appeared to have the distinctive slope from the shoulders down to the hind legs. I raised my rifle and fired two rounds. Costello, who was following, stepped forward and loosed one round from the shotgun. We went forward together and found, beside the path, a jackal, mortally wounded apparently by the shotgun. Costello's second barrel was used to deliver a *coup de grace*.

It was then, as the rain began to fall with increased force, the two intrepid hunters assessed their position. Having determined not to pursue further their attempt to bag a leopard, all ammunition had been left in the car, with the exception of one cartridge in each barrel of Costello's 12 gauge, and one clip of five rounds in my rifle. Here we were, in the middle of (literally) darkest Africa, with only three rounds of .303 ammunition for the one rifle. Prudence dictated that the fowl would have to take its chances for the remainder of the night, and we went back to the car and to beds in Blantyre.

The telegram which arrived at Blantyre Police Station some ten days later is still in my possession and reads as follows :

NYASALAND POST OFFICE TELEGRAPHS
BLANTYRE TELS
18 MAR 54
NYASALAND

ZB 136 SG F-M S/CLERK LIRANGWE TO XL POLICE BLANTYRE. LION ROUNDING STATION FROM 1830 HRS. ONE WAS KILLED ON 6/3/54 BY POLICE OFFICER. STILL THERE IS ANOTHER GIVING TROUBLE FROM 1830 HRS UPWARDS XY PLEASE ARRANGE SOME BODY TO STATION AND VILLAGE TO NOTE THAT NO BODY WILL BE AT FACE POINT AT THAT TIME X ADDRESSED WARDEN T S LIMBE AND POLICE BLANTYRE.

Costello and I were vastly amused that the villagers seemed to have such confidence in the police that three shots fired in the night could indicate the killing of a lion. The prospect of another big game hunting expedition, this time after lion, whetted our appetite for further adventure and, rather more appropriately armed on this occasion, we set off once more for the Lower River area. We were escorted from Lirangwe station by an excited man to the same village as that which had received us earlier. Local residents welcomed us and hailed us with much respect, telling us how they had heard our shots and, next day, found the dead lion. At first we played along with them in the assumption that some other misfortune must have overtaken the animal. Other hunters had been active in the area perhaps? No, the villagers were adamant, nobody but ourselves had been around – and when people in the remote areas said that no strangers were there one could be sure that such was indeed the case.

We were still trying to seek an answer to the riddle when one of the villagers offered to lead us to the site where the dead lion had been found. He told us, on the way, that the lion had a wound behind the left ear and another in the side of the chest. As we came to the place where the jackal had been shot, our guide turned off the path and, a few yards into the bush, showed us the remains of what was once a fully grown male lion with jet black mane and huge foreleg bones. Very little apart from those fragments remained; indeed it is quite surprising that even those traces were present ten days or so after discovery. Hyenas and other scavengers make short work of clearing up. It was clear to us then what had happened that night out there in the rain. It was not a hyena which I had seen and fired at, but the lion. The jackal which Costello had killed had been following the lion to scavenge upon its kill. We said nothing more to each other until, having explained to our new friends of the village that lion killing was really the job of the Game Department, we returned to our vehicle, resolved not to tempt fate a second time.

OP 73 (Spring 1997)

Good Advice Will Defeat Your Enemy

by G R P Henton

"**W**e have cornered it at last", said the panting and exhausted messenger arriving at the discussions which were taking place at the foot of the mountains in an African country. They concerned the lack of water and the provision of irrigation ditches as a remedy.

"Cornered what?" said the astonished District Officer, taken aback at this rude interruption to the slow deliberations that had occurred until then. It was about 11 o'clock on a hottish June morning, and the interruption could, it was true, provide a break for some welcome coffee and biscuits.

"The man-eating lion that has been terrorising our villages these last two months", said the new arrival, "and we would like you, Sir, to do something about it."

The District Officer, knowing his own lack of experience, looked at his European colleague, and muttered something about arranging for the game scout. His companion said "I have game rifles, shall we go and have a crack?" and the two agreed to go and investigate. They went in a landrover to a village about 5 miles away (just a collection of huts) and found there quite a crowd gathered. Eric B, the man who had the guns, said to the other, "I have here two guns, I will take the double bore elephant rifle, and you can have the magazine rifle". The two men then followed the crowd out of the village. The African men were talking excitedly. They explained that the lion was an old one which had been attacking the people as well as goats and sheep around the village for the last few months, and that very morning it had jumped on a man going to the fields and killed him. It had been dragging his body away when two others had managed to wound the animal with a musket shot and an arrow. They knew that the lion had not gone far and where it was lying up with the corpse. Two miles or so away in the flat desolate bush and scrub land that was the common topography of that part of Africa, the Africans stopped and pointed to a thicket of rather dense bush, whispering "the lion has gone in there". It was agreed that the large party of villagers should then act as beaters, and the two officials, armed with loaded rifles, went to station themselves at the southern side of the thicket, about 50 yards away from the bushes. The villagers then advanced slowly from the western side, beating tin cans, shouting, throwing stones, and making as much commotion as possible. After some minutes of this, the lion stirred and left the cover of the thicket on the eastern side, loping away across the bushland to get away from the detestable hullabaloo. The two officials fired simultaneously; the lion turned towards them and charged. The double bore gun spoke again and missed presumably, the lion came on. Magazine rifle was on the point of shooting when his companion said "Let me have it, it is mine". It was meekly handed over, and the other, drawing aim on the lion by now about ten yards away, shot it straight between the eyes. It dropped dead. There followed much jubilation and feasting around the body and in the village for the rest of that day. From then on the two officials could do no wrong in those parts.

If there is a moral in this, it must be: in times of danger, do not argue with the voice of authority.

OP 56 (October 1988)

Part 7
PERSONALITIES

A Tribute to Captain A Gibb, DSO, DCM
District Commissioner, British Somaliland

by Roland A Hill

I was recently browsing in a local bookshop when I picked up a book of short stories called *Tales from the Outposts* which had been originally published in Blackwood's Magazine. In a story called *The People without a Pillow*, written by 'Zeres', I recognised the hero named Ian Ross as none other than Mr Allan Gibb, DCM, as he then was, in his capacity as an Assistant District Officer stationed at Zeila on the north coast of British Somaliland in 1911. This clue and the words 'dead 1922' alongside his name on the medal roll for his clasp for Somaliland 1920, coupled with information that there had been a civil disturbance in Somaliland in 1922, indicated that, despite a complete absence of service records on this man, there had to be a good story, and the PRO records on the Somaliland Protectorate provided the missing links.

This remarkable man joined Colonel Swayne's first expedition against the Mad Mullah at the age of 23 as an armourer sergeant, only to be murdered 21 years later by hostile tribesmen when he was District Commissioner, Burao. His group of four medals which surfaced recently is of considerable historical importance. The DSO and DCM, linked to the Africa General Service Medal with all six clasps to British Somaliland (1901-20), and the War Medal (1914-20) for active service against the Mad Mullah for which no clasps to the AGSM were awarded, represent 20 years of continuous active service in both a military and a civilian capacity. Gibb was the only European, and one of only two, who was awarded all six clasps, the other being Risaldar-Major Farah al Somal.

Allan Gibb was born on 28 December 1877, the son of a butler, in the parish of Corstorphine in Edinburgh. He was apprenticed to a firm of gunmakers in Frederick Street, and joined the Volunteers around 1898. In 1900 he decided to make his career in the army, and he duly enlisted in the Army Ordnance Corps. Skilled armourers were much in demand and he was soon earmarked for overseas service in Ashanti. Due to an accident his posting was cancelled and instead he arrived a year later in Somaliland in April 1901 as a Sergeant armourer instructor.

He subsequently took part in the engagements at Erigo in 1902, when he was mentioned in despatches for repairing a Maxim under hot fire, and again for his bravery at Daratolleh in 1903. He was also mentioned in the official history of the operations in Somaliland for his role at Jidballi in 1904. Of the action at Daratolleh, Lt Colonel R E Drake-Brockman wrote in an appreciation of his life in *The Times*, 'His gallantry on all occasions, but particularly during the rear-guard action in which Colonel John Gough and two other officers received the Victoria Cross, earned for him in his humble capacity of a non-commissioned officer the DCM, but I have heard on good authority that no-one on that day earned the coveted VC more than Allan Gibb'. In an obituary notice in *The Scotsman*, it is stated that he had been recommended for the highest military honour, and in yet another reference to his feat of arms on that day, there is a snippet written by the then Governor of Somaliland in 1911 on an internal memo before his secondment to the Camel Corps, which reads, 'In view of Gibb's excellent military record, he saved a British force by coolly sticking to his Maxim', and in another memo, 'we are pledged to Gibb'.

The next mention of Gibb is that he proceeded on leave to the UK in 1905 as a Sergeant-Major. The medal roll for his fourth clasp to his AGS Medal for Somaliland 1908-10 lists him as a Lieut Quartermaster with 6th Bn (Somaliland) KAR when he would have been about 30. When 6 KAR was disbanded, Gibb was in a sense time-expired and redundant, having served for nearly 10 years with a colonial force. However, the Secretary of State for the Colonies, the Rt Hon Lewis Harcourt, approved Gibb's appointment as an Assistant District Officer, despite the fact that all government agencies had been withdrawn from the interior, but more significantly to retain his valuable services in Somaliland. When in 1912 it was decided to form the Camel Constabulary under Richard Corfield, Gibb was asked to be his second-in-command. When Gibb was on leave in 1913, Corfield and the Constabulary had a confrontation with the Mad Mullah's followers at Magala Yer, and Corfield and many of the Constabulary were killed.

It was then decided to form a Camel Corps under military command for the purpose of re-establishing the Government's authority in the interior. There was little active service in the Empire at that time and competition was keen for secondment to Somaliland by both British and Indian Army officers. Gibb, now a District Officer, remained as a civilian still on secondment and was appointed a civilian company commander which, in any circumstances, must have been an unusual appointment.

Gibb was involved in both actions at Shimber Berris in 1914 and in 1915. He was mentioned in Colonel Cubitt's despatch and in the Governor's despatch forwarded to the Colonial Office: 'From beginning to end there was no hitch of any sort and it is due to the capable handling of the CO and his staff and the excellent leading by the Company Commanders responsible, Capt Breading, Mr Gibb and Lt Eales, that the casualty list was kept so low as it was'. At this point it was decided to make Gibb a local Captain in the Camel Corps, and thus rectify his somewhat anomalous position as a civilian company commander. His appointment on 20 August 1915 was backdated to 16 September 1914.

He continued to serve in the Camel Corps on secondment from the administration, as did other regular army officers who were refused permission to serve in other theatres of war, until 1918 when he was duly reabsorbed, but now with the rank of District Commissioner and stationed at Burao in the interior. At the same time he was informed that his entire service in Somaliland would count towards his civil pension, a rather unusual gesture from a normally penny-pinching Colonial Office, but it highlighted the appreciation of the authorities for his outstanding services. When the time came to launch the final offensive against the Mad Mullah in 1920 Gibb was given command of the tribal levy comprising some 1,500 persons, which was to work in close liaison with the Camel Corps. Once again Gibb distinguished himself, and although the Mullah just eluded him, he captured his headquarters at Tale and played his part in the complete rout of the Mullah's forces. For his services he received one of the three DSOs awarded for this campaign, and this in distinguished company.

He returned to his civilian duties in 1920 and in the following year led a delegation of distinguished Somalis to Aden to be presented to the Prince of Wales, who was en route to India for his Indian tour. Towards the end of December 1921 he settled compensation claims with representatives of a Royal Italian Commission as a result of inter-tribal fighting on the Anglo-ltalian border. Only a few weeks later, on 24 February 1922, he was murdered by tribesmen at the Burao Station headquarters, as the direct result of wild protests made against Government proposals to institute a levy to assist in the cost of opening schools, since none existed at that time due to the nomadic existence of these tribes. His death had far-reaching effects. The Governor's despatches covered every aspect surrounding his death, for the Governor had been taking tea with Gibb in his bungalow at Burao a quarter of an hour before his death in company with Risaldar-Major

Farah al Somal. The Governor had lent his car to Gibb to enable him to take appropriate action. Unfortunately, although warned by a Corporal of the Somali Camel Corps, in mufti, not to go ahead, he unwisely albeit gallantly went alone to confront the frenzied mob. This time it was a reaction aimed specifically at the Government which Gibb represented. Gibb must have realised too late that this was not the time for heroics and one rifle shot put paid to his life. The Government authorities reacted and RAF planes from Aden flew over the area a few days later, Gibb's body was taken to Sheikh where he now lies buried. On 5 March 1922 the Governor called in the tribe concerned with the killing and imposed a fine of 3,000 camels for Gibb's death (tribal custom and law allows for the payment of 100 camels for murder). He also informed them that the Burao station, except for the mosque, would be bombed and burnt by the RAF. This drastic action and the unprecedented fine well illustrated the importance given to the law and order aspect but in part represented the reaction of the authorities to the death of Gibb.

There is only one known photograph of Gibb (though no doubt others exist) and a sketch of him behind his Maxim at Daratolleh. It was acknowledged 'that no British officer has ever had such a wonderful insight into the Somali character nor presented so sound a colloquial knowledge of the Somali language'. Gibb, who was a bachelor, had been completely dedicated to his work with the Somalis, and in his continuous travelling in the interior, under sometimes appalling conditions, he must have faced danger and hardships too numerous to mention.

OP 84 (October 2002)

Berkeley of Upper Perak

by Anon

Stories of Old Timers remind me of someone I came to know about when posted in 1948 as ADO at Kroh in the Upper Perak district of Malaya near its border with Thailand, the headquarters of which was at a place called Grik.

Upper Perak will always be associated with one of the most extraordinary Englishmen who ever served the Empire. Hubert Berkeley was appointed its district officer in 1891 and remained there until his retirement to England in 1925, a record thirty-four years. Berkeley believed passionately in rural as opposed to technological economic progress and conceived himself as having a mission in helping Malays to become better *bumiputra* (sons of the soil). One of his achievements was to establish new settlements for Malays in the vicinity of Kroh following its annexation under the treaty of 1909 with Siam; and here he introduced irrigation projects on a large scale, being much interested in the cultivation of wet *padi* (rice) and convinced that good agriculture was the only vocation fit for a Malay. In order to achieve his ideals he refused all offers of promotion out of his beloved district, his post being periodically up-graded to reflect his growing seniority. He knew his people intimately, some of them for three generations, and ruled them as a benevolent autocrat, a role which in my time it would have been impossible to sustain. But in days when the *Hulu* (hinterland) had barely been touched by western ideas – and he had no intention that it should be – it was possible in a remote district to become lost to the outside world for years on end and consequently to do what one liked. More than this, Berkeley spurned interference from the British Resident or from any other quarter, and got away with it.

Once, when the Resident got about half way to Grik, his car was stopped by a tree deliberately felled across the road on Berkeley's orders. Naturally no-one could be found or persuaded to move it, and the Resident gave up the struggle and returned to Ipoli. A successor, a man named Hume, managed to penetrate as far as Grik and noticed that many thoroughfares had names; Whitehall where the district office was situated, Downing Street where Berkeley lived at No 10, Piccadilly, Rotten Row and of course Berkeley Square, where several roads met at the *padang* (open space). Hume enquired why no road was named after himself, and Berkeley promised to put the matter right. Thereafter an observant visitor might have spotted a narrow alley-way running for a few yards between two shops and then soon ending in thick undergrowth, where a rough, wooden sign announced it as Hume's Mews. As one of several reminders of Berkeley's reign, the street signs were still there when I first visited Grik in 1948. As for the High Commissioner, the only time when this potentate plucked up courage to attempt a visit, he received a telegram shortly before leaving Singapore purporting to warn him against floods and containing the cryptic message, 'no bridge at the forty-second mile – Berkeley'. There never was a bridge and His Excellency never came.

Berkeley never married officially nor became a Muslim, but he lived, dressed and ate as a Malay. When acting as DO for a few weeks in 1949, 1 saw at Grik some fair-skinned young Malays who, I was told, were descended from his progeny. His spirit still permeated the district at all levels with elderly Malays recalling wistfully the great days of old as if they had lived in some kind of Arcadia. For the transportation round the district of himself and others Berkeley kept a herd of tame elephants, of which I found two survivors, and noticed that Rotten Row was the path between their grazing ground and the District Office. He introduced an Upper Perak coat-of-arms consisting of an elephant rampant superimposed by a motto in Malay which he compiled – *Koh dahulu* (look before you leap). He had the arms embossed on plates and other things, some of which I found still in use. He caused to be worn by all *penghulus* (village headmen) and other officials a district badge, incorporating the same design, one of which together with a plate remains in my, I suppose, illegal possession.

It was a privilege and quite an experience to be invited to stay at his unusual 'ménage', where European guests had to be prepared for some surprises; for it was full of Malays of both sexes whose life-style Berkeley adopted together with some modifications of his own. There were two thunderboxes (commodes) set together in his bathroom opposite the Shanghai jar (for bathing) – all retained for old-times sake certainly up to 1949, one for himself, the other for his guest, where each morning arrangements for the coming day were discussed as nature took its course.

In addition to roads, machines, motor-cars, newspapers and money-lenders, he especially detested lawyers. There was a rare occasion when a lawyer had the audacity to come to Grik to defend a man charged with theft. Sitting as magistrate, Berkeley listened for a minute or two as evidence was produced, then stopped the proceedings by saying, "I do not want to hear any more. He's guilty". To the lawyer's protest that the defence had not been called, he replied, "Of course he's guilty. He always was a cattle thief, as were his father and grandfather before him". Berkeley's ideas of legal procedure were also idiosyncratic. One day when about to leave on an elephant ride, the Court Clerk came up to him to say that there were some cases for hearing. On Berkeley enquiring how many, the clerk replied that there were twenty-five all pleading guilty to the same offence.

"All right", said Berkeley, "odd numbers discharged, even numbers fined five dollars." Then he rode off. He greatly preferred his own summary justice to that of the Indian Code. When a boundary dispute arose, he adjourned the court and summoned the litigants to accompany him to the site. Here he formed them into two teams and held a tug-of-war contest using rotan creepers from the jungle, awarding the disputed land to the winning team. To an enquiry about the use to which a particular building was put, he replied "This is the court-house. Here we dispense justice but not law".

He affected almost royal airs. Coming as he did from an aristocratic background, he regarded himself as a combination of a Malay chief and English squire. He sometimes went all the way to Kroh to bathe at a spot called Ayer Panas (hot springs), not on an elephant which would have been too slow, but in an English landau and pair with a Malay postilion dressed in a garment coloured to correspond with the Berkeley family livery. Even when outside the district he travelled with liveried guards and a large private tent. Eccentric he undoubtedly was, but as was later testified by one of his Malay subordinates, 'he was a real gentleman who always supported those in need usually from his own pocket', and who was kind and benevolent in his autocratic way. Within the district he was respected and obeyed without question. Outside he evidently had his enemies. Years later I learnt from someone whose father had known Berkeley that there were many who considered his eccentricities to go well beyond the bounds of propriety.

OP 57 (April 1989)

Serving Mallam Abubakar Tafawa Balewa,
Nigerian Minister of Works and Transport in 1951

by R L Armstrong

O ne afternoon early in 1951, I found myself at the Ikeja Airport, Lagos, awaiting the arrival of Mallam Abubakar Tafawa Balewa, who had just been appointed Central Minister of Works and Transport in the Nigerian House of Representatives, created under a new Constitution which granted Nigeria internal self-government as a step towards eventual independence. There were twelve ministers in the Council of Ministers who, under the chairmanship of the Governor-General, Sir John Macpherson, formed the Cabinet. Suitably qualified Departmental Officers of the Colonial Service, of whom I was one, were appointed to act as their Private Secretaries. I am a Chartered Civil Engineer and by then had seen over twelve years service with the Nigerian Public Works Department, eleven of them in the Northern Region. This had enabled me to learn something of the Hausa language.

I was born in 1912 and for the first 13 years of my life lived in Alexandria, Egypt, attending Victoria College, the pupils of which were drawn from many nationalities, only a small number being British. Obviously I absorbed the cosmopolitan atmosphere and was taught the rudiments of reading and writing in Arabic which, incidentally, I spoke fairly fluently. Later when I was sent to school in England, my knowledge of the language was largely forgotten, only to be revived when I eventually went to Nigeria and was fascinated to find so many Arabic roots in Hausa. I only mention this in passing as I believe it was an important factor in my subsequent relationship with Mallam Abubakar.

He had been born in 1912 in the little village of Tafawa Balewa in Bauchi Province, Northern Nigeria. After primary education locally he went to Katsina Higher College in 1925 and in 1933 began his career as a teacher by joining the staff of Bauchi Middle School. His promotion was steady and in 1949 he became Education Officer for Bauchi Province. His talents soon led him into wider fields and after the War, when the development of Nigeria was being accelerated, he was appointed to the Northern Self-Development Fund Committee.

I can't remember being given a specification for the job of Private Secretary apart from being told to help the Minister in any way I could. So I acted as his ADC whenever we went on tour. I arranged the catering for our journeys and for cocktail parties. I kept notes and wrote reports of meetings, underlining points of special interest for future study. I was required to undertake research and write papers and briefs for his attendances at the Council of Ministers and his appearances in the 'House'. In the early days, at 'Questions Time' in the House of Representatives, I often accompanied him and, keeping out of sight, I scribbled replies to supplementary questions. As he grew more and more familiar with the workings of his Department, so my need to accompany him to the House declined and finally ceased.

The Minister's Office was in the headquarters building of the PWD in Lagos and a part of my job was to meet visitors who had appointments and take them to the Minister. Only rarely was I asked to leave him alone with the visitor. On one occasion, however, a Lebanese gentleman called and I was asked to leave them together. When the visitor had left, Mallam Abubakar said to me "the reason I did not ask you to stay was that the subject under discussion with our visitor had nothing to do with Government business. To re-assure you, I can tell you that my answer to his request was NO!" Then he said "He will come to my house this evening I shouldn't wonder, but the answer I shall give him will still be NO".

I insert this small incident to show the complete incorruptibility of the mark. He was not interested in money for its own sake. His life-style was simple and sometimes when I had to visit him at his home in the late evening, I would find him sitting on the floor and, on one occasion, sharing a meal with one of his male relatives who cooked for him. On that occasion I was invited to sit down and squatted on my heels beside him which was something I had learnt to do as a boy in Egypt. With his usual candour he said "You see Mr Armstrong, I like to live simply". He was a Mohammedan and having made the pilgrimage to Mecca was entitled to wear the green turban and be addressed as 'Alhaji'.

His rise to eminence in the political field was swift and sure and to list all his achievements is not the purpose of this article; they have been fully documented elsewhere. Sufficient to say that 1948 found him in London as the Nigerian delegate to the African Conference and to the Commonwealth Parliamentary Association. In 1951 he came again to London, this time as the Nigerian delegate to the Festival of Britain. In that same year he was elected Deputy Leader of the Northern Peoples Congress and appointed Central Minister of Works and Transport.

It was at this juncture in his life that I first met him. In appearance he was tall and slim, of dark skin and a quiet air of dignity. Basically shy, it took some time before his reserve was breached, but those of us who came to know him, found him a warm friendly man with a great sense of humour and a keen penetrating mind. He had a beautiful speaking voice, his command of English was remarkable, his diction and the cadence of his delivery made it a pleasure to listen to him.

As I have stated previously, part of my duties was to arrange his official life. My first wife – whom I left sleeping beneath Nigerian skies – was a great help in these matters, especially with cocktail parties, for although a Moslem and a strict teetotaller, his position demanded that he should entertain many people whose religions and tastes were varied. The arrangement of the guest list brought him more than once to our house and my wife was able – as I was not – to ask him about his wife and children. It transpired that, although a Mohammedan and therefore permitted to have up to four wives, he had in fact only one. Quite simply the Minister replied to my wife's question that his wife had been his constant friend and companion over many years and that it would hurt her deeply if he had thought of bringing another woman into the household and that, to him, was the prime consideration. This thoughtfulness for a woman's feeling was rare, but was typical of the man. Shortly after this conversation, I found myself with the pleasurable task of helping in the transfer of his children from their Bauchi School to Lagos to continue their education and still be with their father.

A school-master by profession, Mallam Abubakar had no experience of engineering works or the methods by which they were conceived, designed or constructed. It was one of my duties to escort him to construction sites and offices, first preparing a brief and explaining the project in advance. On one occasion I took him to see the replacement of a junction in the 36 inch water-main to the Lagos water supply. The operation had to be done when demand for water was at its lowest, in fact between 1am and 3am. When we arrived, the excavation and timbering had already been completed, the water had been shut off and the faulty section removed. The work of connecting the new section was in progress and the Minister saw it being lowered into the trench and correctly aligned. In the trench under brilliant arc-lights the operation was being directed by a British Senior

Inspector of Works helped by another British Inspector and his African staff and workforce. The whole operation, well planned in advance, was completed within the time limit and the flow of potable water to Lagos resumed. The Minister appeared to be intensely interested in every detail as the Water Engineer who was in charge and who had been responsible for the planning explained each process as it occurred.

On the way back to Lagos in the car, he was for the most part silent. Suddenly he turned to me, "There were Europeans down that hole with the Africans" he said.

"It happens all the time Minister", I replied. "You see it is not only a question of getting the job done, but of using the opportunity to train staff."

"Do you know," he said, "I never thought that it happened like that."

I was to learn later that before his appointment as Minister of Works and Transport he had been a notable critic of the Public Works Department. By the time I left his service the Department could not have wished for a more understanding champion.

So that he could become acquainted with the problems of his portfolio we toured large areas of the country. The Minister and I travelled in the Ministerial car followed by a station wagon carrying his servant, my steward-boy and all the luggage and provisions. On our long road journeys, the Minister and I were on our own together in the car. Protocol was then waived and we could talk as friends. He spoke of his past and of stories told to him by his parents. He recounted how his grandmother had told him of seeing her husband's throat cut by marauding tribesmen, but that once the British rule was established order was restored. We spoke of the present and plans for the future, of our different cultures and our past experiences and of astronomy in which he and I were deeply interested. When I returned home on leave I made a point of selecting a couple of books on astronomy to send him and I was told that he later installed a telescope on the roof of his house and found relaxation in studying the skies.

It was on one of these tours that the Minister displayed his talents as a mimic. He was telling me about his school-days at Katsina Higher College and regaled me with tales about the idiosyncrasies of some of the masters. He obviously held these past members of the Nigerian Education Department in high regard and affection as he reproduced turns of speech and mannerisms which would have equalled some of Mike Yarwood's best impressions.

His affection for his teachers and his regard for the British were exemplified by the reference he made to them in his speech as Prime

Minister on Nigerian Independence Day on 20th August 1960, when he said, "We are grateful to the British officers we have known first as masters, then as leaders and finally as partners, but always as friends."

OP 48 (November 1984)

"Wote Timamu, Effendi"
("All Present and Correct, Sir")

by Ian D St G Lindsay

Tramp! Tramp! Tramp! Left! Right! Left! As on every other morning at this time, I could hear the single pair of booted feet marching up the concrete footpath towards my office in the Provincial Administration's Divisional District Officer's Headquarters.

Sitting at my desk, out of the corner of my eye, I caught the movement of a shadow in the doorway. I looked up as a grinning Tribal Police Sergeant Suleimani made his daily report.

"Wote timamu (All present and correct), *Effendi."*

I thanked him, *"Asante,* Sar' Major."

As usual it was exactly 7.28am, and the immaculately uniformed, stiffly starched and highly 'bulled' Sergeant Suleimani, standing smartly at attention, silver-knobbed Malacca cane under his left armpit and right hand quivering at the salute, was reporting that his detachment of tribal policemen, or *kangas,* were assembled on parade on the road outside my office. At this daily parade I would normally inspect, and occasionally address, the mustered tribal policemen (TPs) before they were dismissed to their allocated duties in the surrounding locations, or village areas, within the Division.

Originally a body of messengers employed by District Commissioners in the earlier days of colonial rule in Uganda, the Tribal Police Force in Kenya was officially constituted in 1929 as an executive force under District Commissioners, and within the Chiefs and Headmen organisation. The Force was tasked with the performance of crime prevention and general policing duties in the tribal reserves, with the investigation of serious crime being the responsibility of the colony's police force, which generally operated outside the tribal reserves. As its name implies, it was basically recruited along tribal lines. Outside the tribal reserves, in the cities and urban areas, for example, where many tribes were represented in the local population, its ranks were a tribal melange.

Suleimani bin (son of) Abu Abdulla, a Nubian whose family originated in the Nuba Mountains of Kordofan in the Sudan, was born in the early

1920s to his father's second wife. He was born in the settlement which had been established on the outskirts of the city for the descendants of Mehmet Emin Pasha's Sudanese soldiers, who were levied at the end of the 19th Century for the opening up of Equatorial Africa. The family had a four-generation tradition of military service. Suleimani's great grandfather was one of Emin Pasha's soldiers. His grandfather served in the Uganda Rifles in the early 1900s; his father was in the King's African Rifles in World War I and Suleimani himself, also in the King's African Rifles, served in Burma in World War II with the 11th East African Division. At war's end, Suleimani, by then a Sergeant, stayed on in the army. He left the King's African Rifles towards the end of 1952 with the rank of Company Sergeant-Major, and two months later, in response to a recruiting drive, joined the Tribal Police with the rank of Acting Sergeant.

From the outset Suleimani was held in high regard by everyone who worked with him and, although the establishment structure for TPs limited the senior rank to Sergeant, the presence, demeanour and general stamp of the man were such that both his subordinates and superiors, indeed even his contemporaries in rank, addressed him by his former military rank. This manifested itself as either 'Sar' Major' or, more usually, from his fellow TPs at any rate, the complimentary 'Major'.

Some years earlier, when he was a soldier, Suleimani had met and married a 16 year old Boran girl, who had been given into prostitution by her father to pay some pressing family debts. On her first night in the brothel she had been assigned to Suleimani. It must have been love at first sight for, early in the morning, the pair stole away and wed. Two attempts by the girl's family and the bordello keeper to get her back from a very determined Suleimani were aborted in the face of a ferocious defence. Eventually, when reason prevailed, Suleimani undertook to pay the family debts in place of the customary bride price for his wife. By the time I met him, Suleimani was the proud and very protective father of two sets of twin daughters. He and his wife were the only Africans I ever knew whose obvious love for each other showed in their eyes.

Thoroughly loyal, absolutely trustworthy and always respectful, he was the ideal mentor for a new and untried DO. Remarkably though – in view of the ranks he reached, first as a soldier and then as a tribal policeman – Sergeant Suleimani was only partially literate. Moreover, his English was not very good, though clearly he understood more than he spoke. This lack of formal education, however, was scarcely a handicap, for he was above all a thinker. Problems for him were mere irritations interrupting the orderly and disciplined flow of life. When any hitch or difficulty presented itself, he would apply himself immediately and assiduously to its solution and elimination using, I imagine, a sort of NCO's mental military appreciation process.

There was the time the 'Nubian gin' court exhibit went missing. A man and his two adult sons had been arrested for the umpteenth time for manufacturing this particularly potent and often lethal high-proofed spirit. The distillation and consumption of the cloudy liquor, which was produced on illicit stills hidden in the bush, was strictly against the law, notwithstanding its extreme popularity amongst some tribes despite its capacity to blind, paralyse and kill. The profits however were great, but so too were the personal risks and the punishments.

The three accused, as usual, pleaded not guilty and the case was remanded for hearing with the exhibits – some one dozen or so bottles of gin – being placed in a cupboard for safekeeping. On the day after the case was eventually heard and the three accused convicted, Sergeant Suleimani returned the exhibits to my office for destruction. As he put them on my desk, I absent-mindedly removed the cork from one of the bottles and sniffed the contents.

"What's this Sar' Major?", I queried, surprised. "It's not gin."

"Yes *Effendi*, it is Jin, *Effendi*", he insisted. "Jin-ja beer,* *Effendi*".

"Jin-ja beer? Never heard of it." Then the fog began to clear. "Oh, you mean ginger beer."

"That's right," he agreed, "Jin-ja beer, *Effendi*."

And so I learned that on the day before the case was to come to trial, every one of the bottles of gin was found to have been broached and, worse, emptied. The presence of the liquor had been too strong a temptation for those responsible for its custody. And, normally, that would have been that; no gin, no case. But Sergeant Suleimani had had other ideas, solving the problem with a few bottles of ginger beer. Fortunately, the court had not been as nosy as I.

Still on the subject of Nubian gin, some time later I was on patrol with a party of TPs, and we visited an area where stone was quarried and dressed. The stonecutters and their families lived alongside the quarry where they

---

*Jinja is a major commercial town in Uganda

also grew and smoked *bhang* and manufactured and drank Nubian gin. Permanently under the influence of drink or a drug, these people were considered by the rest of the population as belonging to another tribe.

The blasting technique used for extracting the stone was very crude. Consequently the area around the quarry was a mass of rubble, in which the stonecutters would hide their illicit liquor by burying it in 44 gallon drums, and covering the lids with a layer of rubble, making it fairly difficult to find. On this particular day, though, the quarrymen were out of luck. We uncovered 12 full drums buried in the rubble. But we immediately had a problem; how to get rid of their contents, for it was impossible for us to lift them out of the ground. After giving it some thought, I told Sergeant Suleimani to get the TPs to collect shovels from the stonecutters' camp, gather up any faeces they could find – cattle, dog, human, it didn't matter – and put it into the drums of gin. If we couldn't take it away, I reasoned, we could at least make it undrinkable.

"Yes, *Effendi*," he said. "But," he paused respectfully.

"But what, Sar' Major?" I asked.

He went on to explain that he believed the gin we had found had been made for sale; there was just too much for the stonecutters to be able to drink on their own.

"And so?" I persisted.

"When we have left," he continued, "they will simply remove whatever we have put into the gin, and sell it without saying anything to the people who buy it."

"All right," I said, "what do you suggest?"

Turning, he called to the TPs to look for a crowbar. When one had been found he instructed his men to punch holes in the bottom of each uncovered drum. After one or two holes had been made, the contents began to drain away and soon the drums were empty, and the problem was solved. Of course, when we returned on a follow-up visit, we found that the holes in the drums had been plugged with tar – the distillers would not give up that easily. Continued treatments with the crowbar, however, eventually ensured that the drums could no longer be used.

A few months before I quit the colony and the Colonial Service, the decision was made to include a contingent of Tribal Police in what was to be the last Queen's Birthday Parade before the grant of independence. Sergeant Suleimani was given the task of training and preparing the squad of 60 TPs. Daily inspections and practices were held to refine and fine-tune drill movements and dress.

Finally the day arrived and, as the men formed up, ready to march on to the parade ground at Government House, it was obvious that Sergeant Suleimani had again done a first-rate job. The squad's turn-out was faultless; brass and leather gleamed, puttees were wound precisely and khaki drill uniforms starched and ironed to a glazed perfection. Now, as anyone who has worn starched drill will know, a uniform without a stray crease or two is practically unattainable. Sergeant Suleimani had managed it for his whole squad, however, through the simple expedient of not allowing his men to sit down once they were dressed. And when they set off for Government House they had travelled standing up in the back of the DC's lorry. As they marched onto the parade ground behind the leading military band, and under the command of Sergeant Suleimani bin Abu Abdulla, the men of the Tribal Police that day seemed second to none.

It was some years before I returned to Kenya on a visit to the colony, now a republic. I went to see Suleimani, who by then was no longer a Tribal Policeman. It seems that though he tried for a couple of years, he just could not come to terms with the new order. For men like Suleimani, old loyalties do die hard. Unable to switch his allegiance and, I suspect, unwilling to compromise his principles, he retired and opened a small general goods shop among his people in the settlement where he was born. When finally it was time for me to go, I took Suleimani's hand, thanked him again for his loyal service and wished him well for the future.

"Goodbye Sar' Major, and thank you", I said, my voice quavering somewhat emotionally, as I bade him farewell. As I turned to leave, the old askari snapped to attention, tucked his walking stick under his arm and, raising his hand in salute, answered :

"Goodnight *Effendi.*" Then he added, with a grin : "*Wote timamu, Effendi.*"

OP 67 (Spring 1994)

APPENDICES

1. Colonial Emblems and Badges

2. British colonial territories (or groupings) administered since WWII by the Colonial Service / HMOCS (or similar)

APPENDIX I

Colonial Emblems and Badges

by David Le Breton

Every colonial territory had its unique emblem which was displayed and used for various official and ceremonial purposes. The emblem was usually a badge, often of the same design as on the Public Seal which every colonial government had to have. Some territories also obtained coats of arms, which the College of Arms would design and register in return for a fee to be paid by the government concerned. Many governments decided that a coat of arms was not necessary.

The badge, or coat of arms, was depicted on the Governor's flag, surrounded by a laurel wreath or garland, in the centre of the Union Jack. The emblem could be used as the territory's own distinctive flag, carried on the fly of the Blue Ensign (usually) or the Red Ensign in some cases.

The design of the badge would normally be conceived by the colonial government. It would need to be approved by the Colonial Office, though there was no department with specific authority for badges or flags so correspondence about a territory's badge would be done with the relevant geographical department within the Colonial Office.

In order to be shown on the Blue or Red Ensign the badge or coat of arms had to be registered with the Admiralty. The *Admiralty Flag Book* was consequently the best consolidated record of colonial emblems, on the flags.

Most emblems – whether badge or coat of arms – were commonly shown on the Blue or Red Ensign in the form of a disc, or in some cases a shield. This corresponded with how it looked on the Governor's flag within the laurel garland. In 1918 the Colonial Office and the Admiralty agreed that the white discs were not necessary in all cases, but in practice they were often retained. Here are two examples of ensigns defaced with the badges, of Aden (disc) and Northern Rhodesia (shield).

The territories whose emblems are depicted, with short accompanying explanations, are:

Aden	Page 199
Barbados	Page 266
Ceylon	Page 271
Hong Kong	Page 78
Kenya	Page 129
Leeward Islands	Page 90
Nigeria	Page 52
North Borneo	Page 48
Northern Rhodesia	Page 77
Nyasaland	Page 132
Sarawak	Page 290
Sierra Leone	Page 35
Somaliland Protectorate	Page 183
Tanganyika	Page 102

With acknowledgement to FOTW Flags of the World website at :
http://www.flagspot.net/flags
and to Lt Col A R Tinson (for badge of Aden)

APPENDIX II

**British colonial territories (or groupings) administered since
WWII by the Colonial Service / HMOCS (or similar – see #)**

Name of Territory (or grouping)	Year of Independence (or end of British responsibility)	Present Name (if different)
Aden	1967	Yemen (part)
Bahamas	1973	
Barbados	1966	
Basutoland	1966	Lesotho
Bechunaland	1966	Botswana
Bermuda	*	
British Guiana	1966	Guyana
British Honduras	1981	Belize
British Indian Ocean Territory (since 1965) #	*	
Brunei	1984	Negara Brunei Darussalam
Cameroons :		
Northern Cameroons	1960	Nigeria (part)
Southern Cameroons	1961	Republic of Cameroon (part)
Cayman Islands	*	
Central African Federation (of Rhodesia & Nyasaland) †	1964 (dissolved)	
Ceylon	1948	Sri Lanka
Cyprus	1960	
East Africa High Commission (& Departments)	na	
East African Railways & Harbours	na	
Falkland Islands (with Dependencies)	*	
Fiji	1970	

Gambia	1965	The Gambia
Gibraltar	*	
Gold Coast	1957	Ghana
Hong Kong	1997 (to China)	
Jamaica	1962	
Kenya	1963	
Leeward Islands :		
Anguilla	*	
Antigua	1981	Antigua & Barbuda
British Virgin Islands	*	
Montserrat	*	
St Kitts-Nevis	1983	St Christopher & Nevis
Malaya	1957	Malaysia (part)
Malta	1964	
Mauritius	1968	
Nigeria	1960	
North Borneo	1963	Sabah, Malaysia
Northern Rhodesia	1964	Zambia
Nyasaland	1964	Malawi
Palestine	1948	Israel / Palestine
St Helena (with Ascension & Tristan da Cunha)	*	
Sarawak	1963	Malaysia (part)
Seychelles	1976	
Sierra Leone	1961	
Singapore	1965 (ex Malaysia)	
Somaliland Protectorate	1960 (to Somalia)	Somalia (part)
Southern Rhodesia #	1980	Zimbabwe
Sudan (*Anglo-Egyptian Condominium*) #	1956	
Swaziland	1968	
Tanganyika	1961	Tanzania (part)
Trinidad & Tobago	1962	
Turks & Caicos Islands	*	
Uganda	1962	
West Indies Federation	1962 (dissolved)	

Western Pacific Territories :		
British Solomon Islands	1978	Solomon Islands
Gilbert & Ellice Islands	1978 / 79	Kiribati / Tuvalu
New Hebrides (*Anglo-French Condominium*)	1980	Vanuatu
Pitcairn #	*	
Tonga	1970	
Windward Islands :		
Dominica	1978	
Grenada	1974	
St Lucia	1979	
St Vincent	1979	St Vincent & the Grenadines
Zanzibar	1963	Tanzania (part)

* now remaining as UK Overseas Territories

\# not administered by Colonial Service / HMOCS

† Colonial Service / HMOCS officers served the Federal Government but did not control it

INDEXES

CONTRIBUTORS

Ainley, John M; b.1925, d. 2009; Field Officer, Agriculture, Tanganyika, 1949; Agricultural Officer, 1958-65.

Armstrong, Robert L, OBE; b. 1912, d. 1994; Engineer, Public Works Department, Nigeria 1938; Executive Engineer, 1939; Senior Engineer, 1951; Chief Engineer, Southern Cameroons, 1954; Director of Public Works, Sierra Leone, 1957-62.

Babb, B Arthur; b. 1907, d. 2001; Superintendent, Education, Nigeria, 1929; Education Officer, Tanganyika, 1945; Director of Education, Zanzibar, 1951-54.

Barkway, Mrs M C; b.?, d.?; Domestic Science Supervisor, Malaya, 1939.

Barnett, Muriel; d. 2001; w/o **D E Barnett**; b. 1917, d. 1992; Asst. Auditor, Nyasaland, 1939; Tanganyika 1942; Senior Auditor, Palestine, 1947; Nigeria, 1948; Kenya, 1953; Asst. Director of Audit, 1954; Director of Audit, East Africa Common Services Organisation, 1954; Controller and Auditor-General, Kenya, 1965-69.

Bird, J Ronald; b. 1920; Administrative Officer, Northern Nigeria, 1944; Senior District Officer, 1957-63.

Brent, David L; b. 1930; Asst. Superintendent of Police, Malaya, 1952-58.

Bult, Eric W; b. 1926; Asst. Inspector of Police, Nyasaland, 1951; Asst. Superintendent, 1955; Superintendent, 1961-64.

Burbrook, J Peter C; b.1922; District Officer, North Borneo, 1948; Asst. District Commissioner, Cyprus, 1955-57; District Officer, North Borneo, 1958-68.

Cooke, John; b. 1927; District Officer, Tanganyika, 1951; Education Officer, 1962-69.

Cunningham, Eric O; b. 1927; Education Officer, Gold Coast, 1952; Senior Education Officer, 1957-62.

Dennis, **Faith**; w/o **Philip W C Dennis**; b.1917, d. 2005; Asst. District Commissioner, Gold Coast, 1940; District Commissioner, 1949; Administrative Officer Class II, 1952-56.

Everard, **A Colin J**; b. 1930; Locust Officer, Desert Locust Control Organisation, 1952; Administrative Officer, 1954; Senior Field Officer, 1957; Executive Secretary, 1962; Logistics Adviser, 1966-67; Chief Supplies Officer, East African Community, 1968-70.

Fletcher, **Mary**; w/o **P D Fletcher**, MBE; b. 1916, d. 1978; Political Officer, Aden Protectorate, 1940; Education Officer, 1944-46; Deputy British Government Agent, Eastern Aden Protectorate, 1948; Famine Relief Commissioner, 1949; Administrative Officer, Nigeria, 1950; Asst. Chief Secretary, Aden, 1952; Permanent Secretary, Ministry of Works, Northern Nigeria, 1955-62.

Forder, **Kenneth**; b. 1925, d. 2001; District Officer, Northern Rhodesia, 1951-64.

Gullick, **John M**; b. 1916; District Officer, Uganda, 1939; Military Service 1940-46; Secretary to Resident Commissioner, Negri Sembilan, 1946; Secretary to UK Police Mission to Malaya, 1949; Secretary, R.I.D.A., 1950; Controller, Trade Division, 1953; Acting Deputy Federation Establishment Officer, 1955-56.

Harris, **John H**; b. 1912, d. 2004; Asst. Chemist, Tanganyika, 1935; Metallurgist, 1939; Senior Metallurgist, 1948; Asst. Director & Acting Deputy Director, Geological Survey, 1952-55; Chief Research Officer, Mines Department, Malaya, 1955-60.

Henton, **G Robin P**; b. 1927, d. 1989; District Officer, Tanganyika, 1951; District Commissioner, 1961-63.

Hill, **Roland A**, MBE; b. 1925; District Officer, Northern Rhodesia, 1949; Senior District Officer, 1964-65.

Holliday, **Leslie (Jock)**; b. 1925; Air Traffic Control Officer, Palestine, 1947; Singapore, 1948; Operations Officer, Sarawak; North Borneo, 1953-64.

Horsley, **Roger R H**, MBE; b. 1909, d. 2002; Inspector of Mines, Malaya, 1948; Deputy Senior Inspector of Mines, 1957-58.

Kelsall, J Desmond; b. 1920; Fisheries Officer, Lake Victoria Fisheries Service, 1948; Chief Fisheries Officer, 1955-61.

Kirk-Greene, Anthony H M, CMG, MBE; b. 1925; Administrative Officer, Northern Nigeria, 1950; Senior District Officer, 1960-65.

Lang-Brown, James R: b. 1931; Asst. Conservator of Forests, Uganda, 1955-64.

Le Breton, David F B, CBE; b. 1931; District Officer, Tanganyika, 1954; Private Secretary to Governor, 1959-60; Judiciary, Magistrate and Local Courts Officer, 1962-63.

Lever, R J A W; b. 1905, d. 1993; Entomologist, British Solomon Islands Protectorate, 1930; Fiji, 1937; Malaya, 1946-56.

Lewis, J S A, OBE; b. 1909, d. 2003; Customs Cadet, Federated Malay States, 1928; Asst. Superintendent, 1931; Superintendent, 1936; Senior Customs Officer & Harbourmaster, 1939; interned, Singapore, 1942; Asst. Comptroller of Customs, 1946; Singapore, 1949; Deputy Comptroller 1954-57; Deputy Head, Overseas Service Resettlement Bureau, 1957.

Lewis-Barned, John F de S; b. 1927; District Officer, Tanganyika, 1951; Judiciary, Local Courts Appeals Officer, 1962-63.

Lindsay, Ian D St G; b. 1931; Asst. Inspector of Police, Kenya, 1952; Inspector of Police, 1956; District Assistant, 1959; District Officer, 1961-63.

Lloyd, G Peter, CMG, CVO; b. 1926, d. 2007; District Officer, Kenya, 1951-60; Colonial Office, 1960-61; Colonial Secretary, Seychelles, 1961-66; Chief Secretary, Fiji, 1966-70; Defence Secretary, Hong Kong, 1971-74; Deputy Governor, Bermuda, 1974-81; Governor, Cayman Islands, 1982-87.

McClintock, Nicholas C; b. 1916, d. 2001; Administrative Officer, Nigeria, 1939; War Service 1939-46; Colonial Office, 1946; Administrative Officer, Northern Nigeria, 1946; Private Secretary to Governor, 1949-50; Senior District Officer, 1955; Administrative Officer Class I, 1960-63.

McCormack, Duncan D; b. 1933; Cartographer, Kenya, 1958-63.

Moman, Kuldip Rai; b. 1919, d. 2007; Postal Officer, East African Posts & Telegraphs, 1938; Postal Overseer, 1961-64.

Moon, Justin T, OBE; b. 1908, d. 1977; Agricultural Officer, Kenya, 1934; Provincial Agricultural Officer, 1947; Asst. Director of Agriculture, Uganda, 1952; Deputy Director, 1954-60.

Nicholl, Samuel; b. 1922; Borehole Maintenance Officer, Geological Survey Department, Uganda, 1950-64.

O'Dwyer, Francis G (Pat); b. 1910, d. 1993; Administrative Officer, Sierra Leone, 1933-46.

O'Mahony, Winifred K; d. 1994; w/o **Dr J P O'Mahony**; b. 1901, d. ?; Medical Officer, Leeward Islands, 1931; Medical Officer in Charge, St Kitts-Nevis, 1943; Chief Medical Officer, Barbados, 1948; Director of Medical Services, 1950.

Owens, Donald J; b. 1923, d. 2007; Chargehand, East African Railways & Harbours, 1949; Locomotive Foreman, 1950; Shedmaster, 1954; Shedmaster, Senior Executive, 1963; Depot Superintendent, 1968-73.

Reavill, J Brian; b. 1931; Administrative and Executive Officer, External Affairs, Central African Federal Service, 1956; Principal, 1959-63; Senior Administrative Officer, Foreign Affairs, Southern Rhodesia, 1963; Assistant Secretary, 1968; Under Secretary, 1977; Deputy Secretary, 1980-81.

Reid, E Mary; d. 2002; w/o **Crawford R Reid**, OBE; b. 1921, d. 1996; Overseas Audit Service, Nigeria, 1946; Asst. Auditor, 1950; Auditor, Basutoland, 1950; Swaziland, 1951; Tanganyika, 1952; Senior Auditor, Hong Kong, 1957; Northern Nigeria, 1958; Principal Auditor, Aden, 1961; Director of Audit, Federation of South Arabia, 1963-68.

Russell, Joan; b. 1912; Education Officer, Nigeria, 1946; Inspector of Education, 1955; Chief Education Officer, 1957-59.

Shadbolt, Jane; w/o **Kenneth E Shadbolt**; b. 1927; District Officer, Tanganyika, 1952-61.

Smith, **Roderick E N**; b. 1922, d. 2005; Administrative Officer, Nyasaland, 1950; Administrative Officer, New Hebrides, 1961; Administrative Officer, Gilbert & Ellice Islands, 1967-76.

Tedder, James L O'N, MBE; b. 1926; Administrative Officer, British Solomon Islands Protectorate, 1952; Administrative Officer Class B, 1955; Administrative Officer Class A, 1967; Director of Information and Broadcasting, 1972-74.

Templer, **Simon**; b. 1932, d. 2009; Principal Collector, East African Customs & Excise Department, 1950-71.

Thompson, **Basil W**; b. 1918; Scientific Officer, Royal Observatory, Hong Kong, 1946-51; Colonial Insecticide Research (secondment), Tanganyika, 1951; Meteorologist, East African Meteorological Dept, 1951; Regional Representative, Kenya, 1956-59; Deputy Director, 1959-62; Director, 1962-66.

Webb, **Astor S**; b. 1914, d. 1989; Asst. Engineer, Railways, Nigeria, 1948; Senior Engineer, 1949; District Engineer, 1952; Engineer, Public Works Department, Hong Kong, 1957; Asst. Chief Engineer, 1979, Chief Engineer 1960; Asst. Director of Public Works, 1961-65.

Wilmot, Edward T, OBE; b. 1924; Agricultural Officer, Nyasaland, 1950; Chief Agricultural Officer, 1962; Chief Agricultural Planning Officer, Malawi, 1965; Under Secretary, Natural Resources, 1969; Deputy Secretary, 1970; Acting Secretary, Natural Resources, 1972; Agricultural Adviser, ODA, 1972-76.

Wilson, **Brian D**, CBE; b. 1924; Administrative Officer, Hong Kong, 1948; Senior Administrative Officer, 1959; Administrative Officer Staff Grade, 1961; Director of Urban Services, 1975; Secretary Grade, 1979; retired 1983 as Director of Urban Services.

Wimbush, Janet; w/o **Michael D Wimbush**, OBE; b. 1905, d. 1999; Surveyor, Nigeria, 1928-51.

Yearley, **Ronald R**; b. 1919, d. 2002; Accountant, Posts & Telegraphs, Gold Coast, 1948; Controller, Savings Bank, 1955-57.

Note: Four contributors have not revealed their names – BH, Iddo Huddo, PC 49 and Anon.

TERRITORIES INDEX

Aden	2.3	Children of Arabia, 1944-46	97
	3.11	Journey in the Hadhramaut	193
Barbados	4.9	Hurricane Janet, Barbados 1955	262
Central African Federation	1.17	Two Knights and a Chief in Central Africa	79
Ceylon	5.1	How Do You Do?	269
Gold Coast	2.14	A Learning Experience	137
	3.7	Massa Gets Transport	174
	4.8	One Christmas in the Gold Coast	260
	5.2	Massa Gets to Speak Propa	272
Hong Kong	1.2	A Course of Fun (the First Devonshire)	25
	1.16	Signing Off	78
Kenya	1.9	Lamu Town	53
	2.2	The Making of a Colonial Agriculturalist	91
	2.6	Season of Green Leaves	107
	2.11	Rain Stimulation in East Africa	126
	3.14	A Kenya Journey	210
	3.18	Railways and Motive Power	227
	4.3	It's a Dog's Life	243
	7.4	*"Wote Timamu, Effendi"* ("All Present and Correct, Sir")	311
Leeward Islands	2.1	Reminiscences of the Leeward Islands, 1931-34	85
Malaya	1.6	Emergency Days, Malaya 1948-50	40
	1.10	Malayan Opium Tales	56
	1.14	Signed, Sealed and Delivered	71
	2.5	How Government Officers Became Official Opium Dealers in the old Federated Malay States	103
	3.4	Jungle Trip from Grik to Temengor	158
	4.6	Bumps in the Night	253
	7.2	Berkeley of Upper Perak	303

Nigeria	1.8	A New Town Plan for Zuru	49
	1.11	The Day's Work and Odd Jobs :	
		Rescue up the Niger	59
	1.12	The Day's Work and Odd Jobs :	
		No Tax? No Bridge!	64
	2.7	A Woman Education Officer on the Niger	111
	3.1	Journey to Yola, 1929	145
	4.2	A Nigerian Garden	239
	4.7	Who's Afraid?	256
	5.5	He Needs a White Cloth	280
	6.1	Golf in the Nigerian Bush, 1948-65	285
	7.3	Serving Mallam Abubakar Tafawa Balewa,	
		Nigerian Minister of Works & Transport, 1951	306
North Borneo	1.7	Fish Bombs and Copra	44
Northern Rhodesia	1.15	Africa Past and Present	74
	1.17	Two Knights and a Chief in Central Africa	79
	3.12	Journey to Mongu	200
Nyasaland	1.3	Checking the Books	28
	2.12	First Foot *Ulendo*	130
	3.3	*Ulendo*	153
	4.1	The Lap of Luxury	233
	5.4	Witchcraft	277
	6.3	The Lion	291
Sarawak	6.2	Cricket in Sarawak	288
Sierra Leone	1.4	The White Man's Grave	31
Somaliland	3.8	Journeying to Cape Guardafui	178
	7.1	A Tribute to Captain A Gibb, DSO, DCM	
		District Commissioner, British Somaliland	299

Tanganyika

1.1	Vacancy Tanganyika		21
2.4	A War Effort in Tanganyika		99
2.8	Magnet Brand		116
2.10	Resettlement of Suspected Mau Mau Sympathisers in Tanganyika		121
3.2	First Footsteps		149
3.5	Lake Victoria Passage		165
3.10	Not a Wisdom Tooth		189
3.17	The Silver Handshake		225
5.3	How Not to Speak Swahili		275
6.4	Good Advice Will Defeat Your Enemy		295

Uganda

2.9	Dura Camp		118
2.13	Train to Iganga		133
2.15	A Matter of Understanding		139
3.6	Karamoja Journey		169
3.16	By Motorcycle in Uganda		221

Western Pacific

1.5	The Solomon Islands in the 1930s		36
1.13	*"Vive Le Royaume Uni!"*		67
3.9	Anuta – An Island from Paradise?		184
3.13	Stomach Ache in the Solomons		205
3.15	On Being a Pacific Sea-Dog		216
4.1	The Lap of Luxury		233
4.4	Mail Day		246
4.5	Supermarket – Island Style		250

SUBJECT INDEX

Accounting	1.3	Checking the Books	28
Agriculture	1.15	Africa Past and Present	74
	2.2	The Making of a Colonial Agriculturalist	91
	2.10	Resettlement of Suspected Mau Mau Sympathisers in Tanganyika	121
	2.12	First Foot *Ulendo*	130
Barotseland	1.17	Two Knights and a Chief in Central Africa	79
	3.12	Journey to Mongu	200
Boats	1.7	Fish Bombs and Copra	44
	1.11	The Day's Work and Odd Jobs : Rescue up the Niger	59
	1.17	Two Knights and a Chief in Central Africa	79
	2.1	Reminiscences of the Leeward Islands, 1931-34	85
	2.2	The Making of a Colonial Agriculturalist	91
	2.7	A Woman Education Officer on the Niger	111
	3.1	Journey to Yola, 1929	145
	3.3	*Ulendo*	153
	3.5	Lake Victoria Passage	165
	3.9	Anuta – An Island from Paradise?	184
	3.13	Stomach Ache in the Solomons	205
	3.15	On Being a Pacific Sea-Dog	216
	3.17	The Silver Handshake	225
	4.4	Mail Day	246
	4.5	Supermarket – Island Style	250
	6.2	Cricket in Sarawak	288
Carriers *(see Porters)*			
Customs Dept	1.7	Fish Bombs and Copra	44
	2.5	How Government Officers Became Official Opium Dealers in the old Federated Malay States	103
	2.15	A Matter of Understanding	139
	4.6	Bumps in the Night	253

Disorder	1.4	White Man's Grave	31
	1.6	Emergency Days, Malaya 1948-50	40
	1.11	The Day's Work and Odd Jobs :	
		Rescue up the Niger	59
	1.12	The Day's Work and Odd Jobs :	
		No Tax? No Bridge!	64
	2.1	Reminiscences of the Leeward Islands, 1931-34	85
Dogs	4.3	It's a Dog's Life	243
Education	1.5	The Solomon Islands in the 1930s	36
	2.3	Children of Arabia, 1944-46	97
	2.7	A Woman Education Officer on the Niger	111
	2.14	A Learning Experience	137
	3.1	Journey to Yola, 1929	145
	3.4	Jungle Trip from Grik to Temengor	158
Elephants	1.15	Africa Past and Present	74
	2.2	The Making of a Colonial Agriculturalist	91
	3.4	Jungle Trip from Grik to Temengor	158
Fish / Fisheries	1.7	Fish Bombs and Copra	44
	2.8	Magnet Brand	116
	3.5	Lake Victoria Passage	165
Forestry	2.9	Dura Camp	118
French Authorities	1.13	*"Vive Le Royaume Uni!"*	67
	3.15	On Being a Pacific Sea-Dog	216
	6.1	Golf in the Nigerian Bush, 1948-65	285
Game *(see Wildlife)*			
Gardens	4.2	A Nigerian Garden	239
Golf	1.5	The Solomon Islands in the 1930s	36
	6.1	Golf in the Nigerian Bush, 1948-65	285

Guns / Firearms	1.4	The White Man's Grave	31
	1.7	Fish Bombs and Copra	44
	1.15	Africa Past and Present	74
Housing	1.1	Vacancy Tanganyika	21
	1.9	Lamu Town	53
	4.1	The Lap of Luxury	233
	4.6	Bumps in the Night	253
India / Indians	2.6	Season of Green Leaves	107
	2.13	Train to Iganga	133
	3.10	Not a Wisdom Tooth	189
	4.1	The Lap of Luxury	233
Languages	1.5	The Solomon Islands in the 1930s	36
	2.12	First Foot *Ulendo*	130
	5.1	How Do You Do?	269
	5.2	Massa Gets to Speak Propa	272
	5.3	How Not to Learn Swahili	275
Leeches	3.4	Jungle Trip from Grik to Temengor	158
Lions	6.3	The Lion	291
	6.4	Good Advice Will Defeat Your Enemy	295
Local Customs	1.8	A New Town Plan for Zuru	49
	1.14	Signed, Sealed and Delivered	71
	2.1	Reminiscences of the Leeward Islands, 1931-34	85
Locusts	3.8	Journeying to Cape Guardafui	178
Meals	3.11	Journey in the Hadhramaut	193
Medical	1.4	The White Man's Grave	31
	2.1	Reminiscences of the Leeward Islands, 1931-34	85
	3.13	Stomach Ache in the Solomons	205
	4.9	Hurricane Janet, Barbados 1955	262
	5.4	Witchcraft	277
Meteorology	2.11	Rain Stimulation in East Africa	126

Subject Index

Mines / Mining

Minerals

1.4	The White Man's Grave	31
1.6	Emergency Days, Malaya 1948-50	40
1.11	The Day's Work and Odd Jobs :	
	Rescue up the Niger	59
2.4	A War Effort in Tanganyika	99
2.9	Dura Camp	118
5.3	How Not to Learn Swahili	275

Monkeys

2.1	Reminiscences of the Leeward Islands, 1931-34	85
4.2	A Nigerian Garden	239
4.3	It's a Dog's Life	243

Police

1.10	Malayan Opium Tales	56
1.11	The Day's Work and Odd Jobs :	
	Rescue up the Niger	59
1.12	The Day's Work and Odd Jobs :	
	No Tax? No Bridge!	64
6.3	The Lion	291

Porters

1.1	Vacancy Tanganyika	21
2.2	The Making of a Colonial Agriculturalist	91
2.7	A Woman Education Officer on the Niger	111
2.12	First Foot *Ulendo*	130
3.1	Journey to Yola, 1929	145
3.3	*Ulendo*	153

Postal Service

2.6	Season of Green Leaves	107
2.13	Train to Iganga	133
3.7	Massa Gets Transport	174
4.4	Mail Day	246
4.5	Supermarket – Island Style	250

Railways

1.1	Vacancy Tanganyika	21
3.18	Railways and Motive Power	227
5.5	He Needs a White Cloth	280

Recruitment

1.1	Vacancy Tanganyika	21
2.2	The Making of a Colonial Agriculturalist	91
3.1	Journey to Yola, 1929	145

Riot *(see Disorder)*

Ships *(see Boats)*

Snakes	1.4	The White Man's Grave	31
	4.1	The Lap of Luxury	233
Taxation	1.3	Checking the Books	28
	1.12	The Day's Work and Odd Jobs : No Tax? No Bridge!	64
Training	1.1	Vacancy Tanganyika	21
	1.2	A Course of Fun (the First Devonshire)	25
	1.3	Checking the Books	28
	2.2	The Making of a Colonial Agriculturalist	91
Troops / Military Wartime	1.4	The White Man's Grave	31
	2.4	A War Effort in Tanganyika	99
Water (development)	3.6	Karamoja Journey	169
Wildlife	1.4	The White Man's Grave	31
	1.15	Africa Past and Present	74
	2.1	Reminiscences of the Leward Islands, 1931-34	85
	2.15	A Matter of Understanding	139
	3.18	Railways and Motive Power	227
	6.3	The Lion	291
	6.4	Good Advice Will Defeat Your Enemy	295
Wives	2.1	Reminiscences of the Leeward Islands, 1931-34	85
	2.3	The Children of Arabia, 1944-46	97
	3.6	Karamoja Journey	169
	3.10	Not a Wisdom Tooth	189
	3.11	Journey in the Hadhramaut	193
	3.12	Journey to Mongu	200
	3.16	By Motorcycle in Uganda	221

4.2	A Nigerian Garden	239
4.7	Who's Afraid?	256
4.8	One Christmas in the Gold Coast	260
4.9	Hurricane Janet, Barbados 1955	262
5.2	Massa Gets to Speak Propa	272

Witchcraft

1.4	The White Man's Grave	31
2.1	Reminiscences of the Leeward Islands, 1931-34	85
5.4	Witchcraft	277

About the Editor

David Le Breton grew up in the Kenya Highlands where his father had settled in 1921. Educated in Kenya and in England, he joined the Colonial Administrative Service and was posted to Tanganyika as a District Officer in 1954. He served up-country and in the capital Dar es Salaam, including a spell as Private Secretary to the Governor. A year after Tanganyika's independence he took the early retirement option for expatriate officers. Seeking another career overseas he joined the Commonwealth Relations Office and then the Diplomatic Service, with postings in Central, East and West Africa and in Europe, with one late colonial assignment in the Caribbean island of Anguilla, still one of Britain's overseas territories.

In 1992 after leaving the Foreign and Commonwealth Office he became Secretary / Treasurer of the Overseas Service Pensioners' Association, which made an apt re-connection with his colonial background. The job included being the Editor of the Association's biannual journal, *the Overseas Pensioner*. He has carried on that work for 18 years now, a longer period than any of his three predecessors since OSPA's formation in 1960.

Sovereign World Ltd
&
Ellel Ministries International

In a stroke of divine master planning both Sovereign World and Ellel Ministries were independently founded in the same year – 1986.

Sovereign World, founded by Chris Mungeam, has become a widely respected Christian publishing imprint and Ellel Ministries, founded by Peter Horrobin, has developed a world-wide network of Centres, each designed to resource and equip the Church through healing retreats, courses and training schools.

Twenty years later, in April 2006, Ellel Ministries purchased Sovereign World Ltd to continue the precious work of publishing outstanding Christian teaching, as well as to create a publishing arm for Ellel Ministries. It was a divine knitting together of these two organizations both of which share the vision to proclaim the Kingdom of God by preaching the good news, healing the broken-hearted and setting the captives free.

If you would like to know more about Ellel Ministries their UK contact information is:

International Headquarters
Ellel Grange
Ellel
Lancaster
LA2 0HN
UK

Tel: +44 (0)1524 751651
Fax: +44 (0)1524 751738
Email: info@grange.ellel.org.uk

For details of other Centres please refer to the website at:
www.ellelministries.org

We hope you enjoyed reading this Sovereign World book.
For more details of other Sovereign books and
new releases see our website:

www.sovereignworld.com

If you would like to help us send a copy of this book
and many other titles to needy pastors in developing
countries, please write for further information
or send your gift to:

**Sovereign World Trust
PO Box 777
Tonbridge, Kent TN11 0ZS
United Kingdom**

You can also visit **www.sovereignworldtrust.com**.
The Trust is a registered charity.